Introduction to MATLAB® 7

Delores M. Etter and David C. Kuncicky
with Holly Moore

PEARSON

Prentice
Hall

Upper Saddle River, NJ 07458

Library of Congress Cataloging-in-Publication Data

Etter, D. M.
  Introduction to MATLAB 7/ Delores M. Etter and David C. Kuncicky with Holly Moore
    p. cm. -- (The Prentice Hall engineering source)
  Includes bibliographical reference and index.
  ISBN 0-13-147492-8
   1. Engineering mathematics--Data processing. 2. MATLAB. 3. Numerical
    analysis--data processing. I. Kuncicky, David C. II. Moore, Holly. III. Title.
  TA345.E8726 2004
  620'.001'51--dc22   2004040106

Vice President and Editorial Director, ECS: *Marcia J. Horton*
Executive Editor: *Eric Svendsen*
Associate Editor: *Dee Bernhard*
Vice President and Director of Production and Manufacturing, ESM: *David W. Riccardi*
Executive Managing Editor: *Vince O'Brien*
Managing Editor: *David A. George*
Production Editor: *Scott Disanno*
Art Director: *Jayne Conte*
Cover Designer: *Bruce Kenselaar*
Art Editor: *Greg Dulles*
Manufacturing Manager: *Trudy Pisciotti*
Manufacturing Buyer: *Lisa McDowell*
Marketing Manager: *Holly Stark*

© 2005, 2004, 2002 Pearson Education, Inc.
Pearson Prentice Hall
Pearson Education, Inc.
Upper Saddle River, NJ 07458

MATLAB is a registered trademark of The MathWorks, Inc., 3 Apple Hill Drive, Natick, MA 01760-2098.

The author and publisher of this book have used their best efforts in preparing this book. These efforts include the development, research, and testing of the theories and programs to determine their effectiveness. The author and publisher make no warranty of any kind, expressed or implied, with regard to these programs or the documentation contained in this book. The author and publisher shall not be liable in any event for incidental or consequential damages in connection with, or arising out of, the furnishing, performance, or use of these programs.

Printed in the United States of America
10 9 8 7 6 5 4 3 2 1

0-13-147492-8

Pearson Education Ltd., *London*
Pearson Education Australia Pty. Ltd., *Sydney*
Pearson Education Singapore, Pte. Ltd.
Pearson Education North Asia Ltd., *Hong Kong*
Pearson Education Canada, Inc., *Toronto*
Pearson Educación de Mexico, S.A. de C.V.
Pearson Education—Japan, *Tokyo*
Pearson Education Malaysia, Pte. Ltd.
Pearson Education, Inc., *Upper Saddle River, New Jersey*

About ESource

ESource—The Prentice Hall Engineering Source— www.prenhall.com/esource

ESource—The Prentice Hall Engineering Source gives professors the power to harness the full potential of their text and their first-year engineering course. More than just a collection of books, ESource is a unique publishing system revolving around the ESource website—www.prenhall.com/esource. ESource enables you to put your stamp on your book just as you do your course. It lets you:

Control You choose exactly which chapters are in your book and in what order they appear. Of course, you can choose the entire book if you'd like and stay with the authors' original order.

Optimize Get the most from your book and your course. ESource lets you produce the optimal text for your students needs.

Customize You can add your own material anywhere in your text's presentation, and your final product will arrive at your bookstore as a professionally formatted text. Of course, all titles in this series are available as stand-alone texts, or as bundles of two or more books sold at a discount. Contact your PH sales rep for discount information.

ESource ACCESS

Professors who choose to bundle two or more texts from the ESource series for their class, or use an ESource custom book will be providing their students with an on-line library of intro engineering content—ESource Access. We've designed ESource ACCESS to provide students a flexible, searchable, on-line resource. Free access codes come in bundles and custom books are valid for one year after initial log-on. Contact your PH sales rep for more information.

ESource Content

All the content in ESource was written by educators specifically for freshman/first-year students. Authors tried to strike a balanced level of presentation, an approach that was neither formulaic nor trivial, and one that did not focus too heavily on advanced topics that most introductory students do not encounter until later classes. Because many professors do not have extensive time to cover these topics in the classroom, authors prepared each text with the idea that many students would use it for self-instruction and independent study. Students should be able to use this content to learn the software tool or subject on their own.

While authors had the freedom to write texts in a style appropriate to their particular subject, all followed certain guidelines created to promote a consistency that makes students comfortable. Namely, every chapter opens with a clear set of **Objectives**, includes **Practice Boxes** throughout the chapter, and ends with a number of **Problems**, and a list of **Key Terms**. **Applications Boxes** are spread throughout the book with the intent of giving students a real-world perspective of engineering. **Success Boxes** provide the student with advice about college study skills, and help students avoid the common pitfalls of first-year students. In addition, this series contains an entire book titled *Engineering Success* by Peter Schiavone of the University of Alberta intended to expose students quickly to what it takes to be an engineering student.

Creating Your Book

Using ESource is simple. You preview the content either on-line or through examination copies of the books you can request on-line, from your PH sales rep, or by calling 1-800-526-0485. Create an on-line outline of the content you want, in the order you want, using ESource's simple interface. Insert your own material into the text flow. If you are not ready to order, ESource will save your work. You can come back at any time and change, re-arrange, or add more material to your creation. Once you're finished you'll automatically receive an ISBN. Give it to your bookstore and your book will arrive on their shelves four to six weeks after they order. Your custom desk copies with their instructor supplements will arrive at your address at the same time.

To learn more about this new system for creating the perfect textbook, go to www.prenhall.com/esource. You can either go through the on-line walkthrough of how to create a book, or experiment yourself.

Supplements

Adopters of ESource receive an instructor's CD that contains professor and student resources and **350 PowerPoint transparencies** created by Jack Leifer of University of Kentucky–Paducah for various books in the series. Professors can either follow these transparencies as pre-prepared lectures or use them as the basis for their own custom presentations.

Titles in the ESource Series

Design Concepts for Engineers, 2/e
0-13-093430-5
Mark Horenstein

Engineering Success, 2/e
0-13-041827-7
Peter Schiavone

Engineering Design and Problem Solving, 2E
0-13-093399-6
Steven K. Howell

Exploring Engineering
0-13-093442-9
Joe King

Engineering Ethics
0-13-784224-4
Charles B. Fleddermann

Introduction to Engineering Analysis, 2/e
0-13-145332-7
Kirk D. Hagen

Introduction to Engineering Communication
0-13-146102-8
Hillary Hart

Introduction to Engineering Experimentation
0-13-032835-9
Ronald W. Larsen, John T. Sears, and Royce Wilkinson

Introduction to Mechanical Engineering
0-13-019640-1
Robert Rizza

Introduction to Electrical and Computer Engineering
0-13-033363-8
Charles B. Fleddermann and Martin Bradshaw

Introduction to MATLAB 7
0-13-147492-8
Delores Etter and David C. Kuncicky with Holly Moore

MATLAB Programming
0-13-035127-X
David C. Kuncicky

Introduction to Mathcad 2000
0-13-020007-7
Ronald W. Larsen

Introduction to Mathcad 11
0-13-008177-9
Ronald W. Larsen

Introduction to Maple 8
0-13-032844-8
David I. Schwartz

Mathematics Review
0-13-011501-0
Peter Schiavone

Power Programming with VBA/Excel
0-13-047377-4
Steven C. Chapra

Introduction to Excel 2002
0-13-008175-2
David C. Kuncicky

Introduction to Excel, 2/e
0-13-016881-5
David C. Kuncicky

About the Authors

No project could ever come to pass without a group of authors who have the vision and the courage to turn a stack of blank paper into a book. The authors in this series, who worked diligently to produce their books, provide the building blocks of the series.

Martin D. Bradshaw was born in Pittsburg, KS in 1936, grew up in Kansas and the surrounding states of Arkansas and Missouri, graduating from Newton High School, Newton, KS in 1954. He received the B.S.E.E. and M.S.E.E. degrees from the University of Wichita in 1958 and 1961, respectively. A Ford Foundation fellowship at Carnegie Institute of Technology followed from 1961 to 1963 and he received the Ph.D. degree in electrical engineering in 1964. He spent his entire academic career with the Department of Electrical and Computer Engineering at the University of New Mexico (1961-1963 and 1991-1996). He served as the Assistant Dean for Special Programs with the UNM College of Engineering from 1974 to 1976 and as the Associate Chairman for the EECE Department from 1993 to 1996. During the period 1987-1991 he was a consultant with his own company, EE Problem Solvers. During 1978 he spent a sabbatical year with the State Electricity Commission of Victoria, Melbourne, Australia. From 1979 to 1981 he served an IPA assignment as a Project Officer at the U.S. Air Force Weapons Laboratory, Kirkland AFB, Albuquerque, NM. He has won numerous local, regional, and national teaching awards, including the George Westinghouse Award from the ASEE in 1973. He was awarded the IEEE Centennial Medal in 2000.

Acknowledgments: Dr. Bradshaw would like to acknowledge his late mother, who gave him a great love of reading and learning, and his father, who taught him to persist until the job is finished. The encouragement of his wife, Jo, and his six children is a never-ending inspiration.

Stephen J. Chapman received a B.S. degree in Electrical Engineering from Louisiana State University (1975), the M.S.E. degree in Electrical Engineering from the University of Central Florida (1979), and pursued further graduate studies at Rice University. Mr. Chapman is currently Manager of Technical Systems for British Aerospace Australia, in Melbourne, Australia. In this position, he provides technical direction and design authority for the work of younger engineers within the company. He also continues to teach at local universities on a part-time basis.

Mr. Chapman is a Senior Member of the Institute of Electrical and Electronics Engineers (and several of its component societies). He is also a member of the Association for Computing Machinery and the Institution of Engineers (Australia).

Steven C. Chapra presently holds the Louis Berger Chair for Computing and Engineering in the Civil and Environmental Engineering Department at Tufts University. Dr. Chapra received engineering degrees from Manhattan College and the University of Michigan. Before joining the faculty at Tufts, he taught at Texas A&M University, the University of Colorado, and Imperial College, London. His research interests focus on surface water-quality modeling and advanced computer applications in environmental engineering. He has published over 50 refereed journal articles, 20 software packages and 6 books. He has received a number of awards including the 1987 ASEE Merriam/Wiley Distinguished Author Award, the 1993 Rudolph Hering Medal, and teaching awards from Texas A&M, the University of Colorado, and the Association of Environmental Engineering and Science Professors.

Acknowledgments: To the Berger Family for their many contributions to engineering education. I would also like to thank David Clough for his friendship and insights, John Walkenbach for his wonderful books, and my colleague Lee Minardi and my students Kenny William, Robert Viesca and Jennifer Edelmann for their suggestions.

Mark Dix began working with AutoCAD in 1985 as a programmer for CAD Support Associates, Inc. He helped design a system for creating estimates and bills of material directly from AutoCAD drawing databases for use in the automated conveyor industry. This system became the basis for systems still widely in use today. In 1986 he began collaborating with Paul Riley to create AutoCAD training materials, combining Riley's background in industrial design and training with Dix's background in writing, curriculum development, and programming. Mr. Dix received the M.S. degree in education from the University of Massachusetts. He is currently the Director of Dearborn Academy High School in Arlington, Massachusetts.

Delores M. Etter is a Professor of Electrical and Computer Engineering at the University of Colorado. Dr. Etter was a faculty member at the University of New Mexico and also a Visiting Professor at Stanford University. Dr. Etter was responsible for the Freshman Engineering Program at the University of New Mexico and is active in the Integrated Teaching Laboratory at the University of Colorado. She was elected a Fellow of the Institute of Electrical and Electronics Engineers for her contributions to education and for her technical leadership in digital signal processing.

Charles B. Fleddermann is a professor in the Department of Electrical and Computer Engineering at the University of New Mexico in Albuquerque, New Mexico. All of his degrees are in electrical engineering: his Bachelor's degree from the University of Notre Dame, and the Master's and Ph.D. from the University of Illinois at Urbana-Champaign. Prof. Fleddermann developed an engineering ethics course for his department in response to the ABET requirement to incorporate ethics topics into the undergraduate engineering curriculum. *Engineering Ethics* was written as a vehicle for presenting ethical theory, analysis, and problem solving to engineering undergraduates in a concise and readily accessible way.

Acknowledgments: I would like to thank Profs. Charles Harris and Michael Rabins of Texas A & M University whose NSF sponsored workshops on engineering ethics got me started thinking in this field. Special thanks to my wife Liz, who proofread the manuscript for this book, provided many useful suggestions, and who helped me learn how to teach "soft" topics to engineers.

Kirk D. Hagen is a professor at Weber State University in Ogden, Utah. He has taught introductory-level engineering courses and upper-division thermal science courses at WSU since 1993. He received his B.S. degree in physics from Weber State College and his M.S. degree in mechanical engineering from Utah State University, after which he worked as a thermal designer/analyst in the aerospace and electronics industries. After several years of engineering practice, he resumed his formal education, earning his Ph.D. in mechanical engineering at the University of Utah. Hagen is the author of an undergraduate heat transfer text.

Mark N. Horenstein is a Professor in the Department of Electrical and Computer Engineering at Boston University. He has degrees in Electrical Engineering from M.I.T. and U.C. Berkeley and has been involved in teaching engineering design for the greater part of his academic career. He devised and developed the senior design project class taken by all electrical and computer engineering students at Boston University. In this class, the students work for a virtual engineering company developing products and systems for real-world engineering and social-service clients.

Acknowledgments: I would like to thank Prof. James Bethune, the architect of the Peak Performance event at Boston University, for his permission to highlight the competition in my text. Several of the ideas relating to brainstorming and teamwork were derived from a workshop on engineering design offered by Prof. Charles Lovas of Southern Methodist University. The principles of estimation were derived in part from a freshman engineering problem posed by Prof. Thomas Kincaid of Boston University.

 **Steven Howell** is the Chairman and a Professor of Mechanical Engineering at Lawrence Technological University. Prior to joining LTU in 2001, Dr. Howell led a knowledge-based engineering project for Visteon Automotive Systems and taught computer-aided design classes for Ford Motor Company engineers. Dr. Howell also has a total of 15 years experience as an engineering faculty member at Northern Arizona University, the University of the Pacific, and the University of Zimbabwe. While at Northern Arizona University, he helped develop and implement an award-winning interdisciplinary series of design courses simulating a corporate engineering-design environment.

 **Douglas W. Hull** is a graduate student in the Department of Mechanical Engineering at Carnegie Mellon University in Pittsburgh, Pennsylvania. He is the author of *Mastering Mechanics I Using Matlab 5*, and contributed to *Mechanics of Materials* by Bedford and Liechti. His research in the Sensor Based Planning lab involves motion planning for hyper-redundant manipulators, also known as serpentine robots.

 **Scott D. James** is a staff lecturer at Kettering University (formerly GMI Engineering & Management Institute) in Flint, Michigan. He is currently pursuing a Ph.D. in Systems Engineering with an emphasis on software engineering and computer-integrated manufacturing. He chose teaching as a profession after several years in the computer industry. "I thought that it was really important to know what it was like outside of academia. I wanted to provide students with classes that were up to date and provide the information that is really used and needed."

Acknowledgments: Scott would like to acknowledge his family for the time to work on the text and his students and peers at Kettering who offered helpful critiques of the materials that eventually became the book.

 **Joe King** received the B.S. and M.S. degrees from the University of California at Davis. He is a Professor of Computer Engineering at the University of the Pacific, Stockton, CA, where he teaches courses in digital design, computer design, artificial intelligence, and computer networking. Since joining the UOP faculty, Professor King has spent yearlong sabbaticals teaching in Zimbabwe, Singapore, and Finland. A licensed engineer in the state of California, King's industrial experience includes major design projects with Lawrence Livermore National Laboratory, as well as independent consulting projects. Prof. King has had a number of books published with titles including *Matlab*, MathCAD, Exploring Engineering, and Engineering and Society.

 **David C. Kuncicky** is a native Floridian. He earned his Baccalaureate in psychology, Master's in computer science, and Ph.D. in computer science from Florida State University. He has served as a faculty member in the Department of Electrical Engineering at the FAMU–FSU College of Engineering and the Department of Computer Science at Florida State University. He has taught computer science and computer engineering courses for over 15 years. He has published research in the areas of intelligent hybrid systems and neural networks. He is currently the Director of Engineering at Bioreason, Inc. in Sante Fe, New Mexico.

Acknowledgments: Thanks to Steffie and Helen for putting up with my late nights and long weekends at the computer. Finally, thanks to Susan Bassett for having faith in my abilities, and for providing continued tutelage and support.

Ron Larsen is a Professor of Chemical Engineering at Montana State University, and received his Ph.D. from the Pennsylvania State University. He was initially attracted to engineering by the challenges the profession offers, but also appreciates that engineering is a serving profession. Some of the greatest challenges he has faced while teaching have involved non-traditional teaching methods, including evening courses for practicing engineers and teaching through an interpreter at the Mongolian National University. These experiences have provided tremendous opportunities to learn new ways to communicate technical material. Dr. Larsen views modern software as one of the new tools that will radically alter the way engineers work, and his book *Introduction to MathCAD* was written to help young engineers prepare to meet the challenges of an ever-changing workplace.

Acknowledgments: To my students at Montana State University who have endured the rough drafts and typos, and who still allow me to experiment with their classes— my sincere thanks.

Sanford Leestma is a Professor of Mathematics and Computer Science at Calvin College, and received his Ph.D. from New Mexico State University. He has been the long-time co-author of successful textbooks on Fortran, Pascal, and data structures in Pascal. His current research interest are in the areas of algorithms and numerical computation.

Jack Leifer is an Assistant Professor in the Department of Mechanical Engineering at the University of Kentucky Extended Campus Program in Paducah, and was previously with the Department of Mathematical Sciences and Engineering at the University of South Carolina–Aiken. He received his Ph.D. in Mechanical Engineering from the University of Texas at Austin in December 1995. His current research interests include the analysis of ultra-light and inflatable (Gossamer) space structures.

Acknowledgments: I'd like to thank my colleagues at USC–Aiken, especially Professors Mike May and Laurene Fausett, for their encouragement and feedback; and my parents, Felice and Morton Leifer, for being there and providing support (as always) as I completed this book.

Richard M. Lueptow is the Charles Deering McCormick Professor of Teaching Excellence and Associate Professor of Mechanical Engineering at Northwestern University. He is a native of Wisconsin and received his doctorate from the Massachusetts Institute of Technology in 1986. He teaches design, fluid mechanics, an spectral analysis techniques. Rich has an active research program on rotating filtration, Taylor Couette flow, granular flow, fire suppression, and acoustics. He has five patents and over 40 refereed journal and proceedings papers along with many other articles, abstracts, and presentations.

Acknowledgments: Thanks to my talented and hard-working co-authors as well as the many colleagues and students who took the tutorial for a "test drive." Special thanks to Mike Minbiole for his major contributions to Graphics Concepts with SolidWorks. Thanks also to Northwestern University for the time to work on a book. Most of all, thanks to my loving wife, Maiya, and my children, Hannah and Kyle, for supporting me in this endeavor. (Photo courtesy of Evanston Photographic Studios, Inc.)

Holly Moore is a professor of engineering at Salt Lake Community College, where she teaches courses in thermal science, materials science engineering, and engineering computing. Dr. Moore received the B.S. degree in chemistry, the M.S. degree in chemical engineering from South Dakota School of Mines and Technology, and the Ph.D. degree in chemical engineering from the University of Utah. She spent 10 years working in the aerospace industry, designing and analyzing solid rocket boosters for both defense and space programs. She has also been active in the development of hands-on elementary science materials for the state of Utah.

Acknowledgments: Holly would like to recognize the tremendous influence of her father, Professor George

Moore, who taught in the Department of Electrical Engineering at the South Dakota School of Mines and Technology for almost 20 years. Professor Moore earned his college education after a successful career in the United States Air Force, and was a living reminder that you are never too old to learn.

Larry Nyhoff is a Professor of Mathematics and Computer Science at Calvin College. After doing bachelor's work at Calvin, and Master's work at Michigan, he received a Ph.D. from Michigan State and also did graduate work in computer science at Western Michigan. Dr. Nyhoff has taught at Calvin for the past 34 years—mathematics at first and computer science for the past several years.

Paul Riley is an author, instructor, and designer specializing in graphics and design for multimedia. He is a founding partner of CAD Support Associates, a contract service and professional training organization for computer-aided design. His 15 years of business experience and 20 years of teaching experience are supported by degrees in education and computer science. Paul has taught AutoCAD at the University of Massachusetts at Lowell and is presently teaching AutoCAD at Mt. Ida College in Newton, Massachusetts. He has developed a program,

Computer-aided Design for Professionals that is highly regarded by corporate clients and has been an ongoing success since 1982.

Robert Rizza is an Assistant Professor of Mechanical Engineering at North Dakota State University, where he teaches courses in mechanics and computer-aided design. A native of Chicago, he received the Ph.D. degree from the Illinois Institute of Technology. He is also the author of *Getting Started with Pro/ENGINEER*. Dr. Rizza has worked on a diverse range of engineering projects including projects from the railroad, bioengineering, and

aerospace industries. His current research interests include the fracture of composite materials, repair of cracked aircraft components, and loosening of prostheses.

Peter Schiavone is a professor and student advisor in the Department of Mechanical Engineering at the University of Alberta, Canada. He received his Ph.D. from the University of Strathclyde, U.K. in 1988. He has authored several books in the area of student academic success as well as numerous papers in international scientific research journals. Dr. Schiavone has worked in private industry in several different areas of engineering including aerospace and systems engineering. He founded the first Mathematics Resource Center at the University of Alberta, a unit designed specifically to teach new students the necessary *survival skills* in mathematics and the physical sciences required for success in first-year engineering. This led to the Students' Union Gold Key Award for outstanding contributions to the university. Dr. Schiavone lectures regularly to freshman engineering students and to new engineering professors on engineering success, in particular about maximizing students' academic performance.

Acknowledgements: Thanks to Richard Felder for being such an inspiration; to my wife Linda for sharing my dreams and believing in me; and to Francesca and Antonio for putting up with Dad when working on the text.

David I. Schneider holds an A.B. degree from Oberlin College and a Ph.D. degree in Mathematics from MIT. He has taught for 34 years, primarily at the University of Maryland. Dr. Schneider has authored 28 books, with one-half of them computer programming books. He has developed three customized software packages that are supplied as supplements to over 55 mathematics textbooks. His involvement with computers dates back to 1962, when he programmed a special purpose computer at MIT's Lincoln Laboratory to correct errors in a communications system.

David I. Schwartz is an Assistant Professor in the Computer Science Department at Cornell University and earned his B.S., M.S., and Ph.D. degrees in Civil Engineering from State University of New York at Buffalo. Throughout his graduate studies, Schwartz combined principles of computer science to applications of civil engineering. He became interested in helping students learn how to apply software tools for solving a variety of engineering problems. He teaches his students to learn incrementally and practice frequently to gain the maturity to tackle other subjects. In his spare time, Schwartz plays drums in a variety of bands.

Acknowledgments: I dedicate my books to my family, friends, and students who all helped in so many ways.

Many thanks go to the schools of Civil Engineering and Engineering & Applied Science at State University of New York at Buffalo where I originally developed and tested my UNIX and Maple books. I greatly appreciate the opportunity to explore my goals and all the help from everyone at the Computer Science Department at Cornell.

John T. Sears received the Ph.D. degree from Princeton University. Currently, he is a Professor and the head of the Department of Chemical Engineering at Montana State University. After leaving Princeton he worked in research at Brookhaven National Laboratory and Esso Research and Engineering, until he took a position at West Virginia University. He came to MSU in 1982, where he has served as the Director of the College of Engineering Minority Program and Interim Director for BioFilm Engineering. Prof. Sears has written a book on air pollution and economic development, and over 45 articles in engineering and engineering education.

Michael T. Snyder is President of Internet startup company Appointments 123.com. He is a native of Chicago, and he received his Bachelor of Science degree in Mechanical Engineering from the University of Notre Dame. Mike also graduated with honors from Northwestern

University's Kellogg Graduate School of Management in 1999 with his Masters of Management degree. Before Appointments123.com, Mike was a mechanical engineer in new product development for Motorola Cellular and Acco Office Products. He has received four patents for his mechanical design work. "Pro/ ENGINEER was an invaluable design tool for me, and I am glad to help students learn the basics of Pro/ ENGINEER."

Acknowledgments: Thanks to Rich Lueptow and Jim Steger for inviting me to be a part of this great project. Of course, thanks to my wife Gretchen for her support in my various projects.

Jim Steger is currently Chief Technical Officer and cofounder of an Internet applications company. He graduated with a Bachelor of Science degree in Mechanical Engineering from Northwestern University. His prior work included mechanical engineering assignments at Motorola and Acco Brands. At Motorola, Jim worked on part design for two-way radios and was one of the lead mechanical engineers on a cellular phone product line. At Acco Brands, Jim was the sole engineer on numerous office product designs. His Worx stapler has won design awards in the United States and in Europe. Jim has been a Pro/ENGINEER user for over six years.

Acknowledgments: Many thanks to my co-authors, especially Rich Lueptow for his leadership on this project. I would also like to thank my family for their continuous support.

Royce Wilkinson received his undergraduate degree in chemistry from Rose-Hulman Institute of Technology in 1991 and the Ph.D. degree in chemistry from Montana State University in 1998 with research in natural product isolation from fungi. He currently resides in Bozeman, MT and is involved in HIV drug research. His research interests center on biological molecules and their interactions in the search for pharmaceutical advances.

ESource Reviewers

We would like to thank everyone who helped us with or has reviewed texts in this series.

Christopher Rowe, *Vanderbilt University*
Steve Yurgartis, *Clarkson University*
Heidi A. Diefes-Dux, *Purdue University*
Howard Silver, *Fairleigh Dickenson University*
Jean C. Malzahn Kampe, *Virginia Polytechnic Institute and State University*
Malcolm Heimer, *Florida International University*
Stanley Reeves, *Auburn University*
John Demel, *Ohio State University*
Shahnam Navee, *Georgia Southern University*
Heshem Shaalem, *Georgia Southern University*
Terry L. Kohutek, *Texas A & M University*
Liz Rozell, *Bakersfield College*
Mary C. Lynch, *University of Florida*
Ted Pawlicki, *University of Rochester*
James N. Jensen, *SUNY at Buffalo*
Tom Horton, *University of Virginia*
Eileen Young, *Bristol Community College*
James D. Nelson, *Louisiana Tech University*
Jerry Dunn, *Texas Tech University*
Howard M. Fulmer, *Villanova University*
Naeem Abdurrahman, *University of Texas, Austin*
Stephen Allan, *Utah State University*
Anil Bajaj, *Purdue University*
Grant Baker, *University of Alaska–Anchorage*
William Beckwith, *Clemson University*
Haym Benaroya, *Rutgers University*
John Biddle, *California State Polytechnic University*
Tom Bledsaw, *ITT Technical Institute*
Fred Boadu, *Duk University*
Tom Bryson, *University of Missouri, Rolla*
Ramzi Bualuan, *University of Notre Dame*
Dan Budny, *Purdue University*
Betty Burr, *University of Houston*
Dale Calkins, *University of Washington*
Harish Cherukuri, *University of North Carolina –Charlotte*
Arthur Clausing, *University of Illinois*
Barry Crittendon, *Virginia Polytechnic and State University*
James Devine, *University of South Florida*

Ron Eaglin, *University of Central Florida*
Dale Elifrits, *University of Missouri, Rolla*
Patrick Fitzhorn, *Colorado State University*
Susan Freeman, *Northeastern University*
Frank Gerlitz, *Washtenaw College*
Frank Gerlitz, *Washtenaw Community College*
John Glover, *University of Houston*
John Graham, *University of North Carolina–Charlotte*
Ashish Gupta, *SUNY at Buffalo*
Otto Gygax, *Oregon State University*
Malcom Heimer, *Florida International University*
Donald Herling, *Oregon State University*
Thomas Hill, *SUNY at Buffalo*
A.S. Hodel, *Auburn University*
James N. Jensen, *SUNY at Buffalo*
Vern Johnson, *University of Arizona*
Autar Kaw, *University of South Florida*
Kathleen Kitto, *Western Washington University*
Kenneth Klika, *University of Akron*
Terry L. Kohutek, *Texas A&M University*
Melvin J. Maron, *University of Louisville*
Robert Montgomery, *Purdue University*
Mark Nagurka, *Marquette University*
Romarathnam Narasimhan, *University of Miami*
Soronadi Nnaji, *Florida A&M University*
Sheila O'Connor, *Wichita State University*
Michael Peshkin, *Northwestern University*
Dr. John Ray, *University of Memphis*
Larry Richards, *University of Virginia*
Marc H. Richman, *Brown University*
Randy Shih, *Oregon Institute of Technology*
Avi Singhal, *Arizona State University*
Tim Sykes, *Houston Community College*
Neil R. Thompson, *University of Waterloo*
Raman Menon Unnikrishnan, *Rochester Institute of Technology*
Michael S. Wells, *Tennessee Tech University*
Joseph Wujek, *University of California, Berkeley*
Edward Young, *University of South Carolina*
Garry Young, *Oklahoma State University*
Mandochehr Zoghi, *University of Dayton*

Contents

1

An Introduction to Engineering Problem Solving

1.1 GRAND CHALLENGES

Engineers solve real-world problems using scientific principles from disciplines that include computer science, mathematics, physics, and chemistry. It is this variety of subjects, and the challenge of solving real problems, that makes engineering so interesting and so rewarding. In this section, we present a group of **grand challenges**—fundamental problems in science and engineering with broad potential impact. The grand challenges were identified by the Office of Science and Technology Policy, in Washington, DC, as part of a research and development strategy for high-performance computing. The next set of paragraphs briefly presents some of these grand challenges and outlines the types of benefits that will come with their solutions; additional discussion of the individual challenges is presented at the beginning of each chapter. Just as the computer played an important part in the engineering achievements of the last 35 years, it will play an even greater role in solving problems related to these grand challenges.

The **prediction of change in weather, climate**, and **the global environment** requires that we understand the coupled atmosphere and ocean biosphere system. This includes understanding CO_2 dynamics in the atmosphere and ocean, ozone depletion, and climatological changes that are due to the release of chemicals or energy. These complex processes also include solar interactions. A major eruption from a solar storm near a "coronal hole" (a venting point for the solar wind) can eject vast amounts of hot gases from the sun's surface toward the earth's surface at speeds of over a million miles per hour. This ejection of hot gases bombards the earth with X rays and can interfere with communication

OBJECTIVES

After reading this chapter, you should

- be acquainted with the fundamental problems in science and engineering in today's society
- understand the relationship of MATLAB to computer hardware and software, and
- understand a process for solving engineering problems.

and cause fluctuations in power lines. Learning to predict changes in weather, climate, and the global environment involves collecting large amounts of data for study and developing new mathematical models that can represent the interdependency of many variables.

Computerized speech understanding could revolutionize our communication systems, but many problems are involved with its development and implementation. It is currently possible to teach a computer to understand words from a small vocabulary spoken by one person. However, it is much more difficult to develop systems that are speaker independent and that understand words from large vocabularies and from different languages. In addition, subtle changes in one's voice, such as those caused by a cold or stress, can affect the performance of speech recognition systems. Even assuming that the computer can recognize the words, it may not be simple for the computer to determine their meaning. Many words are context dependent and thus cannot be analyzed independently. Intonation, such as raising one's voice, can change a statement into a question. While there are still many difficult problems to be addressed in the field of automatic speech recognition and understanding, exciting applications are everywhere. For example, imagine a telephone system that determines the languages being spoken over its lines and translates the speech signals so that each person hears the conversation in his or her native language.

The goals of the **Human Genome Project** are to locate, identify, and determine the functions of each of the 30,000+ human genes that are contained in the primary human genetic material, DNA or deoxyribonucleic acid. The majority of the human genome was sequenced in the year 2000 and 90 percent of the sequence of the genome's three billion base-pairs was published February 2001.

Now that most of the human genome has been mapped, the mission of researchers includes studies aimed at understanding how the human genome functions in the role of creating gene products, most notably the many proteins for which genes code.

The deciphering of the human genetic code and the determination of the function of each gene may lead to many technical advances, including the ability to detect, treat, and prevent many of the over 4,000 known human genetic diseases such as sickle-cell anemia and cystic fibrosis.

Substantial **improvements in vehicle performance** require more complex physical modeling in the areas of fluid dynamic behavior for three-dimensional flow fields and flow inside engine turbomachinery and ducts. Turbulence in fluid flows impacts the stability and control, thermal characteristics, and fuel performance of aerospace vehicles; modeling of this flow is necessary for the analysis of new configurations. The analysis of the aeroelastic behavior of vehicles also affects the development of new designs. The efficiency of combustion systems is related to vehicle performance as well, because attaining significant improvements in combustion efficiency requires an understanding of the relationships between the flows of the various substances and the chemistry that causes the substances to react. Vehicle performance is also being addressed through the use of onboard computers and microprocessors. For example, transportation systems in which small video screens are mounted on the dashboards of cars are currently being studied. The driver enters the destination into the computer, and the video screen shows the path, including street names, to get from the current location to the desired location. A communication network keeps the car's computer aware of any traffic jams along the path, so that it can automatically reroute the car if necessary. Other research on transportation addresses totally automated driving, with computers and networks handling all of the control and information interchange.

Enhanced oil and gas recovery will allow us to locate the estimated 300 billion barrels of oil reserves in the United States. Current techniques for identifying structures likely to contain oil and gas use seismic technology that can evaluate structures down to 20,000 feet below the surface. These techniques use a group of sensors, called a *sensor array*, that is located near the area to be tested. A ground shock signal is sent into the earth and is then reflected by the different geological layer boundaries and received by the sensors. Using sophisticated signal processing, the layer boundaries can be mapped, and some estimate can be made as to the materials in the various layers, such as sandstone, shale, and water. The ground shock signals can be generated in several ways: A hole can be drilled, and an explosive charge can be made in the hole; an explosive charge can be made on the surface; or a special truck that uses a hydraulic hammer can be used to pound the earth several times per second. Continued research is needed to improve the resolution of the information and to find methods of production and recovery that are economical and ecologically sound.

These grand challenges are only a few of the many interesting problems waiting to be solved by engineers and scientists. The solutions to problems of this magnitude will be the result of organized approaches that combine ideas and technologies. The use of computers and engineering problem-solving techniques will be a key element in the solution process.

1.2   COMPUTING SYSTEMS

Before we begin discussing MATLAB, we provide a brief discussion on computing, which is especially useful for those who have not had prior experience with computers. A **computer** is a machine designed to perform operations that are specified with a set of instructions, called a **program**. Computer **hardware** refers to the computer equipment, such as the keyboard, the mouse, the terminal, the hard disk, and the printer. Computer **software** refers to the programs that describe the steps we want the computer to perform.

1.2.1   Computer Hardware

All computers have a common internal organization, as shown in Figure 1.1. The **processor** is the part of the computer that controls all the other parts. It accepts input values (from a device such as a keyboard) and stores them in the computer's **memory**. It also interprets the instructions in a computer program. If we want to add two values, the processor will retrieve the values from memory and send them to the **arithmetic logic unit**, or ALU. The ALU performs the addition, and the processor then stores the result in memory. The processing unit and the ALU use internal memory composed of read-only memory (ROM) and random access memory (RAM) in their processing. Most data are stored in external memory or secondary memory using hard disk drives or floppy disk drives that are attached to the processor. The processor and ALU together are called the **central processing unit**, or CPU. A **microprocessor** is a CPU, which is contained in a single integrated circuit chip that contains millions of components in an area smaller than a postage stamp.

We usually instruct a computer to print the values that it has computed on the terminal screen or on paper, using a printer. Dot matrix printers use a matrix (or grid) of pins to produce the shape of a character on paper, whereas a laser printer uses a light beam to transfer images to paper. The computer can also write information to

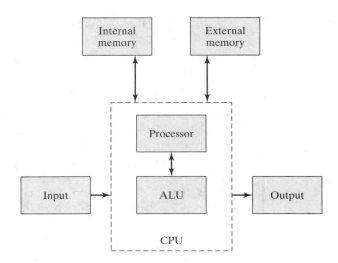

Figure 1.1. Internal organization of a computer.

diskettes, which store the information magnetically. A printed copy of information is called a **hard copy**, and a magnetic copy of information is called an **electronic copy** or a soft copy.

Computers come in all sizes, shapes, and forms. (See Figure 1.2.) Personal computers (**PCs**) are small, inexpensive computers that are commonly used in offices, homes, and laboratories. PCs are also referred to as **microcomputers**. Their design is built around a microprocessor, such as the Pentium microprocessor, which can process millions of instructions per second (mips). Minicomputers are more powerful than microcomputers. Mainframes are even more powerful computers that are often used in businesses and research laboratories. A **workstation** is a minicomputer or mainframe computer that is small enough to fit on the top of a desk. **Supercomputers** are the fastest of all computers and can process billions of instructions per second. Because of their speed, supercomputers are capable of solving very complex problems that cannot feasibly be solved on other computers. Mainframes and supercomputers require special facilities and a specialized staff to run and maintain the computer systems.

The type of computer needed to solve a particular problem depends on the requirements of the problem. If the computer is part of a home security system, a microprocessor is sufficient; if the computer is running a military grade flight simulator, a mainframe is probably needed. Computer **networks** allow computers to communicate with each other, so that they can share resources and information. For example, Ethernet is a commonly used local area network (LAN).

1.2.2 Computer Software

Computer software contains the instructions or commands that we want the computer to perform. There are several important categories of software, including operating systems, software tools, and language compilers. Figure 1.3 illustrates the interactions among these categories of software and the computer hardware. We now discuss each of these software categories in more detail.

Courtesy of Johnson Space Center   *Courtesy of Getty Images, Inc.*

Courtesy of Apple Computer, Inc.   *Courtesy of Getty Images/EyeWire, Inc.*

Courtesy of Boeing Commercial Airplane Group   *Courtesy of PhotoEdit*

Figure 1.2. A variety of computers for a variety of uses.

Operating Systems

The program that controls or "operates" a computer is called the operating system. The operating system manages the computer's hardware such as the disk drives, terminal, keyboard, and modem. Other programs that want to access the computer's hardware must pass their requests to the operating system.

The operating system also manages the programs that are running on the computer. Modern computers may have tens or hundreds of programs running at any one time. The operating system is the traffic cop that schedules one program at a time to have access to the CPU.

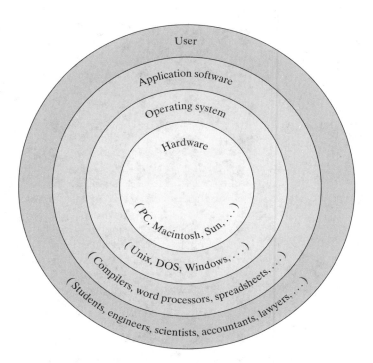

Figure 1.3. Interactions between software and hardware.

Part of the operating system, called the kernel, is loaded when the computer is turned on. The kernel remains running until the computer is turned off. Common modern operating systems are Microsoft® Windows 2000, Microsoft® Windows XP, Linux, UNIX, and Apple Mac OS.

Operating systems also contain a group of programs called **utilities** that allow you to perform functions such as printing files, copying files from one disk to another, and listing the files that you have saved on a disk. Although these utilities are common to most operating systems, the commands themselves vary from operating system to operating system. For example, to list your files using DOS (a disk operating system used mainly with PCs), the command is *dir*; to list your files using UNIX (a powerful operating system frequently used with workstations) or linux (a powerful free operating system that is ported to many different hardware platforms), the command is *ls*. Some operating systems are referred to as *user-friendly*, because they simplify the interface with the user. Examples of user-friendly operating systems are the Macintosh environment and the Windows environment.

Because MATLAB programs can be run on many different platforms or hardware systems and because an individual computer can use different operating systems, it is not feasible to discuss the wide variety of operating systems that you might use while taking this course. We assume that your professor will provide you with information on the specific operating system that you need to use the computers available at your university. This information is also contained in the user's manual for the operating system.

Software Tools Software tools are programs that have been written to perform common operations. For example, **word processors**, such as Microsoft® Word and Corel™ Word-Perfect®, are programs that have been written to help you enter and format text. Word processors allow you to move sentences and paragraphs and often have capabilities that enable you to enter mathematical equations and to check your spelling and grammar. Word processors are also used to enter computer programs and store them in files. Very sophisticated word processors allow you to produce well-designed pages that combine elaborate charts and graphics with text and headlines. These word processors use a technology called **desktop publishing**, which combines a very powerful word processor with a high-quality printer to produce professional-looking documents.

Spreadsheet programs are software tools that allow you to work easily with data that can be displayed in a grid of rows and columns. Spreadsheets were initially used for financial and accounting applications, but many science and engineering problems can be solved using spreadsheets as well. Most spreadsheet packages include plotting capabilities, so they can be especially useful in analyzing and displaying information. LOTUS 1-2-3 and Microsoft® Excel are popular spreadsheet programs.

Another popular group of software tools are database management programs such as Microsoft® Access, Microsoft® SQL Server, and ORACLE®. These programs allow you to store a large amount of data and then easily retrieve pieces of the data and format them into reports. Databases are used by large organizations, such as banks, hospitals, universities, hotels, and airlines, to store and organize crucial information. Databases are also used to analyze large amounts of scientific data. Meteorology and oceanography are examples of scientific fields that commonly require large databases for storage and analysis of data.

Computer-aided design (CAD) packages, such as AutoCAD®, ProE®, and Uni-graphics®, allow you to define objects and then manipulate them graphically. For example, you can define an object and then view it from different angles or observe a rotation of the object from one position to another. CAD packages are frequently used in engineering applications.

MATLAB®, Mathematica®, Mathcad®, and Maple® are very powerful **mathematical computation** tools. Not only do these tools enable very powerful mathematical commands, but they also provide extensive capabilities for generating graphs. This combination of computational power and visualization power make them particularly useful tools for engineers.

If an engineering problem can be solved using a software tool, it is usually more efficient to use the software tool than to write a program in a computer language to solve the problem. However, many problems cannot be solved using software tools, or a software tool may not be available on the computer system that must be used for solving the problem. Thus, we also need to know how to write programs using computer languages. The distinction between a software tool and a computer language is becoming less clear as some of the more powerful tools, such as MATLAB and Mathematica, include their own languages in addition to specialized operations.

Computer Languages   A computer programming language is a notational form for relating instructions to a computer. Computer languages can be described in terms of levels. Low-level languages, or machine languages, are the most primitive languages. **Machine language** is tied closely to the design of the computer hardware. Because computer designs are based on two-state technology (i.e., computers are devices with two states, such as open or closed circuits, on or off switches, or positive or negative charges), machine language is written using two symbols, which are usually represented by the digits 0 and 1. Therefore, machine language is a binary language, and the instructions are written as sequences of 0s and 1s, called *binary strings*. Because machine language is closely tied to the design of the computer hardware, the machine language for a Sun Microsystems, Inc. computer is different from the machine language for a Silicon Graphics, Inc. computer.

An **assembly language** is a means of programming symbolically in machine language. Each line of code usually produces a single machine instruction. Assembly language is closely tied to the architecture of a specific processor such as the Intel Corporation 80×86 series or the Sun Microsystems, Inc., SPARC series. Programming in assembly language is certainly easier than programming in binary language, but it is still a tedious process.

EXAMPLE 1.1

The assembly code listed here demonstrates typical assembly-language syntax. Each instruction is listed on a separate line and consists of an operation, or **opcode**, followed by its operands.

```
mov     cx,bx
shl     cx,8
shl     bx,6
add     bx,cx
add     ax,bx
mov     cx,es: [ax]
```

■

High-level languages are computer languages that have English-like commands and instructions and include languages such as C, Fortran, Ada, Pascal, COBOL, and BASIC. Writing programs in high-level languages is certainly easier than writing programs in machine language or in assembly language. However, a high-level language contains a large number of commands and an extensive set of **syntax** (or grammar) rules for using the commands. To illustrate the syntax and punctuation required by both software tools and high-level languages, we compute the area of a circle with a specified diameter in Table 1.1 using several different languages and tools. Notice both the similarities and the differences in this simple computation. Although we have included C as a high-level language, many people like to describe C as a midlevel language, because it allows access to low-level routines and is often used to define programs that are converted to assembly language.

Languages are also defined in terms of **generations**. The first generation of computer languages is machine language, the second generation is assembly language, and the third generation is high-level language. Fourth-generation languages, also referred to as **4GLs**, have not been developed yet and are described only in terms of characteristics and programmer productivity. The fifth generation of languages is called *natural languages*. To program in a fifth-generation language, one would use the syntax of natural speech. Clearly, the implementation of a natural language would require the achievement of one of the grand challenges: computerized speech understanding.

Fortran (FORmula TRANslation) was developed in the mid-1950s for solving engineering and scientific problems. New standards updated the language over the years, and the current standard, Fortran 90, contains strong numerical computation

TABLE 1.1 Comparison of Software Statements

Software	Example Statement
MATLAB	area = pi*((diameter/2)^2);
C	area = 3.141593*(diameter/2)*(diameter/2);
Fortran	area = 3.141593*(diameter/2.0)**2
Ada	area: = 3.141593*(diameter/2)**2;
Pascal	area: = 3.141593*(diameter/2)*(diameter/2)
BASIC	let a = 3.141593*(d/2)*(d/2)
COBOL	compute area = 3.141593*(diameter/2)*(diameter/2).

capabilities, along with many of the new features and structures in languages such as C. **COBOL** (COmmon Business-Oriented Language) was developed in the late 1950s to solve business problems. Many legacy COBOL programs exist today and were a common source of the Year 2000 (Y2K) programming bug. **BASIC** (Beginner's All-purpose Symbolic Instruction Code) was developed in the mid-1960s and was used as an educational tool; in the 1980s, a BASIC interpreter was often included with the system software for a PC. **Pascal** was developed in the early 1970s and during the 1980s was widely used in computer science programs to introduce students to computing. **Ada** was developed at the initiative of the U.S. Department of Defense with the purpose of developing a high-level language appropriate to embedded computer systems that are typically implemented using microprocessors. The final design of the language was accepted in 1979. The language was named in honor of Ada Lovelace, who developed instructions for doing computations on an analytical machine in the early 1800s. **C** is a general-purpose language that evolved from two languages, BCPL and B, that were developed at Bell Laboratories, Inc. in the late 1960s. In 1972, Dennis Ritchie developed and implemented the first C compiler on a DEC PDP-11 computer at Bell Laboratories, Inc. The language was originally developed in order to write the UNIX operating system. Until that time, most operating systems were written in assembly language. C became very popular for system development because it was hardware independent (unlike assembly code). Because of its popularity in both industry and in academia, it became clear that a standard definition of it was needed. A committee of the American National Standards Institute (ANSI) was created in 1983 to provide a machine-independent and unambiguous definition of C. In 1989, the C ANSI standard was approved. **C++** is an object-oriented programming language that is a superset of the C language. Much of the early development of C++ was made in the mid-1980s by Bjarne Stroustrup at Bell Laboratories, Inc. The major features that C++ adds to C are inheritance, abstract classes, overloaded operators, and a form of dynamic type binding (virtual functions). During the 1990s, C++ became the dominant programming language for applications in such diverse fields as engineering, finance, telecommunications, embedded systems, and computer-aided design. In 1997, the International Standards Organization (ISO) approved a standard for C++.

Executing a Computer Program

A program written in a high-level language, such as C, must be translated into machine language before the instructions can be executed by the computer. A special program called a **compiler** is used to perform this translation. Thus, in order to be able to write and execute C programs on a computer, the computer's software must include a C compiler.

If any errors (often called **bugs**) are detected by the compiler during compilation, corresponding error messages are printed. We must correct our program statements and then perform the compilation step again. The errors identified during this stage are called **compile errors**, or **compile-time errors**. For example, if we want to divide the value stored in a variable called *sum* by 3, the correct expression in C is **sum/3**. If we incorrectly write the expression using the backslash, as in **sum\3**, we will have a compiler error. The process of compiling, correcting statements (or **debugging**), and recompiling must often be repeated several times before the program compiles without compiler errors. When there are no compiler errors, the compiler generates a program in machine language that performs the steps specified by the original C program. The original C program is referred to as the **source program**, and the machine-language version is called an **object program**. Thus, the source program and the object program specify

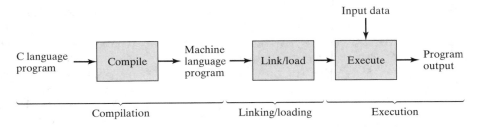

Figure 1.4. Program compilation/loading, linking, and execution.

the same steps, but the source program is specified in a high-level language, and the object program is specified in machine language.

Once the program has compiled correctly, additional steps are necessary to prepare the object program for **execution**. This preparation involves **linking** other machine-language statements to the object program and then **loading** the program into memory. After these linking and loading steps have been performed, the program's commands are then executed by the computer. New errors, called **execution errors, runtime errors, logic errors**, or **program bugs**, may be identified in this stage. Execution errors often cause the termination of a program. For example, the program statements may attempt to perform a division by zero, which generates an execution error. Some execution errors do not stop the program from executing, but they cause incorrect results to be computed. These types of errors can be caused by programmer errors in determining the correct steps in the solutions and by errors in the data processed by the program. When execution errors occur because of errors in the program statements, we must correct the errors in the source program and then begin again with the compilation step. Even when a program appears to execute properly, we must check the results carefully to be sure that they are correct. The computer will perform the steps precisely as we specify. If we specify the wrong steps, the computer will execute these wrong (but syntactically legal) steps and present us with an answer that is incorrect.

The processes of compilation, linking/loading, and execution are outlined in Figure 1.4. The process of converting an assembly language program to binary language is performed by an **assembler** program, and the corresponding processes are called assembly, linking/loading, and execution.

Executing a MATLAB Program

In the MATLAB environment, we can develop and execute programs, or scripts, that contain MATLAB commands. We can also execute a MATLAB command, observe the results, and then execute another MATLAB command that interacts with the information in memory, observe its results, and so on. This **interactive environment** does not require the formal compilation, linking/loading, and execution process that we described for high-level computer languages. However, errors in the syntax of a MATLAB command are detected when the MATLAB environment attempts to translate the command, and logic errors can cause execution errors when the MATLAB environment attempts to execute the command.

Software Life Cycle

In 1955, the cost of a typical computer solution was estimated to be broken down as follows: 15% for the software development and 85% for the associated computer hardware. Over the years, the cost of hardware has dramatically decreased, while the cost of software has

TABLE 1.2 Software Life Cycle Phases

Life Cycle	Percent of Effort
Definition	3%
Specification	15%
Coding and Modular Testing	14%
Integrated Testing	8%
Maintenance	60%

increased. In 1985, it was estimated that these numbers had essentially switched, with 85% of the cost being for the software and 15% for the hardware. With the majority of the cost of a computer solution residing in the development of software, a great deal of attention has been given to understanding the development of a software solution.

The development of a software project generally follows defined steps, or cycles, which are collectively called the **software life cycle**. These steps typically include project definition, detailed specification, coding and modular testing, integrated testing, and maintenance. Data indicate that the corresponding percentages of effort involved can be estimated as shown in Table 1.2. From these estimates, it is clear that software maintenance contributes a significant part of the cost of a software system. This maintenance includes adding enhancements to the software, fixing errors identified as the software is used, and adapting the software to work with new hardware and software. The ease of providing maintenance is directly related to the original definition and specification of the solution, because these steps lay the foundation for the rest of the project. The problem-solving process that we present in the next section emphasizes the need to define and specify the solution carefully before beginning to code or test it.

One of the techniques that has been successful in reducing the cost of software development, in terms of both time and money is the development of **software prototypes**. Instead of waiting until the software system has been developed to let users work with it, a prototype of the system is developed early in the life cycle. This prototype does not have all the functions required of the final software, but it allows the user to use it early in the life cycle and to make desired modifications to the specifications. Making changes earlier in the life cycle is both cost effective and time effective. Because of its powerful commands and its graphics capabilities, MATLAB is especially effective in developing software prototypes. Once the MATLAB prototype is correctly performing the desired operations and the users are happy with the user–software interaction, the final solution may be the MATLAB program, or the final solution may be converted to another language for implementation with a specific computer or piece of instrumentation.

As an engineer, it is very likely that you will need to modify or add additional capabilities to existing software. These modifications will be much simpler if the existing software is well structured and readable and if the documentation that accompanies the software is up-to-date and clearly written. Even with powerful tools such as MATLAB, it is important to write well-structured and readable code. For these reasons, we stress the importance of developing good habits that make software more readable and self-documenting.

1.3 AN ENGINEERING PROBLEM-SOLVING METHODOLOGY

Problem solving is a key part not only of engineering courses, but also of courses in computer science, mathematics, physics, and chemistry. Therefore, it is important to have a consistent approach to solving problems. It is also helpful if the approach is general enough to work for all these different areas, so that we do not have to learn one technique for solving mathematics problems, a different technique for solving physics problems, and so on. The problem-solving technique that we present works for engineering problems and can be tailored to solve problems in other areas as well. However, it does assume that we are using a computer to help solve the problem.

The process, or methodology, for problem solving that we will use throughout this text has **five steps**:

1. State the problem clearly.
2. Describe the input and output information.
3. Work the problem by hand (or with a calculator) for a simple set of data.
4. Develop a MATLAB solution.
5. Test the solution with a variety of data.

We now discuss each of these steps, using data collected from a physics laboratory experiment as an example. Assume that we have collected a set of temperatures from a sensor on a piece of equipment that is being used in an experiment. The temperature measurements are taken every 30 seconds, for 5 minutes, during the experiment. We want to compute the average temperature, and we also want to plot the temperature values.

1.3.1 Problem Statement

The first step is to state the problem clearly. It is extremely important to give a clear, concise statement of the problem, in order to avoid any misunderstandings. For this example, the statement of the problem is as follows:

Compute the average of a set of temperatures. Then plot the time and temperature values.

1.3.2 Input/Output Description

The second step is to describe carefully the information that is given to solve the problem and then to identify the values to be computed. These items represent the input and the output for the problem and collectively can be called **input/output**, or **I/O**. For many problems, it is useful to create a diagram that shows the input and output. At this point, the program is called an **abstraction** because we are not defining the steps to determine the output; instead, we are only showing the information that is used to compute the output. The **I/O diagram** for this example is as follows:

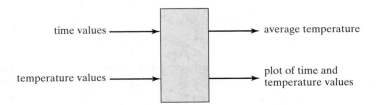

1.3.3 Hand Example

The third step is to work the problem by hand or with a calculator, using a simple set of data. This step is very important and should not be skipped, even for simple problems. This is the step in which you work out the details of the solution to the problem. If you cannot take a simple set of numbers and compute the output (either by hand or with a calculator), you are not ready to move on to the next step. You should reread the problem and perhaps consult reference material. For this problem, the only calculation is computing the average of a set of temperature values. Assume that we use the following data for the hand example:

Time (Minutes)	Temperature (Degrees F)
0.0	105
0.5	126
1.0	119

By hand, we compute the average to be (105 + 126 + 119)/3, or 116.6667 degrees F.

1.3.4   MATLAB Solution

Once you can work the problem for a simple set of data, you are ready to develop an **algorithm**, which is a step-by-step outline of the solution to the problem. For simple problems such as this one, the algorithm can be written immediately using MATLAB commands. For more complicated problems, it may be necessary to write an outline of the steps and then decompose the steps into smaller steps that can be translated into MATLAB commands. One of the strengths of MATLAB is that its commands match very closely to the steps that we use to solve engineering problems. Thus, the process of determining the steps to solve the problem also determines the MATLAB commands. Observe that the MATLAB steps match closely to the solution steps from the hand example:

```
%    Compute average temperature and
%    plot the temperature data.
%
time = [0.0, 0.5, 1.0];
temps = [105, 126, 119];
average = mean(temps)
plot (time,temps),title('Temperature Measurements'),
xlabel ('Time, minutes'),
ylabel ('Temperature, degrees F'),grid
```

The words that follow percent signs are comments to help us in reading the MATLAB statements. If a MATLAB statement assigns or computes a value, it will also print the value on the screen if the statement does not end in a semicolon. Thus, the values of **time** and **temps** will not be printed, because the statements that assign them values end with semicolons. The value of the average will be computed and printed on the screen, because the statement that computes it does not end with a semicolon. Finally, a plot of the time and temperature data will be generated.

1.3.5   Testing

The final step in our problem-solving process is testing the solution. We should first test the solution with the data from the hand example, because we have already computed the solution to it. When the previous statements are executed, the computer displays the following output:

```
average =
    116.6667
```

A plot of the data points is also shown on the screen. Because the value of the average computed by the program matches the value from the hand example, we now replace the data from the hand example with the data from the physics experiment, yielding the following program:

```
%  Compute average temperature and
%  plot the temperature data.
%
time  =  [0.0,  0.5,  1.0,  1.5,  2.0,  2.5,  3.0,  . . .
          3.5, 4.0, 4.5, 5.0];
temps =  [105,  126,  119,  129,  132,  128,  131,  . . .
          135, 136, 132, 137];
average = mean(temps)
plot (time,temps),title('Temperature Measurements'),
xlabel ('Time, minutes'),
ylabel ('Temperature, degrees F'),grid
```

When these commands are executed, the computer displays the following output:

```
average =

    128.1818
```

The plot in Figure 1.5 is also shown on the screen.

SUMMARY

A set of grand challenges was presented to illustrate some of the exciting and difficult problems that currently face engineers and scientists. Because the solutions to most engineering problems, including the grand challenges, involve the use of computers, we also presented a summary of the components of a computer system, from computer hardware to computer software. We then introduced a five-step problem-solving

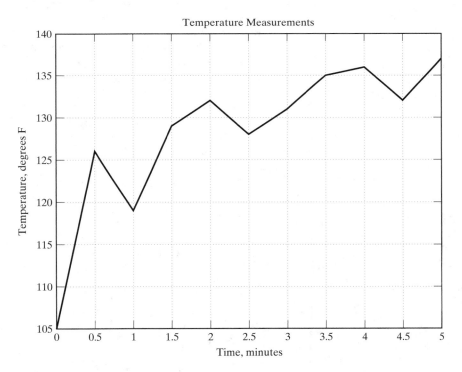

Figure 1.5. Temperatures collected in the physics experiment.

methodology that we will use to develop computer solutions to problems. The five steps are as follows:

    a. State the problem clearly.

    b. Describe the input and output information.

    c. Work the problem by hand (or with a calculator) for a simple set of data.

    d. Develop a MATLAB solution.

    e. Test the solution with a variety of data.

This process will be used throughout the text as we develop solutions to problems.

KEY TERMS

algorithm	hard copy	soft copy
assembly language	hardware	software
bugs	high-level languages	software life cycle
central processing unit	logic errors	software prototypes
compile errors	machine language	syntax
compiler	microprocessor	utilities
debugging	opcode	workstation
electronic copy	operating system	

Problems

1.   Match the following terms:

    _____ CPU   A. low-level language

    _____ kernel   B. operating system

    _____ MATLAB   C. steps for solving a problem

    _____ assembler D. hardware

    _____ algorithm E. high-level language

    _____ Java   F. mathematical computation tool

2.   Create an I/O diagram for the following description of a problem:

Each monitoring station in a group of five stations produces representative quality assurance ratings for that station. Compute the mean quality assurance rating for each of the five monitoring stations. Present the results in a bar graph. Then find the station with the maximum rating and compute the mean of the five station means.

3.   Solve the previous problem by hand for the following data:

Station 1	Station 2	Station 3	Station 4	Station 4
10.6	5.6	1.3	6.5	3.4
9.8	7.2	1.5	6.2	
4.5	3.4	1.8		
	5.8	2.1		
	5.9	1.2		
		1.1		

4.   Write an algorithm that describes the steps that you used to solve the previous problem. Write the algorithm in plain English.

2

MATLAB Environment

GRAND CHALLENGE: VEHICLE PERFORMANCE

Wind tunnels are test chambers built to generate precise wind speeds. Accurate scale models of new aircraft can be mounted on force-measuring supports in the test chamber, and then measurements of the forces acting on the models can be made at many different wind speeds and angles of the models relative to the wind direction. Some wind tunnels can operate at hypersonic velocities, generating wind speeds of thousands of miles per hour. The sizes of wind tunnel test sections vary from a few inches across to sizes large enough to accommodate a business jet. At the completion of a wind tunnel test series, many sets of data have been collected that can be used to determine the lift, drag, and other aerodynamic performance characteristics of a new aircraft at its various operating speeds and positions.

Many of the example problems in this section are related to wind tunnels and the calculations that are performed with the data collected in them.

2.1   GETTING STARTED

MATLAB is one of a number of commercially available, sophisticated mathematical computation tools, such as MAPLE, Mathematica, and MathCad. Despite what their proponents may claim, no single one of these tools is "the best." They all have strengths and weaknesses. Each will allow you to perform basic mathematical computations, but they differ in the ways that they handle symbolic calculations and more complicated mathematical processes. MATLAB excels at computations involving matrices. In fact its name, MATLAB, is short for **Mat**rix **Lab**oratory. At a very basic level, you can think of these programs as sophisticated, computer-based calculators. They can perform the same functions as your scientific calculator, and **many more**. In many engineering

SECTIONS

2.1   Getting Started
2.2   Solving Problems in MATLAB
2.3   Saving Your Work

OBJECTIVES

After reading this chapter, you should be able to

- understand the MATLAB screen layout, windows, and interactive environments
- initialize and use scalars, vectors, and matrices in computations
- save and retrieve MATLAB data
- create and use script M-files

classes, performing computations with a mathematical computation program is replacing more traditional computer programming. That doesn't mean you shouldn't learn a high-level language such as C++ or FORTRAN; but programs such as MATLAB have become a standard tool for engineers and scientists.

Today's MATLAB has capabilities far beyond the original MATLAB and is an interactive system and programming language for general scientific and technical computation. Its basic element is a matrix. Because MATLAB commands are similar to the way that we express engineering steps in mathematics, writing computer solutions in MATLAB can be much quicker than writing solutions in a high-level language. It's important to understand when to use a computational program such as MATLAB and when to use a general purpose, high-level programming language. MATLAB excels at numerical calculations, especially matrix calculations, and graphics. However, you wouldn't want to write a word processing program in MATLAB. C++ and FORTRAN are general purpose programs, and would be the programming tool of choice for large application programs such as operating systems or drafting software. (In fact, MATLAB, which is a large application program, was written in C, a precursor to C++.) Usually, high-level programs do not offer easy access to graphing. The primary area of overlap between MATLAB and high-level programs is in "number crunching"—programs that require repetitive calculations or processing of large quantities of data. Both MATLAB and high-level languages are good at processing numbers. It is usually easier to write a "number crunching" program in MATLAB, and it usually executes faster in C++ or FORTRAN. The one exception to this rule is with matrices. Because MATLAB is optimized for matrices, if a problem can be formulated with a matrix solution, MATLAB executes substantially faster than a similar program in a high-level language.

MATLAB is available in both a professional version and a student version. The professional version is probably installed in your college or university computer laboratory, but you may enjoy having a student version at home.

2.1.1   Student Edition of MATLAB

In this section, we explain the differences between the professional and student versions of MATLAB, and introduce you to the MATLAB environment. A number of examples are presented. We encourage you to type the example problems into MATLAB as you read the book, and observe the results.

> *Hint:* You may think some of the examples are too simple to type in yourself—that just reading the material is sufficient. However, you will remember the material better if you both read it and type it!

The MathWorks provides an inexpensive student version of MATLAB, for the Microsoft Windows, McIntosh, and Linux operating systems. The student version of MATLAB includes the following components of the professional version:

- The basic MATLAB engine and development environment
- The MATLAB notebook
- Simulink
- The symbolic math toolbox functions

You probably won't be able to tell the difference between the student and professional versions. Matrix sizes are unlimited in both; the amount of memory in your computer is the limiting factor. The Simulink toolbox for the student version is limited to 300 modeling blocks, but that is usually more than adequate.

Other toolboxes besides the included symbolic math toolbox must be purchased separately; however, most problems can be solved with the standard software. Not all toolboxes are available for the student version. For more information, please see the MATLAB website, www.themathworks.com.

The only difference you should notice is the command prompt. In the professional version the prompt is >>, but in the student version it is **EDU>>.**

2.1.2   MATLAB Windows

To begin MATLAB, use your mouse to click on the MATLAB icon (which should be located on the desktop) or use the start menu. If you are using a UNIX operating system, type **matlab** at the shell prompt. You should see the MATLAB prompt (>> or **EDU**>>), which tells you that MATLAB is waiting for you to enter a command. To exit MATLAB, type **quit** or **exit** at the MATLAB prompt, choose **EXIT MATLAB** from the file menu, or select the close icon (x) from the upper right-hand corner of the screen. (See Figure 2.1.)

MATLAB uses several display windows. The default view includes a large **command window** on the right, and stacked on the left are the **current directory, workspace**, and **command history windows**. Notice the tabs at the bottom of the windows on the left, which allow you to access the hidden windows. Older versions of MATLAB also included a **launch pad** window, which has been replaced by the **start** button in the lower left-hand corner. In addition, **document windows, graphics windows**, and **editing windows** will automatically open when needed.

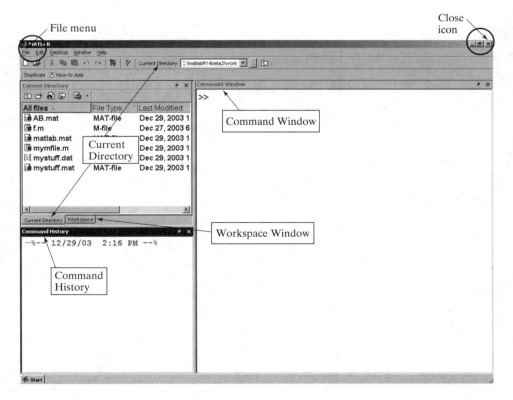

Figure 2.1.   MATLAB opening window.

Command Window

You can use MATLAB in two basic modes. The command window offers an environment similar to a scratch pad. Using the command window allows you to save the values you calculate, but not the commands used to generate those values. If you want to save the command sequence, you'll need to use the editing window to create an **M-file**. (M-Files are MATLAB files that contain programming code. An M-File is an ASCII text file similar to a C or FORTRAN source code file.) Both approaches are valuable. Here, we will concentrate on using the command window.

You can perform calculations in the command window in a manner very similar to the way you perform calculations on a scientific calculator. Most of the syntax is even the same. For example, to compute the value of 5 squared, type the command

```
5^2
```

The following output will be displayed:

```
ans =
      25
```

Or, to find the value of $\cos(\pi)$, type

```
cos(pi)
```

which results in the following output:

```
ans =
     -1
```

MATLAB uses the standard algebraic rules for order of operation, which becomes important when you chain calculations together.

Hint: You may find it frustrating to discover that when you make a mistake, you can't just overwrite your command after you have executed it. This is because the command window is creating a list of all the commands you've entered. You can't "un-execute" a command, or "un-create" it. What you can do is enter the command correctly, and then execute your new version. MATLAB offers several ways to make this easier for you. One way is to use the arrow keys, usually located on the right-hand side of your keyboard. The up arrow, ↑, allows you to move through the list of commands you have executed. Once you find the appropriate command, you can edit it, and then execute your new version. This can be a real time-saver. However, you can also always just retype the command.

Command History

The command history window records the commands you issued in the command window. When you exit MATLAB, or when you issue the **clc** command, the command window is cleared. However, the command history window retains a list of all of your commands. You may clear the command history using the file menu if you need to. If you work on a public computer, as a security precaution MATLAB's defaults may be set to clear the history when you exit MATLAB. If you entered the example commands above, notice that they are repeated in the command history window. This window is valuable for a number of reasons. It allows you to review previous MATLAB sessions, and it can be used to transfer commands to the command window. For example, in the command window, type

```
clc
```

This should clear the command window, but leave the data in the command history window intact. You can transfer any command from the command history window to the command window by double clicking (which also executes the command) or by clicking and dragging the line of code into the command window. Try double clicking

```
cos(pi)
```

which should return

```
ans =
        -1
```

Click and drag

```
5^2
```

from the command history window into the command window. The command won't execute until you hit enter, and then you'll get the following result:

```
ans =
        25
```

You'll find the command history useful as you perform more and more complicated calculations in the command window.

Workspace Window

The workspace window keeps track of the variables you have defined as you execute commands in the command window. As you do the examples, the workspace window should just show one variable, **ans**, and tell us that it has a value of 25 and is a double array:

Name	Value	Class
ans	25	double array

Set the workspace window to show us more about this variable by right-clicking on the bar with the column labels. (This is new to MATLAB 7.) Check **size** and **bytes**, in addition to **name, value**, and **class**. Your workspace window should now display:

Name	Value	Size	Bytes	Class
ans	25	1 × 1	8	double array

The yellow grid-like symbol indicates the variable **ans** is an array. The size, 1 × 1, tells us that it is a single value (one row by one column) and therefore a scalar. The array uses 8 bytes of memory. MATLAB was written in C, and the class designation tells us that in the C language **ans** is a double precision, floating point array. For our needs it is enough to know that the variable **ans** can store a floating point number (one with a decimal point). MATLAB considers every number you enter to be a floating point number, whether you put a decimal in the number or not.

You can define additional variables in the command window and they will be listed in the workspace window. For example, type

```
A = 5
```

which returns

```
A =
        5
```

Notice that the variable A has been added to the workspace window, which lists variables in alphabetical order. Variables beginning with capital letters are listed first, followed by variables starting with lowercase letters:

Name	Value	Size	Bytes	Class
⊞ A	5	1×1	8	double array
⊞ ans	25	1×1	8	double array

Entering matrices into MATLAB is not discussed in detail in this section. However, you can enter a simple one-dimensional matrix by typing

```
B = [1, 2, 3, 4]
```

which returns

```
B =
     1     2     3     4
```

The commas are optional. You'd get the same result with

```
B = [ 1   2   3   4]
B =
     1     2     3     4
```

Notice that the variable B has been added to the workspace window and that its size is a 1×4 array:

Name	Value	Size	Bytes	Class
⊞ A	5	1×1	8	double array
⊞ B	[1 2 3 4]	1×4	32	double array
⊞ ans	25	1×1	8	double array

You define two-dimensional matrices in a similar fashion. Semicolons are used to separate rows. For example,

```
C = [ 1 2 3 4; 10 20 30 40; 5 10 15 20]
```

returns

```
C =
      1     2     3     4
     10    20    30    40
      5    10    15    20
```

Notice that C appears in the workspace window as a 3×4 matrix. You can recall the values for any variable by just typing in the variable name. For example, entering

```
A
```

returns

```
A =
      5
```

Name	Value	Size	Bytes	Class
⊞ A	5	1×1	8	double array
⊞ B	[1 2 3 4]	1×4	32	double array
⊞ C	<3×4 *double*>	3×4	96	double array
⊞ ans	25	1×1	8	double array

Although we have only introduced variables that are matrices, other types of variables, such as symbolic variables, are possible.

If you prefer to have a less cluttered desktop, you may close any of the windows (except the command window) by selecting the x in the upper right-hand corner of each window. You can also personalize which windows you prefer to keep open by selecting **View** from the menu bar and checking the appropriate windows. If you suppress the workspace window, you can still find out what variables have been defined by using the command

whos

which returns

```
Name        Size        Bytes       Class
A           1x1             8       double array
B           1x4            32       double array
C           3x4            96       double array
ans         1x1             8       double array
Grand total is 18 elements using 144 bytes
```

Current Directory Window

When MATLAB either accesses files or saves information onto your computer, it uses the current directory. The default for the current directory varies, depending on your version of the software and how it was installed. However, the current directory is listed at the top of the main window. The current directory can be changed by selecting another directory from the drop-down list located next to the directory listing, or by browsing through your computer files using the browse button located next to the drop-down list (circled on Figure 2.2).

Document Window

Double clicking on any variable listed in the workspace window automatically launches a document window containing the **array editor**. Values stored in the variable are displayed in a spreadsheet format. You can change values in the array editor, or you can add new values. For example, if you haven't already entered the two-dimensional matrix **C**, enter the following command in the command window:

```
C = [ 1 2 3 4; 10 20 30 40; 5 10 15 20];
```

Placing a semicolon at the end of the command suppresses the output so that it is not repeated back in the command window; however, C should now be listed in the workspace window. Double click it. A document window will open above the command window, as shown in Figure 2.3.

You can now add additional values to the C matrix, or change existing values.

The document window that displays the array editor can also be used in conjunction with the workspace window to create entirely new arrays. Run your mouse slowly over the icons in the shortcut bar at the top of the workspace window. The function of each icon should appear, if you are patient. The new-variable icon looks like a page with a large asterisk behind it. Select the new-variable icon. A new variable called **unnamed** should appear on the variable list. You can change its name by right-clicking and selecting **rename** from the pop-up menu. To add values to this new variable, double click on it and add your data from the document window.

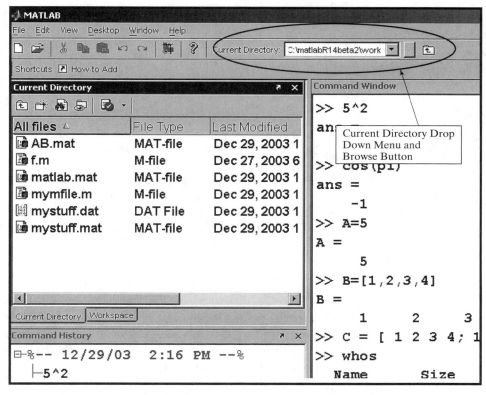

Figure 2.2.   The **Current Directory Window** lists all the files in the current directory.

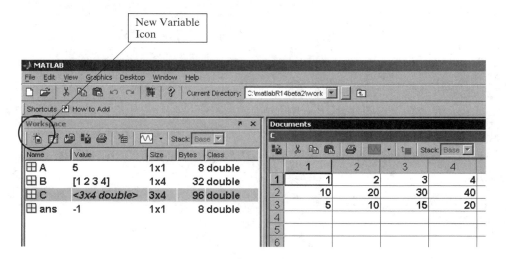

Figure 2.3.   The document window displays the array editor.

Graphics Window

The graphics window(s) launches automatically when you request a graph. To create a simple graph first, create an array of *x* values:

```
x = [ 1 2 3 4 5];
```

(Remember, the semicolon suppresses the output from this command; however, a new variable *x*, appears in the workspace window.) Now create a list of *y* values:

```
y = [10 20 30 40 50];
```

To create a graph, use the plot command:

```
plot(x,y)
```

The graphics window opens automatically. (See Figure 2.4.) Notice that a new window label also appears on the task bar at the bottom of the windows screen. It will either be titled **<Student Version> Figure** . . . , or simply **Figure 1**, depending on whether you are using the student or professional version of the MATLAB software. Any additional graphs you create will overwrite Figure 1 unless you specifically command MATLAB to open a new graphics window.

MATLAB makes it easy to modify graphs by adding titles, *x* and *y* labels, multiple lines, and more.

Edit Window

The editing window is opened by choosing **File** from the menu bar, then **New**, and finally **m-file** (**File** → **New** → **m-file**). This window allows you to type and save a series of commands without executing them. You may also open the edit window by typing **edit** at the command prompt.

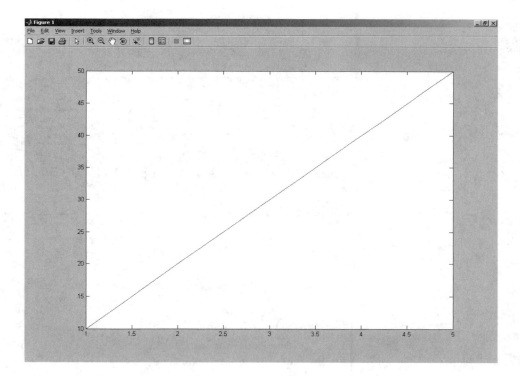

Figure 2.4. MATLAB makes it easy to create graphs.

Start Button

The start button is located in the lower left-hand corner of the MATLAB window. It offers alternative access to the MATLAB toolboxes and to the various MATLAB windows, help function, and Internet products. Toolboxes provide additional MATLAB functionality for specific content areas. The start button is new to MATLAB 7 and replaces the launch pad window used in MATLAB 6.

2.2   SOLVING PROBLEMS IN MATLAB

The command window environment is a powerful tool for solving engineering problems. To use it effectively, you'll need to understand more about how MATLAB works.

2.2.1   Variables

In MATLAB we assign names to the scalars, vectors and matrices we use. The following rules apply to these variable names:

- Variable names must start with a letter.
- Variable names are case sensitive. The names **time, Time,** and **TIME** all represent different variables.
- Other than the first letter, variable names can contain letters, digits, and the underscore (_) character. To test whether a name is a legitimate variable name, use the isvarname command. The answer 1 means true, and the answer 0 means false. For example,

```
isvarname  Vector
ans =
        1
```

  means that Vector is a legitimate variable name.
- Variable names can be any length, but only the first N characters are used by MATLAB. The value of N varies, depending on the version of MATLAB that you are using. For Version 7, Release 14, the value of N is 63. You can see the value of N on your system by typing

```
namelengthmax
```

- Variables cannot have the same name as any of MATLAB's keywords. To see a list of all MATLAB keywords, type

```
iskeyword
```

- MATLAB allows you to use the names of its built-in functions as variable names. This is a dangerous practice, since you can overwrite the meaning of a function, such as **sin**. To check whether a name is a built-in function, use the **which** command. For example, typing

```
which sin
```
  returns
```
sin is a built in function.
```

2.2.2   Working with Matrices

When solving engineering problems, it is important to visualize the data related to the problem. Sometimes the data is just a single number, such as the radius of a circle. Other times, the data may be a coordinate on a plane that can be represented as a pair of numbers, with one number representing the *x*-coordinate and the other number representing the *y*-coordinate. In another problem, we might have a set of four *x-y-z* coordinates that represent the four vertices of a pyramid with a triangular base in a three-dimensional space. We can represent all of these examples using a special type of data structure called a matrix. A matrix is a set of numbers arranged in a rectangular grid of rows and columns. Thus, a single point can be considered a matrix with one row and one column—often referred to as a scalar. An *x-y* coordinate can be considered a matrix with one row and two columns, and is often called a vector. A set of four *x-y-z* coordinates can be considered a matrix with four rows and three columns:

$$\mathbf{A} = [3.5] \qquad\qquad \mathbf{B} = [1.5 \quad 3.1]$$

$$\mathbf{C} = \begin{bmatrix} -1 & 0 & 0 \\ 1 & 1 & 0 \\ 1 & -1 & 0 \\ 0 & 0 & 2 \end{bmatrix}$$

Note that the data within a matrix are written inside brackets.

Scalar Operations

The arithmetic operations between two scalars are shown in Table 2.1. They include addition, subtraction, multiplication, division, and exponentiation. The command

```
a = 1 + 2
```

should be read as **a** is assigned a value of 1 plus 2, which is the addition of two scalar quantities. Assume, for example, that you have defined **a** in the previous statement and that **b** has a value of 5:

```
b = 5
```

Then

```
x = a + b
```

will return the following result:

```
x =
    8
```

A single equals sign (=) is known in MATLAB as the assignment operator. The assignment operator causes the result of your calculations to be stored in a computer memory

TABLE 2.1 Arithmetic Operations Between Two Scalars

Operation	Algebraic Form	MATLAB Form
Addition	$a + b$	**a + b**
Subtraction	$a - b$	**a − b**
Multiplication	$a \times b$	**a ° b**
Division	$\dfrac{a}{b}$	**a / b**
Exponentiation	a^b	**a ^ b**

location. In the example above, **x** is assigned a value of eight, and is stored in computer memory. If you enter the variable name

        x

into MATLAB, you get the result

        x =
            8

which should be read as "**x** is assigned a value of 8." If we interpret assignment statements in this way, we are not disturbed by the valid MATLAB statement

        x = x + 1

which, since the value stored in **x** was originally 8, returns

        x =
            9

indicating that the value stored in the memory location named **x** has been changed to 9. Clearly, this statement is not a valid algebraic statement, but is understandable when viewed as an assignment rather than as a statement of equality. The assignment statement is similar to the familiar process of saving a file. When you first save a word processing document, you assign it a name. Subsequently, when you've made changes, you resave your file, but still assign it the same name. The first and second versions are not equal; you've just assigned a new version of your document to an existing memory location.

Precedence of Arithmetic Operations

Because several operations can be combined in a single arithmetic expression, it is important to know the order in which operations are performed. Table 2.2 contains the precedence of arithmetic operations performed in MATLAB. Note that this precedence follows the rules of standard algebraic precedence.

Assume that we want to calculate the area of a trapezoid, where the base is horizontal and the two edges are vertical. We know that the equation for the area of this trapezoid is

```
area = 0.5 * base * (height_1 + height_2)
```

There are two equally valid approaches to solving this problem. First, assume some values for base, height_1, and height_2, and enter them into MATLAB:

```
base = 5;
height_1 = 12;
height_2 = 6;
```

Now you can solve the problem by entering the equation for area in MATLAB:

```
area = 0.5 * base * (height_1 + height_2)
```

TABLE 2.2 Precedence of Arithmetic Operations

Precedence	Operation
1	Parentheses, innermost first
2	Exponentiation, left to right
3	Multiplication and division, left to right
4	Addition and subtraction, left to right

This equation returns

```
area =
    45
```

Understanding the order of operation is important. MATLAB will first add the two height values together:

```
height_1 + height_2
```

Then the program will perform the multiplication operations, starting from the left. An alternative approach would be to simply enter the numerical values directly into the formula:

```
area = 0.5 * 5 * (12 + 6)
```

This will return

```
area =
    45
```

In either case, neglecting the parentheses will result in the wrong answer. For example,

```
area = 0.5 * base * height_1 + height_2
```

gives

```
area =
    36
```

In this case, MATLAB will first perform the multiplications, working from left to right:

```
0.5 * base * height_1
```

Then it will add the result to height_2. Clearly, it is important to be very careful when converting equations into MATLAB statements. Adding extras parentheses is an easy way to ensure that computations are performed in the order you want.

If an expression is long, break it into multiple statements. For example, consider the equation

$$f = \frac{x^3 - 2x^2 + x - 6.3}{x^2 + 0.05005x - 3.14}$$

The value of f could be computed with the following MATLAB statements:

```
numerator = x^3 - 2*x^2 + x - 6.3;
denominator = x^2 + 0.05005*x - 3.14;
f = numerator/denominator;
```

It is better to use several statements that are easy to understand than to use one statement that requires careful thought to figure out the order of operations.

> *Hint:* MATLAB does not read "white space," so it doesn't matter if you add spaces to your commands. It is easier to read a long expression if you add a space before and after plus (+) and minus (−) signs, but not multiplication (*) and division (/) signs.

EXAMPLE 2.1

SCALAR OPERATIONS

Wind tunnels are used to evaluate high performance aircraft. (See Figure 2.5.) To interpret wind tunnel data, the engineer needs to understand how gases behave. The basic equation describing gas properties is the ideal gas law,

$$PV = nRT$$

Figure 2.5.   Wind tunnels are used to test aircraft designs.

where

P = pressure, kPa

V = volume, m^3

n = number of kmoles of gas in the sample

R = ideal gas constant, 8.314 kPa m^3/kmole K

T = temperature, expressed on an absolute scale (i.e., in degrees K)

In addition, we know that the number of kmoles of gas is equal to the mass of gas divided by the molar mass (also known as the molecular weight); that is,

$$n = m/\text{MW}$$

where

m = mass, kg

MW = molar mass, kg/kmole

Different units can be used in the equations, if the value of R is changed accordingly. Assume that the volume of air in the wind tunnel is 1000 m^3. Before the wind tunnel is turned on, the temperature of the air is 300 K and the pressure is 100 kPa. The molar mass (molecular weight) of air is approximately 29 kg/kmole. Find the mass of air in the wind tunnel.

SOLUTION

To solve this problem, use the following problem-solving methodology:

1.   State the Problem

When you solve a problem, it is a good idea to restate it in your own words:
Find the mass of air in the wind tunnel.

2.   Describe the Input and Output

Input

$$V = 1000 \text{ m}^3$$
$$T = 300 \text{ K}$$
$$P = 100 \text{ kPa}$$
$$MW = 29 \text{ kg/kmole}$$
$$R = 8.314 \text{ kPa m}^3/\text{kmole K}$$

Output

mass kg

3.   Hand Example

Working the problem by hand (or with a calculator) allows you to outline an algorithm, which you can translate to MATLAB code later. You should choose simple data that make it easy to check your work.

Solve the ideal gas law for n, and plug in the given values. This results in

$$n = PV/RT$$
$$= (100 \text{ kPa} \times 1000 \text{ m}^3)/(8.314 \text{ kPa m}^3/\text{kmole K}) \times 300 \text{ K})$$
$$= 40.0930 \text{ kmoles}$$

Convert moles to mass by multiplying by the molar mass:

$$m = n \times MW = 40.0930 \text{ kmoles} \times 29 \text{ kg/kmole}$$
$$m = 1162.70 \text{ kg}$$

4.   Develop a MATLAB solution

```
P = 100
P =
        100
T = 300
T =
        300
V = 1000
V =
          1000
MW = 29
MW =
        29
R = 8.314
R =
        8.3140
n = (P*V)/(R*T)
n =
        40.0930
m = n*MW
m =
          1.1627e+003
```

There are several things you should notice about this MATLAB solution. Because there were no semicolons used to suppress the output, the variable values are repeated back to

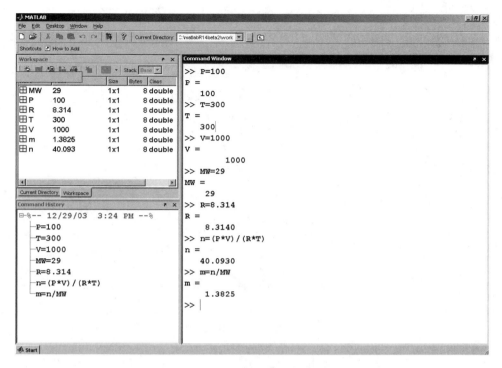

Figure 2.6.   MATLAB screen used to solve the ideal gas problem.

us after each assignment statement. Notice also the use of parentheses in the calculation of n. They are necessary for the denominator, but not for the numerator; however, using parentheses in both makes it easier to read.

5.   Test the Solution

In this case, comparing the result to the hand result is sufficient. More complicated problems solved in MATLAB should use a variety of input data to confirm that your solution works in a variety of cases. A picture of the MATLAB screen used to solve this problem is shown in Figure 2.6.

Notice that the variables defined in the command window are listed in the workspace window. Also notice that the command history lists the commands executed in the command window. If you were to scroll up in the command history window, you would see commands from previous MATLAB sessions. All of these commands are available for you to move to the command window.   ■

Array Operations

Using MATLAB as a glorified calculator is okay, but its real strength is in matrix manipulations. As described previously, the simplest way to define a matrix is to use a list of numbers called an explicit list. The command

        X = [1 2 3 4]

returns the row vector

        X =
            1 2 3 4

Recall that when defining this vector, you may either list the values with or without commas. A new row is indicated by a semicolon, so that a column vector is specified as

```
Y = [ 1; 2; 3; 4]
```

and a matrix that contains both rows and columns would be created with the statement

```
A = [ 1 2 3 4; 2 3 4 5 ; 3 4 5 6]
```

which would return

```
A =
     1 2 3 4
     2 3 4 5
     3 4 5 6
```

Hint: It's easier to keep track of how many values you've entered into a matrix if you enter each row on a separate line:

```
A = [1 2 3 4;
2 3 4 5;
3 4 5 6]
```

While a complicated matrix might have to be entered by hand, evenly spaced matrices can be entered much more readily. The command

```
B = 1:5
```

or the command

```
B = [1:5]
```

returns a row matrix

```
B =
     1 2 3 4 5
```

(The square brackets are optional.) The default increment is 1, but if you want to use a different increment, put it between the first and final values. For example,

```
C = 1:2:5
```

indicates that the increment between values will be 2 and returns

```
C =
     1     3     5
```

If you want MATLAB to calculate the spacing, you must use the **linspace** command. Specify the initial value, the final value, and how many total values you want. For example,

```
D = linspace(1,10,3)
```

returns a vector with three values, evenly spaced between 1 and 10, as follows:

```
D =
     1     5.5     10
```

Matrices can be used in many calculations with scalars. If **A = [1 2 3]**, we can add 5 to each value in the matrix with the calculation

```
B = A + 5
```

which returns

```
B =
     6     7     8
```

This works well for addition and subtraction; however, multiplication and division are slightly different. In matrix mathematics the multiplication operator (*) has a very specific meaning. If you want to do an element-by-element multiplication, the operator .* is used. For example,

        A .* B

results in

    element #1 of matrix **A** being multiplied by element #1 of matrix B,

    element #2 of matrix **A** being multiplied by element #2 of matrix B, etc., and
    element #n of matrix **A** being multiplied by element #n of matrix B.

For the particular case of our **A** (which is [1 2 3]) and our **B** (which is [6 7 8]),

        A .* B

returns

        ans =
            6   14   24

(Be sure to do the math to convince yourself why these are the correct answers.)

Just using * implies a matrix multiplication, which in this case would return an error message, because this particular **A** and **B** do not meet the rules for multiplication in matrix algebra. Just be careful to use the correct operator when you mean element-by-element (also called array) multiplication.

The same syntax holds for element-by-element division (.*/*) and exponentiation (.^) of individual elements:

        A ./B
        A .^2

As an exercise, predict the values resulting from the preceding two expressions, then test out your predictions by executing the commands in MATLAB.

The matrix capability of MATLAB makes it easy to do repetitive calculations. For example, assume you have a list of angles in degrees that you would like to convert to radians. First, put the values into a matrix. For angles of 10, 15, 70, and 90, enter

        D = [10 15 70 90];

To change the values to radians, you must multiply by $\pi/180$:

        R = D*pi/180;

This command returns a matrix **R**, with the values in radians. (Try it!)

Hint: The value of π is built into MATLAB as a floating point number, called pi. Because π is an irrational number, it cannot be expressed exactly with a floating point representation, and the MATLAB constant, pi, is really an approximation. You can see this when you find sin(pi). Based on trigonometry, the answer should be 0. However, MATLAB returns a very small number. The actual value depends on your version of the program—our version returned 1.2246e-016. In most calculations this won't make a difference in the final result.

Another useful matrix operator is transposition. The transpose operator basically changes rows to columns or vice versa. For example,

        D'

returns

```
ans =
      10
      15
      70
      90
```

This makes it easy to create tables. For example, to create a table of degrees to radians, enter

```
table =[D',R']
```

which tells MATLAB to create a matrix named **table**, where column #1 is **D'**, and column #2 is **R'**:

```
table =
        10.0000    0.1745
        15.0000    0.2618
        70.0000    1.2217
        90.0000    1.5708
```

EXAMPLE 2.2

MATRIX CALCULATIONS WITH SCALARS

Scientific data, such as that collected from wind tunnels, are usually in SI (system international) units. However, much of the manufacturing infrastructure in the United States has been tooled in English (sometimes called American Engineering or American Standard) units. Engineers need to be fluent in both systems, and especially careful when sharing data with other engineers. Perhaps the most notorious example of unit confusion problems is the *Mars Climate Orbiter*, which was the second flight of the NASA Mars Surveyor Program. (See Figure 2.7.) The spacecraft burned up in the orbit of Mars in

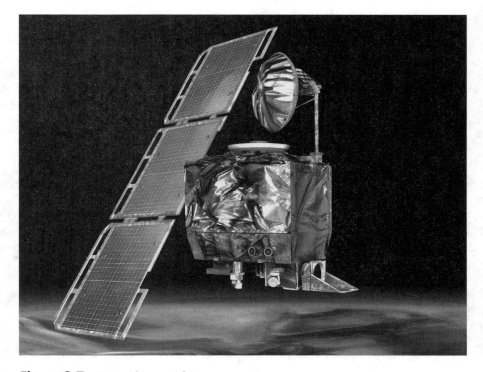

Figure 2.7. Mars Climate Orbiter.

1 lbf = 4.4482216 N

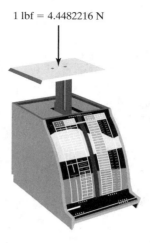

Figure 2.8. A scale measures the applied force.

September 1999 because of a look-up table embedded in the spacecraft's software. The table, probably generated from wind tunnel testing, used pounds force (lbf), when the program expected values in Newtons (N). (See Figure 2.8.)

Use MATLAB to create a conversion table of pounds force (lbf) to Newtons (N). Your table should start at 0 and go to 1000 lbf, at 100 lbf intervals. Use the conversion

$$1 \text{ lbf} = 4.4482216 \text{ N}$$

1. State the Problem

    Create a table converting pound force (lbf) to Newtons (N).

2. Describe the Input and Output

Input

    The starting value in the table is: 0 lbf
    The final value in the table is: 1000 lbf
    The increment between values is: 100 lbf
    The conversion from lbf to N is: 1 lbf = 4.4482216 N

Output

    Table listing pound force (lbf) and Newtons (N)

3. Hand Example

$$0 \times 4.4482216 = 0$$
$$100 \times 4.4482216 = 444.82216$$
$$1000 \times 4.4482216 = 4448.2216$$

4. Develop a MATLAB Solution

```
lbf = [0:100:1000];
N = lbf * 4.44822;
[lbf',N']
```

```
ans =
   1.0e+003  *
          0          0
     0.1000     0.4448
     0.2000     0.8896
     0.3000     1.3345
     0.4000     1.7793
     0.5000     2.2241
     0.6000     2.6689
     0.7000     3.1138
     0.8000     3.5586
     0.9000     4.0034
     1.0000     4.4482
```

It is always a good idea to clear the workspace and the command window before starting a new problem. Notice in the workspace window that lbf and N are 1×11 matrices, and that **ans** (which is where the table we created is stored) is an 11×2 matrix. The output from the first two commands was suppressed by adding a semicolon at the end of each line. It would be very easy to create a table with more entries by changing the increment to 10 or even to 1. Also notice that you'll need to multiply the table results by 1000 to get the correct answers. MATLAB tells you this is necessary directly above the table, as shown in Figure 2.9.

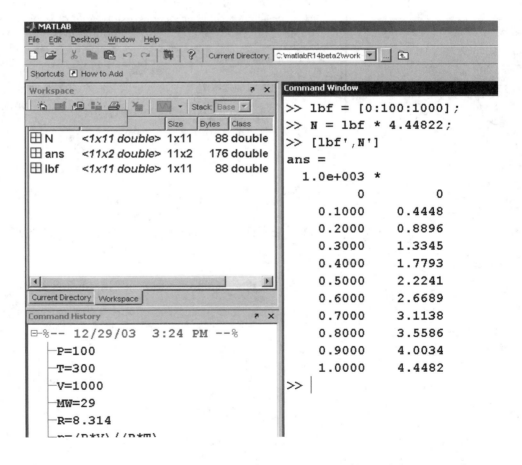

Figure 2.9. The MATLAB workspace window shows the variables as they are created.

5.   Test the Solution

Comparing the results of the MATLAB solution to the hand solution shows the same re-sults. Once we've verified that our solution works, it's easy to use the same algorithm to cre-ate other conversion tables. For example, modify this example to create a conversion table of Newton (N) to pound force, with an increment of 10 N, from 0 N to 1000 N.   ∎

EXAMPLE 2.3

CALCULATING DRAG

One performance characteristic that can be determined in a wind tunnel is drag. The friction related to drag on the Mars Climate Observer (caused by Mars' atmosphere), re-sulted in its burning up during course corrections. Drag is extremely important in the design of terrestrial aircraft as well.

Drag is the force generated as an object, such as an airplane, moves through a fluid. (See Figure 2.10.) Of course, in the case of a wind tunnel, air moves past a station-ary model, but the equations are the same. Drag is a very complex force, depending on many factors. One factor is skin friction, which depends on the surface properties of the aircraft, the properties of the moving fluid (air in this case), and the flow patterns caused by the shape of the aircraft (or in the case of the Mars Climate Observer, by the space-craft). Drag can be calculated with the drag equation

$$\text{Drag} = C_d \frac{rV^2A}{2}$$

where

C_d = drag coefficient, which is determined experimentally, usually in a wind tunnel
r = air density
V = velocity
A = reference area

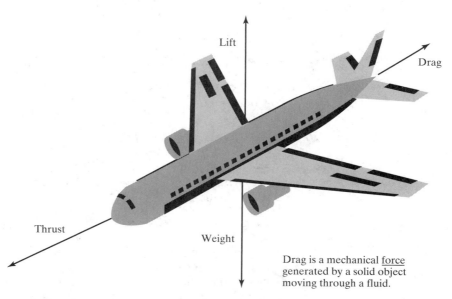

Drag is a mechanical <u>force</u> generated by a solid object moving through a fluid.

Figure 2.10.   Drag is a mechanical force generated by a solid object moving through a fluid.

Although the drag coefficient is not a constant, it can be used as a constant at low speeds (less than 200 mph). Assume the following data were measured in a wind tunnel:

drag	20,000 N
r	1×10^{-6} kg/m^3
V	100 mph (you'll need to convert this to meters per second)
A	1 m^2

Calculate the drag coefficient. Finally, use this experimentally determined drag coefficient to predict how much drag the aircraft will experience at velocities from 0 mph to 200 mph.

1. **State the Problem**

   Calculate the drag coefficient
   Use the drag coefficient to determine the drag at a variety of velocities

2. **Describe the Input and Output**

   Input

drag	20,000 N
r	1×10^{-6} kg/m^3
V	100 mph
A	1 m^2

   Output

   drag coefficient
   drag at a velocities from 0 to 200 mph

3. **Hand Example**

   First find the drag coefficient from the experimental data:

   $$C_d = \text{drag} \times 2/(r \times V^2 \times A) = 2.0019 \text{ e7}$$

   Use the drag coefficient to find the drag at different velocities:

   $$\text{drag} = C_d \times r \times V^2 \times A/2$$

   Calculate the value of drag with $V = 200$ mph, using a calculator

   $$\text{drag} = 80,000 \text{ N}$$

4. **Develop a MATLAB Solution**

   ```
   drag = 20000;
   r = 0.000001;
   V = 100*0.4470;
   A = 1;
   cd = drag*2/(r*V^2*A)
   cd =
      2.0019e+007
   V = 0:20:200;
   V = V*0.4470;
   drag = cd*r*V.^2*A/2;
   table = [V', drag']
   ```

   Define the variables, and change V to SI units

   Calculate the coefficient of drag

   Redefine V as a matrix
   Change it to SI units, and
   calculate the drag

```
table =
  1.0e+004 *
       0          0
  0.0009     0.0800
  0.0018     0.3200
  0.0027     0.7200
  0.0036     1.2800
  0.0045     2.0000
  0.0054     2.8800
  0.0063     3.9200
  0.0072     5.1200
  0.0080     6.4800
  0.0089     8.0000
```

(See Figure 2.11.) Notice that the equation for the drag,

Drag = cd * r * V.^2 * A/2;

uses the .^ operator, because we intend that each value in the matrix **V** be squared, not that the entire matrix **V** be multiplied by itself. Using just the exponentiation operator (^) would result in an error message. Unfortunately, it is possible to compose problems where using the wrong operator does not give us an error message—but does give us a wrong answer. This makes Step 5 in our problem solving methodology especially important.

5.   Test the Solution

By comparing the hand solution to the MATLAB solution, we see that both give the same results. Once we have confirmed with sample data that our algorithm works, we can substitute in new data with confidence that the results will be correct. Ideally, the results should also be compared to experimental data to confirm that the equations we are using accurately model the real physical process. ■

2.2.3   Number Display

Scientific Notation

Although you can enter any number in decimal notation, it isn't always the best way to represent very large or very small numbers. For example, a number that is used frequently in chemistry is Avogadro's constant, whose value to four significant digits is 602,200,000,000,000,000,000,000. The diameter of an iron atom is approximately 140 picometers, which is .000000000140 meters. Scientific notation expresses a value as a number between 1 and 10 (the mantissa) multiplied by a power of 10 (the exponent). In scientific notation, Avogadro's number becomes 6.022×10^{23}, and the diameter of an iron atom becomes 1.4×10^{-10} meters. In MATLAB, values in scientific notation are designated with an e between the mantissa and the exponent. For example,

```
Avogadros_constant = 6.022e23;
Iron_diameter = 140e-12;   or
Iron_diameter = 1.4e-10;
```

It is important to omit blanks between the mantissa and the exponent. For example, MATLAB will interpret

6.022   e23

as two values (6.022 and 10^{23}).

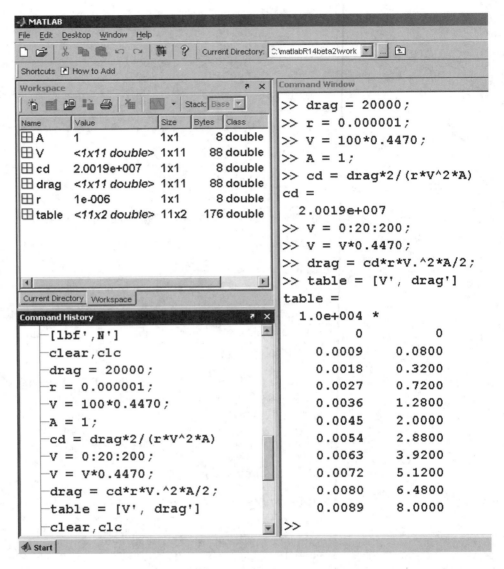

Figure 2.11. The command history window creates a history of previous commands.

Display Format

When elements of a matrix are displayed in MATLAB, integers are always printed as integers. However, values with decimal fractions are printed using a default format that shows four decimal digits. Thus,

        A = 5

returns

        A =
            5

but

        A = 5.1

returns

>   **A =**
>   **5.1000**

and

>   **A = 51.1**

returns

>   **A =**
>   **51.1000**

MATLAB allows you to specify other formats that show more significant digits. For example, to specify that we want values to be displayed in a decimal format with 14 decimal digits, we use the command

>   **format long**

which changes all subsequent displays. For example,

>   **A**

now returns

>   **A =**
>   **51.10000000000000**

We can return the format to four decimal digits by using the command

>   **format short**
>   **A**
>   **A =**
>   **51.1000**

Two decimal digits are displayed when the format is specified as **format bank**. No matter what display format you choose, MATLAB uses double precision, floating-point numbers in its calculations. Exactly how many digits are used in these calculations depends upon your computer. However, changing the display format does not change the accuracy of your results.

When numbers become too large or too small for MATLAB to display using the default format, the program automatically expresses them in scientific notation. For example, if you enter Avogadro's constant into MATLAB in decimal notation,

>   **a = 6020000000000000000000000**

the program returns

>   **a =**
>   **6.0200e+023**

You can force MATLAB to display all numbers in scientific notation with **format short e** (with 5 significant digits) or **format long e** (with 14 significant digits). Thus,

>   **format short e**
>   **x = 10.356789**

returns

>   **x =**
>   **1.0357e+001**

TABLE 2.3 Numeric Display Formats

MATLAB Command	Display	Example
format short	4 decimal digits	15.2345
format long	14 decimal digits	15.23453333333333
format short e	14 decimal digits	1.5234e+01
format long e	15 decimal digits	1.523453333333333e+01
format bank	2 decimal digits	15.23
format +	+, −, blank	+

Another format command is **format +**. When a matrix is displayed with this format, the only characters printed are plus and minus signs. If a value is positive, a plus sign will be displayed; if a value is negative, a minus sign will be displayed. If a value is zero, nothing will be displayed. This format allows us to view a large matrix in terms of its signs:

```
format +
B = [1, -5, 0,12; 10005, 24, -10,4]
B =
    +- +
    ++-+
```

For long and short formats, a common scale factor is applied to the entire matrix if the elements become very large or very small. This scale factor is printed along with the scaled values. For example, when the command window is returned to

```
format short
```

the results from Example 2.3 are displayed as

```
table =
1.0e+005 *          Common Scale Factor

    0          0
    0.0002     0.0400
    0.0004     0.1602
    0.0006     0.3603
    0.0008     0.6406    etc
```

Finally, the command **format compact** suppresses many of the line feeds that appear between matrix displays and allows more lines of information to be seen together on the screen. The command **format loose** will return the command window to the less compact display mode. The examples in this text use the compact format to save space (see Table 2.3 for numeric display formats).

2.3 SAVING YOUR WORK

Working in the command window is similar to performing calculations on your scientific calculator. When you turn off the calculator, or when you exit the program, your work is gone. It *is* possible to save the values of the variables that you defined in the command window and that are listed in the workspace window. Although this may be useful, it is more likely that you will want to save the list of commands that generated your results. In this section, we will first show you how to save and retrieve variables (the results of the assignments you made and the calculations you performed) to MAT-files or to DAT-files.

Then, we'll introduce script M-files, which are created in the edit window. Script M-files allow you to save a list of commands and to execute them later. You will find script M-files especially useful for solving homework problems.

2.3.1   Saving Variables

To preserve the variables you created in the **command window** (check the **workspace window** on the left-hand side of the MATLAB screen for the list of variables) between sessions, you must save the contents of the **workspace window** to a file. The default format is a binary file called a MAT-file. To save the workspace (remember, this is just the set of variables, not the list of commands in the command window) to a file, at the prompt type

```
save < file_name >
```

Although **save** is a MATLAB command, **file_name** is a user defined file name. In this text, we'll indicate user defined names by placing them inside pointed brackets ($<$ $>$). The file name can be any name you choose, as long as it conforms to the variable naming conventions for MATLAB. Actually, you don't even need to supply a file name. If you don't, MATLAB names the file **matlab.mat**. You could also choose **File → Save Workspace As** from the menu bar, which will then prompt you to enter a file name for your data. To restore a workspace, type

```
load < file_name >
```

Again, **load** is a MATLAB command, but **file_name** is the user defined file name. If you just type **load**, MATLAB will look for the default **matlab.mat** file.

The file you save will be stored in the current directory.
For example, type

```
clear, clc
```

This will clear the workspace and the command window. Verify that the work space is empty by checking the workspace window, or by typing

```
whos
```

Now define several variables, such as:

```
A = 5;
B = [1,2,3];
C = [ 1, 2; 3,4];
```

Check the workspace window once again to confirm that the variables have been stored. Now, save the workspace to a file called **my_example_file**:

```
save my_example_file
```

Confirm that a new file has been stored in the current directory. If you prefer to save the file to another directory (for instance, onto a floppy drive), use the browse button (refer to Figure 2.2) to navigate to the directory of your choice. Remember that in a public computer lab, the current directory is probably purged after each user logs off of the system.

Now, clear the workspace and command window by typing

```
clear, clc
```

The workspace window should be empty. Now load the file back into the workspace:

```
load my_example_file
```

Again, the file you want to load must be in the current directory, or else MATLAB won't be able to find it. In the command window, type

A

which returns

A =
            5

Similarly,

B

returns

B =
       1   2   3

and typing

C

returns

C =
           1   2
           3   4

MATLAB can also store individual matrices or lists of matrices into the current directory via the command

save <file_name> <variable_list >

where **file_name** is the user-defined file name where you wish to store the information, and **variable_list** is the list of variables to be stored in the file. For example,

save my_new_file A B

would save just the variables **A** and **B**, into **my_new_file.mat**.

If your saved data will be used by a program other than MATLAB (such as C or C++), the .mat format is not appropriate, because .mat files are unique to MATLAB. The ASCII format is standard between computer platforms and is more appropriate if you need to share files. MATLAB allows you to save files as ASCII files by modifying the save command:

save <file_name> <variable_list> -ascii

The command -ascii tells MATLAB to store the data in a standard 8-digit text format. ASCII files should be saved into a .dat file instead of a .mat file; just be sure to add .dat to your file name—if you don't, it will default to .mat. If more precision is needed, the data can be stored with a 16-digit text format:

save file_name variable_list -ascii -double

It is also possible to delimit the elements (numbers) with tabs:

save <file_name>   <variable_list> -ascii -double -tabs

You can retrieve the data from the current directory with the load command:

load <file_name>

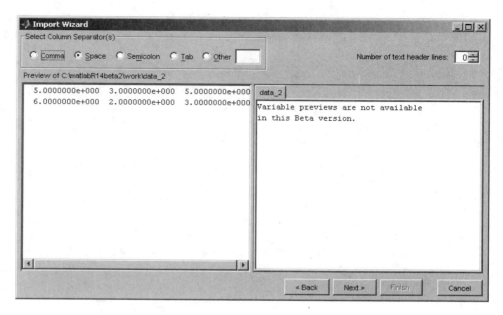

Figure 2.12.   Double clicking the file name in the command directory launches the import wizard.

For example, to create the matrix **Z** and save it to the file **data_2.dat** in 8-digit text format, use the following commands:

```
Z = [5 3 5; 6 2 3];
save data_2.dat Z -ascii
```

This command causes each row of the matrix **Z** to be written to a separate line in the data file. You can view the data_2.dat file by double clicking the file name in the current directory window. (See Figure 2.12.) Follow the directions in the import wizard, which will automatically launch, to load the data into the workspace with the same name as the data file. You can use this same technique to import data from other programs, including Excel spreadsheets, or you can select **File → import data**... from the menu bar.

Perhaps the easiest way to retrieve data from an ASCII. dat file is to enter the **load** command followed by the file name. This will cause the information to be read into a matrix with the same name as the data file.

2.3.2   Script M-Files

In addition to providing an interactive computational environment (using the command window as a scratch pad), MATLAB contains a powerful programming language. As a programmer, you can create and save code in files. The MATLAB files that contain programming code are called M-files. An M-file is an ASCII text file similar to a C or FORTRAN source code file. An M-file can be created and edited using the MATLAB M-file Editor/ Debugger, or you can use another text editor of your choice. The MATLAB editing window is shown in Figure 2.13.

If you choose a different text editor, make sure the files you save are ASCII files. NotePad is an example of a text editor that defaults to an ASCII file structure. Other word processors, such as WordPerfect or Word, will require you to specify the ASCII structure when you save the file. These programs default to proprietary file structures that are not ASCII compliant, and may result in some unexpected results if

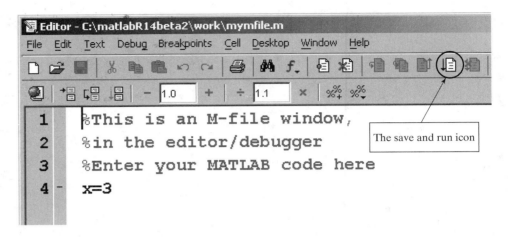

Figure 2.13. The editing window—also called the Editor/Debugger.

you try to use code written in them without specifying that the files are to be saved in ASCII format.

When you save an M-file, it is stored in the current directory. You'll need to name your file with a "legal" MATLAB variable name; that is, one that starts with a letter and contains only letters, numbers, and the underscore (_). Spaces are not allowed.

There are two types of M-files, called scripts and functions. A script M-file is simply a list of MATLAB statements that are saved in a file (typically with a .m file extension). The script has access to workspace variables. Any variables created in the script are accessible to the workspace when the script finishes. A script created in the MATLAB editor window can be executed by selecting the save and run icon from the menu bar. (See Figure 2.13.) Alternately, a script can be executed by typing a filename or by using the run command from the command window.

Assume you have created a script file named myscript.m. You can either run the script from the edit window or use one of the following three ways of executing the script from the command window:

MATLAB Command	Comments
myscript	Type the file name. The .m file extension is assumed.
run myscript	Use the run command with the file name.
run('myscript')	This method uses the functional form of the run command.

All three techniques are equivalent. Which one you choose is strictly a personal preference.

You can find out what M-files and MAT files are in the current directory by typing

    what

into the command window. You can also simply browse through the current directory by looking in the current directory window.

Using script M-files allows you to work on a project and to save the list of commands for future use. Because you will be using these files in the future, it is a good idea to comment them liberally. MATLAB will not execute any code on a commented line. The comment operator is the percentage sign:

    % This is a comment

You can also add comments after a command, but it has to be on the same line:

```
A = 5        %The variable A is defined as 5
```

The MATLAB code that could be used to solve Example 2.3, if it were entered into an M-file, is shown next. It could be run either from the M-file or from the command window. The results will appear in the command window in either case, and the variables will be stored in the workspace. The code is as follows:

```
clear, clc
% A Script M-file to find Drag
%  First define the variables
drag = 20000;            %Define drag in Newtons
r = 0.000001;            %Define air density in kg/m^3
V = 100*0.4470;          %Define velocity in m/s
A = 1;                   %Define area in m^2
% Calculate coefficient of drag
cd = drag *2/(r*V^2*A)
% Find the drag for a variety of velocities
V = 0:20:200;            %Redefine velocity
drag = cd*r*V.^2*A/2;    %Calculate drag
table = [V',drag']       %Create a table of results
```

Example 2.4 uses a script M-file to find the velocity and acceleration of an aircraft using a UDF engine (unducted fan) at different time values.

EXAMPLE 2.4   UDF ENGINE PERFORMANCE

An advanced turboprop engine, called an unducted fan (UDF), is one of the promising new propulsion technologies being developed for future transport aircraft.

    Turboprop engines, which have been in use for decades, combine the power and reliability of jet engines with the efficiency of propellers. They are a significant improvement over earlier piston-powered propeller engines. Their application has been limited to smaller commuter-type aircraft, however, because they are not as fast or powerful as the fanjet engines used on larger airliners. The UDF engine employs significant advancements in propeller technology, narrowing the performance gap between turboprops and fanjets. New materials, blade shapes, and higher rotation speeds enable UDF-powered aircraft to fly almost as fast as fanjets, and with greater fuel efficiency. The UDF is also significantly quieter than the conventional turboprop.

    During the test flight of a UDF-powered aircraft, the test pilot has set the engine power level at 40,000 Newtons, which causes the 20,000 kg aircraft to attain a cruise speed of 180 m/s. The engine throttles are then set to a power level of 60,000 Newtons, and the aircraft begins to accelerate. As the speed of the plane increases, the aerodynamic drag increases in proportion to the square of the air speed. Eventually, the aircraft reaches a new cruise speed, where the thrust from the UDF engines is just offset by the drag. The equations used to estimate the velocity and acceleration of the aircraft from the time the throttle is reset to the time the plane reaches new cruise speed (at approximately 120 s) are the following:

$$\text{velocity} = 0.00001\ \text{time}^3 - 0.00488\ \text{time}^2 + 0.75795\ \text{time} + 181.3566$$

$$\text{acceleration} = 3 - 0.000062\ \text{velocity}^2$$

Figure 2.14. An unducted fan engine (UDF).

Write a MATLAB program, using a script M-file, that calculates the velocity and acceleration of the aircraft at times from 0 to 120 seconds, and at increments of 10 seconds. Assume that time zero represents the point at which the power level was increased. Display the results in a table of time, velocity, and acceleration.

1.   State the Problem

Calculate the velocity and acceleration, using a script M-file.

2.   Describe the Input and Output

Input

Start time is	0 seconds
Final time is	120 seconds
Time increment is	10 seconds

Output

velocity
acceleration

3.   Hand Example

Solve the equations stated in the problem for time = 100 seconds;

$$\text{velocity} = 0.00001\,\text{time}^3 - 0.00488\,\text{time}^2 + 0.75795\,\text{time} + 181.3566$$
$$= 218.35 \text{ m/sec}$$
$$\text{acceleration} = 3 - 0.000062\,\text{velocity}^2$$
$$= 0.04404 \text{ m/sec}^2$$

4. Develop a MATLAB Solution

Create a new script M-file, using the **File → New → m-file** menu selection. Enter these commands:

```
clear, clc
%Example 2.4
%These commands generate velocity and acceleration
%values for a UDF aircraft test
%Define the time matrix
time = 0:10:120;
%Calculate the velocity matrix
velocity = 0.00001*time.^3 - 0.00488*time.^2 ...
                + 0.75795*time + 181.3566;
%Use the calculated velocities to find the acceleration
acceleration = 3 - 6.2e-5*velocity.^2;
%Present the results in a table
[time', velocity', acceleration']
```

Save the file with a name of your choice, using the file selection from the menu bar. Remember that the file name needs to be a legitimate variable name. For example, save the file as **example_4_chapter_2**.

Execute the file by selecting the run icon from the menu bar. The results will be displayed in the command window.

```
ans =
          0        181.3566     0.9608
    10.0000        188.4581     0.7980
    20.0000        194.6436     0.6511
    30.0000        199.9731     0.5207
    40.0000        204.5066     0.4070
    50.0000        208.3041     0.3098
    60.0000        211.4256     0.2286
    70.0000        213.9311     0.1625
    80.0000        215.8806     0.1105
    90.0000        217.3341     0.0715
   100.0000        218.3516     0.0440
   110.0000        218.9931     0.0266
   120.0000        219.3186     0.0178
```

Figure 2.15 is a picture of the MATLAB environment, after the script M-file was executed. Notice the list of variables in the workspace window and the list of files in the current directory window. The current directory window was moved out from under the workspace window by clicking and dragging, so that both could be viewed at the same time. Notice that the command history window *does not* reflect the commands issued and executed in the script M-file.

5. Test the Solution

Compare the MATLAB results to the hand example results. Notice that the velocity and acceleration calculated from the hand example and the MATLAB solution match. Now that you have a MATLAB program that works, you can modify it for other equations chosen to model aircraft behavior. ■

SUMMARY

In this chapter, we introduced you to the MATLAB environment. In particular, we explored the window structure and solved problems in the command window. The primary data structure in MATLAB is a matrix, which can be a single point (a scalar), a

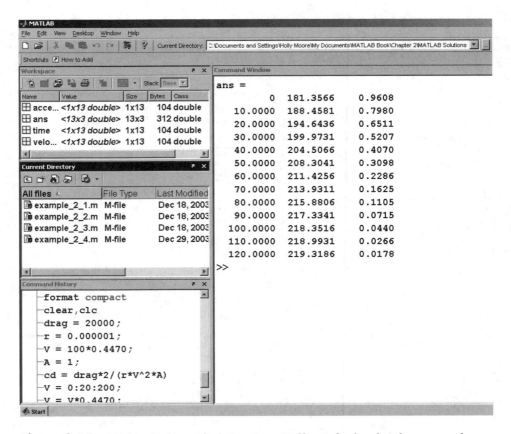

Figure 2.15. The results from calculations in an M-file are displayed in the command window.

list of values (a vector), or a rectangular grid of values with rows and columns. Values can be entered into a matrix by explicitly listing the values or by loading them from MAT files or ASCII files. In addition, we learned how to save values into both MAT files and ASCII files. We explored the various mathematical operations that are performed in an element-by-element manner. Finally, we learned how to use a script M-file to record the sequence of commands used to solve a MATLAB problem.

MATLAB SUMMARY

This MATLAB summary lists all of the special characters, commands, and functions that were defined in this chapter:

Special Characters	
[ ]	forms matrices
( )	used in statements to group operations
	used with a matrix name to identify specific elements
,	separates subscripts or matrix elements
;	separates rows in a matrix definition
	suppresses output when used in commands
:	used to generate matrices
	indicates all rows or all columns

=	assignment operator—assigns a value to a memory location—not the same as an equality
%	indicates a comment in an M-file
+	scalar and array addition
−	scalar and array subtraction
*	scalar multiplication
.*	array multiplication
/	scalar division
./	array division
∧	scalar exponentiation
.∧	array exponentiation

Commands and Functions

`ans`	default variable name for results of MATLAB calculations
`clc`	clears command screen
`clear`	clears workspace
`exit`	terminates MATLAB
`format +`	sets format to plus and minus signs only
`format compact`	sets format to compact form
`format long`	sets format to 14 decimal places
`formal long e`	sets format to 14 exponential places
`format loose`	sets format back to default, non-compact form
`format short`	sets format back to default, four decimal places
`format short e`	sets format to four exponential places
`help`	invokes help utility
`linspace`	linearly spaced vector function
`load`	loads matrices from a file
`pi`	numeric approximation of the value of π
`quit`	terminates MATLAB
`save`	saves variables in a file
`who`	lists variables in memory
`whos`	lists variables and their sizes

KEY TERMS

arguments	document window	prompt
array editor	edit window	scalar
ASCII	function	scientific notation
assignment operator	graphics window	script
command history	M-file	start button
command window	MAT-file	transpose operator
current directory	matrix	vector
DAT-file	operator	workspace

Problems

 1. Which of the following are legitimate variable names in MATLAB?

   a. 3vars

   b. global

    c.   help

    d.   My_var

    e.   sin

    f.   X + Y

    g.   _input

    h.   input

    i.   tax-rate

    j.   example1.1

    k.   example1_1

Test your answers by trying to assign a value to each name by using, for example,

    3vars = 3

or by using **isvarname**, as in

    isvarname 3vars

Remember, **isvarname** returns a 1 if the name is legal and a 0 if it is not. Although it is possible to reassign a function name as a variable name, it's not a good idea. Use **which** to check whether the preceding names are function names, as in

    which sin

In what case would MATLAB tell you that **sin** is a variable name, not a function name?

 2. Predict the outcome of the following MATLAB calculations:

$$1 + 3/4$$
$$5 \times 6 \times 4/2$$
$$5/2 \times 6 \times 4$$
$$5^\wedge 2 \times 3$$
$$5^\wedge(2 \times 3)$$
$$1 + 3 + 5/5 + 3 + 1$$
$$(1 + 3 + 5)/(5 + 3 + 1)$$

Check your results by entering the calculations into the command window.

 3. Create MATLAB code to perform the following calculations:

$$5^2$$
$$\frac{5 + 3}{5 \cdot 6}$$
$$\sqrt{4 + 6^3}$$

Hint: A square root is the same thing as a $\frac{1}{2}$ power.

$$9\frac{6}{12} + 7 \cdot 5^{3+2}$$
$$1 + 5 \cdot 3/6^2 + 2^{2-4} \cdot 1/5.5$$

Check your code by entering it into MATLAB and performing the calculations on your scientific calculator.

4. a. The area of a circle is πr^2. Define r as 5, and then find the area of a circle, using MATLAB.
    b. The surface area of a sphere is $4\pi r^2$. Find the surface area of a sphere with a radius of 10 ft.
    c. The volume of a sphere is $\frac{4}{3}\pi r^3$. Find the volume of a sphere with a radius of 2 ft.

5. a. The volume of a cylinder is $\pi r^2 h$. Define r as 3 and **h** as the matrix

    h = [1,5,12]

    find the volume of the cylinders.
    b. The area of a triangle is $\frac{1}{2}$ base $\times$ height. Define the base as the matrix

    b = [2,4,6]

    and the height h as 12, and find the area of the triangles.
    c. The volume of any right prism is~~base~~ area of base $\times$ vertical_dimension. Find the volume of the triangles in problem (b), for a vertical dimension of 10.

6. a. Generate an evenly spaced vector of values from 1 to 20, in increments of 1.
    b. Generate a vector of values from zero to 2π in increments of $\pi/100$.
    c. Generate a vector containing 15 values, evenly spaced between 4 and 20.

> *Hint:* Use the linspace command. If you can't remember the syntax, type
>
> **help linspace**

7. Generate a table of conversions from degrees to radians. The first line should contain the values for $0°$, the second line should contain the values for $10°$, and so on. The last line should contain the values for $360°$.

8. Generate a table of conversions from centimeters to inches. Start the centimeters column at 0 and increment by 2 centimeters. The last line should contain the value 50 cm.

9. Generate a table of conversions from mi/h to ft/s. The initial value in the mi/h column should be 0 and the final value should be 100. Print 14 values in your table.

10. The general equation for the distance that a free falling body has traveled (neglecting air friction) is

$$d = \tfrac{1}{2}gt^2.$$

Assume that $g = 9.8$ m/s^2. Generate a table of time versus distance traveled.

> *Hint:* Be careful to use the correct operators: t^2 is an array operation!

11. Newton's law of universal gravitation tells us that the force exerted by one particle on another is

$$F = G\frac{m_1 m_2}{r^2}$$

where the universal gravitational constant is found experimentally to be

$$G = 6.673 \times 10^{-11} \text{ N } m^2/\text{kg}^2.$$

take times
btv
0-1 in inc
of 1

The mass of each object is m_1 and m_2, respectively, and r is the distance between the two particles. Use Newton's law of universal gravitation to find the force exerted by the earth on the moon, assuming that

the mass of the earth is approximately 6×10^{24} kg,
the mass of the moon is approximately 7.4×10^{22} kg, and
the earth and the moon are an average of 3.9×10^8 m apart.

12. We know the earth and the moon are not always the same distance apart. Find the force the moon exerts on the earth for 10 distances between 3.8×10^8 m and 4.0×10^8 m.

13. Your instructor will provide you with a file called volatage.dat, which represents data collected during an experiment. We know from Ohm's law that

$$V = I \cdot R.$$

If the resistance in the circuit is constant at 4 ohms, use MATLAB to find the current corresponding to each voltage. First you'll need to load the data into MATLAB, then perform the calculations, and finally create a table of results. Save your table of results into an ASCII file called current.dat.

3

Predefined MATLAB Functions

GRAND CHALLENGE: WEATHER PREDICTION

Weather satellites provide a great deal of information to meteorologists, who attempt to predict the weather. Large volumes of historical weather data can also be analyzed and used to test models for predicting weather. In general, meteorologists can do a reasonably good job of predicting overall weather patterns. However, local weather phenomena, such as tornadoes, water spouts, and microbursts, are still very difficult to predict. Even predicting heavy rainfall or large hail from thunderstorms is often difficult. Although Doppler radar is useful in locating regions within storms that could contain tornadoes or microbursts, the radar detects the events as they occur and thus allows little time for issuing appropriate warnings to populated areas or aircraft passing through the region. Accurate and timely prediction of weather and associated weather phenomena is still an elusive goal.

3.1 USING PREDEFINED FUNCTIONS

Arithmetic expressions often require computations other than addition, subtraction, multiplication, division, and exponentiation. For example, many expressions require the use of logarithms, exponentials, and trigonometric functions. MATLAB includes a built-in library of these useful functions. For example, if we want to compute the square root of **x** and store the result in **b**, we can use the following command:

```
b = sqrt(x);
```

This statement is valid if **x** is a scalar or a matrix. If **x** is a matrix, the function will be applied element by element to the values in the matrix.

SECTIONS

3.1 Using Predefined Functions
3.2 Manipulating Matrices
3.3 Computational Limitations
3.4 Special Values and Functions

OBJECTIVES

After reading this chapter, you should be able to

- apply a variety of mathematical and trigonometric functions to matrices
- compute and use descriptive statistical functions, as they apply to matrices
- generate uniform and Gaussian random sequences
- manipulate matrices
- understand the computational limits inherent in MATLAB
- recognize and be able to use the special values and functions built into MATLAB

For example,

```
x = 9;
b = sqrt(x)
```

returns

```
b =
    3
```

but if **x** is a matrix,

```
x = [4, 9, 16];
b = sqrt(x)
```

returns

```
b =
    2    3    4
```

All functions can be thought of as having three components: a name, input, and output. In this example, the name of the function is **sqrt**, the required input (also called the argument) goes inside the parentheses and can be a scalar or a matrix, and the output is a calculated value or values. The output was assigned the variable name **b**.

Some functions require multiple inputs. For example, the remainder function, **rem**, requires two inputs—a dividend and a divisor. We represent this as **rem(x,y)**. Hence,

rem(10,3)   calculates the remainder of 10 divided by 3

```
ans =
     1
```

The size command is an example of a function that returns two outputs. The size command determines the number of rows and columns in a matrix. Thus,

```
d = [1, 2, 3; 4, 5, 6];
f = size(d)
```

returns

```
f =
    2    3
```

The result of the size function is a matrix with two values. Alternatively, you can assign variable names to each of the answers by representing the left-hand side of the assignment statement as a matrix, as in

```
[x,y] = size(d)
```

which returns

```
x =
    2
y =
    3
```

You can create complex expressions by nesting functions. For example,

```
g = sqrt(sin(x))
```

will find the square root of the sine of whatever values are stored in the matrix named **x**. Since **x** was assigned a value of 2 earlier in this section, the result is

```
g =
    0.9536
```

When one function is used to compute the argument of another function, be sure to enclose the argument of each function in its own set of parentheses. The nesting of **functions** is also called **composition of functions**.

3.1.1   Using the Help Feature

MATLAB includes extensive help tools, which are especially useful for interpreting function syntax. There are three ways to get help from within MATLAB: a command-line help function (**help**), a separate windowed help function (**helpwin**), and an HTML-based documentation set.

To use the command-line help function, type **help** in the command window:

```
help
```

A list of help topics will appear, as follows:

```
HELP topics:

matlab\general   - general purpose commands
matlab\ops       - operators and special characters
matlab\lang      - programming language constructs
matlab\elmat     - elementary matrices and matrix manipulation
matlab\elfun     - elementary math functions
matlab\specfun   - specialized math functions . . .
```

To get help on a particular topic, type **help <topic>**. For example, to get help on the tangent function, type

```
help tan
```

The following should be displayed:

```
TAN  Tangent.
  TAN(X) is the tangent of the elements of X.

  See also ATAN, ATAN2.
```

To use the windowed help screen, select **Help -> MATLAB Help** from the menu bar. A windowed version of the help list will appear.

This help function includes a MATLAB tutorial that you will find extremely useful. As shown in Figure 3.1, the list in the left-hand window is a table of contents. Notice also that the table of contents includes a link to a list of **functions**, organized both by category and alphabetically by name. You can use this link to find out what MATLAB functions are available to solve most problems. For example, you probably are not familiar with a mathematical function called the "error function." One place the error function occurs is in the solution to transient heat transfer problems. Use the MATLAB help window to determine if a MATLAB function is available for the error function.

Select the **MATLAB Functions Listed by Category** link, then the Mathematics link. (See Figure 3.2.)

Near the bottom of the page is the category Specialized Math, which lists the error function. Follow the links to the error function description. The MATLAB function for the error function is **erf**, and it requires a single input. For example,

```
erf(0.8)
```

returns

```
ans =
      0.7421
```

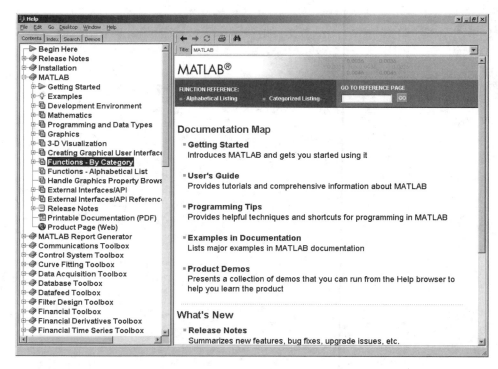

Figure 3.1. The MATLAB Help environment.

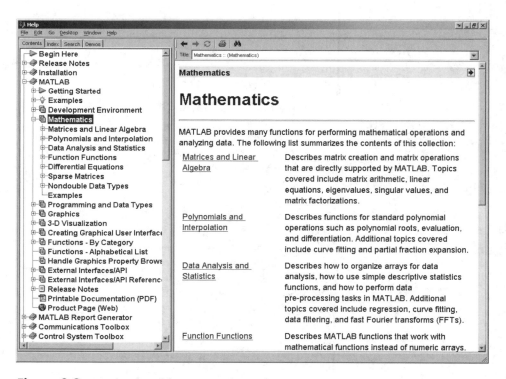

Figure 3.2. Mathematical functions Help window.

Finally, if you are connected to the Internet, use the start button in the lower left-hand corner of the MATLAB window to access MATLAB's online content. You'll also want to check out The MathWorks website at www.mathworks.com.

3.1.2 Elementary Math Functions

The elementary math functions include functions to perform a number of common computations, such as computing the absolute value and the square root of a number. In addition, in this section we include a group of functions used to perform rounding:

abs(x)	Computes the absolute value of **x**.	**abs(−3)** **ans = 3**
sqrt(x)	Computes the square root of **x**.	**sqrt(85)** **ans = 9.2195**
round(x)	Rounds **x** to the nearest integer.	**round(8.6)** **ans = 9**
fix(x)	Rounds (or truncates) **x** to the nearest integer toward zero.	**fix(8.6)** **ans = 8**
floor(x)	Rounds **x** to the nearest integer toward − infinity.	**floor(−8.6)** **ans = −9**
ceil(x)	Rounds **x** to the nearest integer toward + infinity.	**ceil(−8.6)** **ans =−8**
sign(x)	Returns a value of −1 if **x** is less than zero, a value of 0 if **x** equals zero, and a value of +1 if **x** is greater than zero.	**sign(−8)** **ans = −1**
rem(x,y)	Computes the remainder of **x/y**.	**rem(25,4)** **ans = 1**
exp(x)	Computes the value of e^x, where e is the base for natural logarithms, or approximately 2.718282.	**exp(10)** **ans = 2.2026e + 004**
log(x)	Computes the ln(**x**), the natural logarithm of **x** to the base e.	**log(10)** **ans = 2.3026**
log10(x)	Computes the $\log_{10}$(**x**), the common logarithm of **x** to the base 10.	**log10(10)** **ans = 1**

Logarithms deserve special mention in this section. As a rule, the function **log** in all computer languages means the **natural logarithm**. Although not the standard in mathematics text books, this *is* the standard in computer programming. This is a common source of errors, especially for new users. If you want the log base 10, you'll need to use the **log10** function. A **log2** function is also included in MATLAB, but logarithms to any other base will need to be computed; there is no general logarithm function that allows the user to input the base.

You can find the syntax for other common mathematical functions by selecting **Help** from the tool bar, and following the **Mathematics** link.

EXAMPLE 3.1

USING THE CLAUSIUS–CLAPEYRON EQUATION

Meteorologists study the atmosphere in an attempt to understand and ultimately predict the weather. Weather prediction is a complicated process, even with the best data. Meteorologists study chemistry, physics, thermodynamics, and geography, in addition to specialized courses about the atmosphere. (See Figure 3.3.) One equation used by meteorologists is the Clausius–Clapeyron equation, which is usually introduced in chemistry classes and examined in more detail in thermodynamics classes.

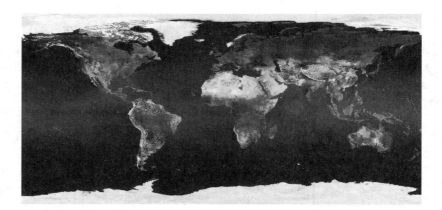

Figure 3.3. View of the earth's weather from space.

In meteorology, the Clausius–Clapeyron equation is used to determine the relationship between saturation water-vapor pressure and the atmospheric temperature. The saturation water-vapor pressure can be used to calculate relative humidity, an important component of weather prediction, when the actual partial pressure of water in the air is known.

The Clausius–Clapeyron equation is.

$$\ln(P^\circ/6.11) = \left(\frac{\Delta H_v}{R_{\text{air}}}\right)\circ\left(\frac{1}{273} - \frac{1}{T}\right)$$

where

P° is the saturation vapor pressure for water, in mbar, at temperature T

ΔH_v is the latent heat of vaporization for water, 2.453×10^6 J/kg

R_{air} is the gas constant for moist air, 461 J/kg

T is the temperature in degrees K

It is rare that temperatures on the surface of the earth are lower than –60°F or higher than 120°F. Use the Clausius–Clapeyron equation to find the saturation vapor pressure for temperatures in this range. Present your results as a table of temperature in Fahrenheit and saturation vapor pressure.

SOLUTION

1.   State the Problem

Find the saturation vapor pressure at temperatures from –60°F to 120°F, using the Clausius–Clapeyron equation.

2.   Describe the Input and Output

Input

$$\Delta H_v = 2.453 \times 10^6 \text{ J/kg}$$

$$R_{air} = 461 \text{ J/kg}$$

$$T = -60°\text{F to } 120°\text{F}$$

Since the number of temperature values was not specified, we'll choose to recalculate every 10°F.

Output

Saturation vapor pressures

3.   Hand Example

The Clausius–Clapeyron equation requires all the variables to have consistent units. That means that temperature (T) needs to be in degrees K. To change Fahrenheit to Kelvin, type

$$T_k = (T_f + 459.6)/1.8$$

(There are many places to find unit conversions. The Internet is one source, as are science and engineering text books.)

Now we need to solve the Clausius–Clapeyron equation for the saturation vapor pressure ($P°$). We have

$$\ln(P°/6.11) = \left(\frac{\Delta H_v}{R_{air}}\right) \cdot \left(\frac{1}{273} - \frac{1}{T}\right)$$

$$P° = 6.11 \cdot \exp\left(\left(\frac{\Delta H_v}{R_{air}}\right) \cdot \left(\frac{1}{273} - \frac{1}{T}\right)\right)$$

Solve for one temperature, for example $T = 0°$F:

$$T = (0 + 459.6)/1.8 = 255.3333$$

$$P° = 6.11 \cdot \exp\left(\left(\frac{2.453 \times 10^6}{461}\right) \cdot \left(\frac{1}{273} - \frac{1}{255.3333}\right)\right) = 1.5836 \text{ mbar}$$

4.   Develop a MATLAB Solution

Create the MATLAB solution in an M-file, and then run it in the command environment:

```
%Example 3.1
%Using the Clausius Clapeyron Equation, find the
%saturation vapor pressure for water at different temperatures
%
TF=[-60:10:120];           %Define temp matrix in F
TK=(TF + 459.6)/1.8;       %Convert temp to K
Delta_H=2.45e6;            %Define latent heat of vaporization
R_air = 461;               %Define ideal gas constant for air
%
%Calculate the Vapor Pressures
Vapor_Pressure = 6.11*exp((Delta_H/R_air)*(1/273 - 1./TK));
%Display the results in a table
my_results = [TF',Vapor_Pressure']
```

When creating a MATLAB program, it is a good idea to comment liberally (**%**). This makes your program easier for others to understand, and may make it easier for you to "debug." Notice that most of the lines of code end with a semicolon, which suppresses the output. Therefore, the only information that displays in the command window is the table **my_results**:

```
my_results =
      -60.0000      0.0698
      -50.0000      0.1252
      -40.0000      0.2184
      -30.0000      0.3714
      -20.0000      0.6163
      -10.0000      1.0000
            0       1.5888
       10.0000      2.4749
       20.0000      3.7847
       30.0000      5.6880
       40.0000      8.4102
       50.0000     12.2458
       60.0000     17.5747
       70.0000     24.8807
       80.0000     34.7729
       90.0000     48.0098
      100.0000     65.5257
      110.0000     88.4608
      120.0000    118.1931
```

5.   Test the Solution

Compare the result from the MATLAB solution with the hand solution when $T = 0°F$:

Hand solution $P° = 1.5888$ mbar

MATLAB solution $\mathbf{P}° = 1.5888$ mbar

The Clausius–Clapeyron equation can be used for more than just humidity problems. By changing the value of ΔH and R, you could generalize the program to any condensing vapor. ∎

3.1.3   Trigonometric Functions

The trigonometric functions assume that angles are represented in radians. To convert radians to degrees or degrees to radians, use the following conversions, which utilize the fact that $180° = \pi$ radians:

```
angle_degrees = angle_radians*(180/pi);
angle_radians = angle_degrees*(pi/180);
```

In trigonometric calculations, the value of π is often needed, so a constant, **pi**, is built into MATLAB. However, since π cannot be expressed as a floating-point number, the constant **pi** in MATLAB is only an approximation of the mathematical quantity π. Usually this is not important; however, you may notice some surprising results—for example,

```
sin(pi)
```

```
ans =
        1.2246e-016
```

when you expect an answer of zero.

Access the Help function from the menu bar and follow the instructions in Section 3.1.1 for a complete list of trigonometric functions available in MATLAB. Here are some of the more common:

sin(x)	Computes the sine of **x**, where **x** is in radians.	**sin(0)** **ans = 0**
cos(x)	Computes the cosine of **x**, where **x** is in radians.	**cos(pi)** **ans = −1**
tan(x)	Computes the tangent of **x**, where **x** is in radians.	**tan(pi)** **ans =** **−1.2246e-016**
asin(x)	Computes the arcsine, or inverse sine, of **x**, where **x** must be between −1 and 1. The function returns an angle in radians between $\pi/2$ and $-\pi/2$.	**asin(−1)** **ans =** **−1.5708**
sinh(x)	Computes the hyperbolic sine of **x**, where **x** is in radians.	**sinh(pi)** **ans =** **11.5487**

EXAMPLE 3.2

USING TRIGONOMETRIC FUNCTIONS

One of the basic calculations in engineering is finding the resulting force on an object that is being pushed and/or pulled in multiple directions. Adding up forces is the primary calculation performed in both statics and dynamics classes. Consider a balloon, such as the one shown in Figure 3.4, that is experiencing the following forces: gravity, wind, and buoyancy.

To find the net force acting on the balloon, we need to add up the force due to gravity, the force due to buoyancy, and the force due to the wind. One approach is to

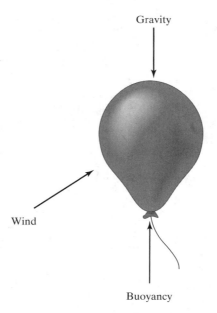

Gravity

Wind

Buoyancy

Figure 3.4. Force balance on a weather balloon.

find the net force in the x direction and the net force in the y direction for each individual force, and then recombine them into a final result.

The force in the x direction can be found using trigonometry:

    F is the total force
    $\mathbf{F}_x$ is the force in the x direction
    $\mathbf{F}_y$ is the force in the y direction

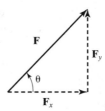

We know from trigonometry that the definition of sine is side opposite over the hypotenuse, so

$$\sin(\theta) = F_y/F \text{ and therefore}$$
$$F_y = F \sin(\theta)$$

Similarly, since the definition of cos is side adjacent over the hypotenuse, $F_x = F \cos(\theta)$.

We can add up all of the forces in the x direction and all of the forces in the y direction, and use these totals to find the resulting force:

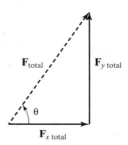

To find the magnitude and angle for F_{total}, we can use trigonometry again. The definition of tangent is side opposite over side adjacent. Therefore,

$$\tan(\theta) = F_{y\,total}/F_{x\,total}$$

We can use an inverse tangent to find θ:

$$\theta = \tan^{-1}(F_{y\,total}/F_{x\,total})$$

(inverse tangent is also called arctangent—you'll see it on your scientific calculator as atan). Once we know θ, we can find F_{total}, using either sine or cosine. We have

$$F_{x\,total} = F_{total} \cos(\theta)$$

and rearranging yields

$$F_{total} = F_{x\,total}/\cos(\theta)$$

Now consider the balloon shown at the outset of this problem. Assume that the force due to gravity on this particular balloon is 100 N, pointed down. Assume further that the buoyant force is 200 N, pointed up. Finally, assume that the wind is pushing on the balloon with a force of 50 N, at an angle of 30 degrees from horizontal. These three assumptions may be depicted as follows:

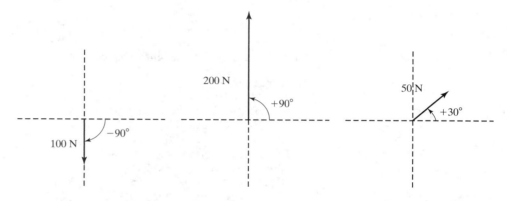

Find the resulting force on the balloon.

SOLUTION

1. State the Problem

Find the resulting force on a balloon. Consider the force due to gravity, buoyancy, and wind.

2. Describe the Input and Output

Input

Force	Magnitude	Direction
Gravity	100 N	−90 degrees
Buoyancy	200 N	+90 degrees
Wind	50 N	+30 degrees

Output

We'll need to find both the magnitude and the direction of the resulting force.

3. Hand Example

First find the x and y components of each force and sum the components:

Force	Horizontal Component	Vertical Component
Gravity	$F_x = F\cos(\theta)$ $F_x = 100\cos(-90°) = 0$ N	$F_y = F\sin(\theta)$ $F_y = 100\sin(-90°) = -100$ N
Buoyancy	$F_x = F\cos(\theta)$ $F_x = 200\cos(+90°) = 0$ N	$F_y = F\sin(\theta)$ $F_y = 200\sin(+90°) = +200$ N
Wind	$F_x = F\cos(\theta)$ $F_x = 50\cos(+30°) = 43.301$ N	$F_y = F\sin(\theta)$ $F_y = 50\sin(+30°) = +25$ N
Sum	$F_{x\,total} = 0 + 0 + 43.301$ $= 43.301$ N	$F_{y\,total} = -100 + 200 + 25$ $= 125$ N

Find the resulting angle:

$$\theta = \tan^{-1}(F_{y\ total}/F_{x\ total})$$
$$\theta = \tan^{-1}(125/43.301) = 70.89°$$

Find the magnitude of the total force:

$$F_{total} = F_{x\ total}/\cos(\theta)$$
$$F_{total} = 43.301/\cos(70.89°) = 132.29\ N$$

4.   Develop a MATLAB Solution

```
%Example 3_2
clear, clc
% Define the input
F =[100, 200, 50];
theta = [-90, +90, +30];
%convert angles to radians
theta = theta*pi/180;
%Find the x components
FX = F.*cos(theta);
%Sum the x components
FXtotal = sum(FX);
%Find and sum the y components in the same step
FYtotal = sum(F.*sin(theta));
%Find the resulting angle in radians
result_angle = atan(FYtotal/FXtotal);
%Find the resulting angle in degrees
result_degrees = result_angle*180/pi
%Find the magnitude of the resulting force
Ftotal = FXtotal/cos(result_angle)
```

returns

```
result_degrees =
        70.8934

Ftotal =
        132.2876
```

Notice that the values for force and the angle were entered into an array. This makes the solution more general. Also notice that the angles were converted to radians. In the final program listed above, the output from all but the final calculations was suppressed. However, while developing the program we left off the semicolons so that we could observe the intermediate results.

5.   Test the Solution

Compare the MATLAB solution to the hand solution. Now that you know it works, you can use the program to find the resultant of multiple forces. Just add the additional information to the definitions of the force vector **F** and the angle vector **theta**. We also assumed a two-dimensional world in this example, but it would be easy to extend our solution to forces in all three dimensions.   ■

3.1.4   Data Analysis Functions

Analyzing data is an important part of evaluating test results. MATLAB contains a number of functions that make it easier to evaluate and analyze data. We first present a number of simple analysis functions, and then functions that compute more complicated measures or "metrics" related to a data set.

Simple Analysis

The following groups of functions are frequently used in evaluating a set of test data:

Maximum and Minimum   This set of functions can be used to determine maximums and minimums, and their locations in a matrix:

max(x)	Returns the largest value in a vector **x**. For example if **x** = [1 5 3], the maximum value is 5.	`x=[1, 5, 3];`
		`max(x)`
		`ans =`
		`        5`

	Returns a row vector containing the maximum element from each column of a matrix **x**. For example if $\mathbf{x} = \begin{bmatrix} 1 & 5 & 3 \\ 2 & 4 & 6 \end{bmatrix}$, the maximum value in column 1 is 2, the maximum value in column 2 is 5, and the maximum value in column 3 is 6	`x=[1, 5, 3; 2, 4, 6];`
		`max(x)`
		
		`ans =`
		
		`    2    5    6`

[a,b] =
   max(x)
	Returns both the largest value in a vector **x** and its location in vector **x**. For **x** =[1 5 3], the maximum value is named **a** and is found to be 5. The location of the maximum value is element 2 and is named **b**.	`x=[1, 5, 3];`
		`[a,b]=max(x)`
		`a =`
		`    5`
		
		`b =`
		`    2`

	Returns a row vector containing the maximum element from each column of a matrix **x**, and returns a row vector of the location of the maximum in each column of matrix **x**. For example, if $\mathbf{x} = \begin{bmatrix} 1 & 5 & 3 \\ 2 & 4 & 6 \end{bmatrix}$, the maximum value in column 1 is 2, the maximum value in column 2 is 5, and the maximum value in column 3 is 6. These maxima occur in row 2, row 1, and row 2, respectively.	`x=[1, 5, 3; 2, 4, 6];`
		`[a,b]=max(x)`
		`a =`
		`    2    5    6`
		
		`b =`
		
		`    2    1    2`

max(x, y)	Returns a matrix the same size as **x** and **y**. (Both **x** and **y** must have the same number of rows and columns.) Each element in the resulting matrix contains the maximum value from the corresponding positions in **x** and **y**. For example if $\mathbf{x} = \begin{bmatrix} 1 & 5 & 3 \\ 2 & 4 & 6 \end{bmatrix}$, and $\mathbf{y} = \begin{bmatrix} 10 & 2 & 4 \\ 1 & 8 & 7 \end{bmatrix}$, the resulting matrix will be $$\mathbf{ans} = \begin{bmatrix} 10 & 5 & 4 \\ 2 & 8 & 7 \end{bmatrix}$$	`x=[1, 5, 3; 2, 4, 6];`
		`y=[10, 2, 4; 1, 8,7];`
		`max(x,y)`
		`ans =`
		`    10    5    4`
		`     2    8    7`

min(x) Returns the smallest value in a vector **x**. For example if **x** = [1 5 3], the minimum value is 1.

```
x=[1, 5, 3];
```

Returns a row vector containing the minimum element from each column of a matrix **x**. For example, if $\mathbf{x} = \begin{bmatrix} 1 & 5 & 3 \\ 2 & 4 & 6 \end{bmatrix}$, the minimum value in column 1 is 1, the minimum value in column 2 is 4, and the minimum value in column 3 is 3.

```
x=[1, 5, 3; 2, 4, 6];
min(x)

ans =

    1    4    3
min    (x)
ans =
```

[a,b]= min(x) Returns both the smallest value in a vector **x** and its location in vector **x**. For **x** = [1 5 3], the minimum value is named **a** and is found to be 1. The location of the minimum value is element 1 and is named **b**.

```
x=[1, 5, 3];
[a, b]=min(x)
a =
    1
b =
    1
```

Returns a row vector containing the minimum element from each column of a matrix **x**, and returns a row vector of the location of the minimum in each column of matrix **x**. For example, if $\mathbf{x} = \begin{bmatrix} 1 & 5 & 3 \\ 2 & 4 & 6 \end{bmatrix}$, the minimum value in column 1 is 1, the minimum value in

column 2 is 4, and the minimum value in column 3 is 3. These minima occur in row 1, row 2, and row 1, respectively.

```
x=[1, 5, 3; 2, 4, 6];
[a,b]=min(x)
a =
    1    4    3
b =
    1    2    1
```

min(x,y) Returns a matrix the same size as **x** and **y**. (Both **x** and **y** must have the same number of rows and columns.) Each element in the resulting matrix contains the minimum value from the corresponding positions in **x** and **y**. For example, if

$$\mathbf{x} = \begin{bmatrix} 1 & 5 & 3 \\ 2 & 4 & 6 \end{bmatrix}, \text{ and } \mathbf{y} = \begin{bmatrix} 10 & 2 & 4 \\ 1 & 8 & 7 \end{bmatrix}, \text{ the}$$

resulting matrix will be **ans** $= \begin{bmatrix} 1 & 2 & 3 \\ 1 & 4 & 6 \end{bmatrix}$

```
x=[1, 5, 3; 2, 4, 6];
y=[10, 2, 4; 1, 8, 7];
min(x,y)
ans =

    1    2    3
    1    4    6
```

Mean and Median The **mean** of a group of values is the average of the values. The Greek symbol μ (mu) is used to represent the value of the mean in many mathematics and engineering applications:

$$\mu = \frac{\sum_{k=1}^{N} x_k}{N}$$

$$\sum_{k=1}^{N} x_k = x_1 + x_2 + x_3 + \cdots + x_N$$

In simple terms, to find the mean, just add up all the values and divide by the total.

The **median** is the value in the middle of the group, assuming that the values are sorted. If there is an odd number of values, the median is the value in the middle position. If there is an even number of values, then the median is the mean of the two middle values. The functions for computing the mean and the median are as follows:

`mean(x)`	Computes the mean value (or average value) of a vector **x**. For example if **x** = [1 5 3], the mean value is 3.	`x=[1, 5, 3];`
		`mean(x)`
		`ans =`
		    `3.0000`

	Returns a row vector containing the mean value from each column of a matrix **x**. For example, if $\mathbf{x} = \begin{bmatrix} 1 & 5 & 3 \\ 2 & 4 & 6 \end{bmatrix}$, the mean value of column 1 is 1.5, the mean value of column 2 is 4.5, and the mean value of column 3 is 4.5.	`x=[1, 5, 3; 2, 4, 6];`
		`mean(x)`
		`ans =`
		   `1.5    4.5    4.5`

`median(x)`	Finds the median of the elements of a vector **x**. For example, if **x** = [1 5 3], the median value is 3.	`x=[1, 5, 3];`
		`median(x)`
		`ans =`
		    `3`

	Returns a row vector containing the median value from each column of a matrix **x**. For example, if $\mathbf{x} = \begin{bmatrix} 1 & 5 & 3 \\ 2 & 4 & 6 \\ 3 & 8 & 4 \end{bmatrix}$, the median value from column 1 is 2, the median value from column 2 is 5, and the median value from column 3 is 4.	`x=[1, 5, 3;`
		`2, 4, 6;`
		`3, 8, 4];`
		`median(x)`
		`ans =`
		   `2    5    4`

Sums and Products   MATLAB contains the following functions for computing the sums and products of vectors (or of the columns in a matrix) and functions for computing the cumulative sums and products of vectors (or the elements of a matrix):

`sum(x)`	Computes the sum of the elements of a vector **x**. For example, if **x** = [1 5 3], the sum is 9.	`x=[1, 5, 3];`
		`sum(x)`
		`ans =`
		    `9`

	Computes a row vector containing the sum of the elements in each column of a matrix **x**. For example, if $\mathbf{x} = \begin{bmatrix} 1 & 5 & 3 \\ 2 & 4 & 6 \end{bmatrix}$, the sum of column 1 is 3, the sum of column 2 is 9, and the sum of column 3 is 9.	`x=[1, 5, 3; 2, 4, 6];`
		`sum(x)`
		`ans =`
		   `3    9    9`

prod(x)
Computes the product of the elements of a vector **x**. For example, if **x** = [1 5 3], the product is 15.

```
x=[1, 5, 3];
prod(x)
ans =
      15
```

Computes a row vector containing the product of the elements in each column of a matrix **x**. For example, if $x = \begin{bmatrix} 1 & 5 & 3 \\ 2 & 4 & 6 \end{bmatrix}$, the product of column 1 is 2, the product of column 2 is 20, and the product of column 3 is 18.

```
x=[1, 5, 3; 2, 4, 6];
prod(x)
ans =
     2    20    18
```

cumsum (x)
Computes a vector of the same size containing cumulative sums of the elements of a vector **x**. For example, if **x** = [1 5 3], the resulting vector is **x** = [1 6 9].

```
x=[1, 5, 3];
cumsum(x)
ans =
     1     6     9
```

Computes a matrix containing the cumulative sum of the elements in each column of a matrix **x**. For example, if $x = \begin{bmatrix} 1 & 5 & 3 \\ 2 & 4 & 6 \end{bmatrix}$, the resulting matrix is $x = \begin{bmatrix} 1 & 5 & 3 \\ 3 & 9 & 9 \end{bmatrix}$

```
x=[1, 5, 3; 2, 4, 6];
cumsum(x)

ans =

     1     5     3
     3     9     9
```

cumprod (x)
Computes a vector of the same size containing cumulative products of the elements of a vector **x**. For example, if **x** = [1 5 3], the resulting vector is $x = [1\ 5\ 15]$.

```
x=[1, 5, 3];
cumprod(x)
ans =
     1     5    15
```

Computes a matrix containing the cumulative product of the elements in each column of a matrix **x**. For example, if $x = \begin{bmatrix} 1 & 5 & 3 \\ 2 & 4 & 6 \end{bmatrix}$, the resulting matrix is $x = \begin{bmatrix} 1 & 5 & 3 \\ 2 & 20 & 18 \end{bmatrix}$

```
x=[1, 5, 3; 2, 4, 6];
cumprod(x)

ans =

     1     5     3
     2    20    18
```

Sorting Values   The **sort** command arranges the values of a vector **x** into ascending order. If **x** is a matrix, the command sorts each column into ascending order:

sort(x)
Sorts the elements of a vector **x** into ascending order. For example, if **x** = [1 5 3], the resulting vector is [1 3 5].

```
x=[1, 5, 3];
sort(x)
ans =
     1     3     5
```

Sorts the elements in each column of a matrix **x** into ascending order. For example, if $x = \begin{bmatrix} 1 & 5 & 3 \\ 2 & 4 & 6 \end{bmatrix}$, the resulting matrix is $\begin{bmatrix} 1 & 4 & 3 \\ 2 & 5 & 6 \end{bmatrix}$

```
x=[1, 5, 3; 2, 4, 6];
sort(x)

ans =

     1     4     3
     2     5     6
```

*Hint:*All of the functions in this section work on the *columns* in two-dimensional matrices. If your data analysis requires you to evaluate data in rows, the data must be transposed—in other words, the rows must become columns and the columns must become rows. The transpose operator is a single quote ('). For example, if you want to find the maximum value in each row of matrix **x**,

$$x = \begin{bmatrix} 1 & 5 & 3 \\ 2 & 4 & 6 \end{bmatrix}$$

use the command

```
max(x')
```

which returns

```
ans =

        5   6
```

Determining Matrix Size   MATLAB offers two functions that allow us to determine how big a matrix is, **size** and **length**:

size(x)	Determines the number of rows and columns in matrix **x**.	`x=[1, 5, 3; 2,4, 6];`
		`size(x)`
		`ans =`
		`      2    3`

[a,b]=
  size(x)
	Determines the number of rows and columns in matrix **x** and assigns the number of rows to **a** and the number of rows to **b**.	`[a,b]=size(x)`
		`a =`
		`   2`
		`b =`
		`   3`

length(x)	Determines the largest dimension of a matrix **x**.	`x=[1, 5, 3; 2, 4, 6];`
		`length(x)`
		`ans =`
		`   3`

EXAMPLE 3.3

WEATHER DATA

The National Weather Service of the National Oceanic and Atmospheric Administration collects massive amounts of weather data. (See Figure 3.5.) That data is available to all of us from their online service at http://cdo.ncdc.noaa.gov/CDO/cdo. Analyzing large amounts of data can be confusing, so it's a good idea to start with a small data set, develop an approach that works, and then apply it to the larger data set.

Extract precipitation information from the National Weather Service for one location (Asheville, North Carolina) for all of 1999, and store it in a file called Weather_Data.xls. (The .xls indicates that this is an Excel spreadsheet.) Each row represents a month, so there should be 12 rows. Each column represents a day of the month, 1 to 31, so there should be 31 columns. Since every month does not have the same number of days, there is no data available for every location in the last several columns. Those locations contain the number –99999. The precipitation information is presented in hundredths of an inch. For example, on February 1st, there was 0.61 inch of precipitation, and on April 1st there were 2.60 inches of precipitation. A sample of the data is displayed in Table 3.1 with labels for clarity. However, **the data in the file contains only numbers**.

Figure 3.5. Satellite photo of a hurricane.

TABLE 3.1 Precipitation Data from Asheville, North Carolina

1999	Day 1	Day 2	Day 3	Day 4		Day 28	Day 29	Day 30	Day 31
January	0	0	272	0	etc.	0	0	33	33
February	61	103	0	2		62	−99999	−99999	−99999
March	2	0	17	27		0	5	8	0
April	260	1	0	0		13	86	0	−99999
May	47	0	0	0		0	0	0	0
June	0	0	30	42		14	14	8	−99999
July	0	0	0	0		5	0	0	0
August	0	45	0	0		0	0	0	0
September	0	0	0	0		138	58	10	−99999
October	0	0	0	14		0	0	0	1
November	1	163	5	0		0	0	0	−99999
December	0	0	0	0		0	0	0	0

Use the data in the file to find the following:

    a.   total precipitation in each month

    b.   total precipitation for the year

    c.   the month and day that recorded the maximum precipitation during the year

SOLUTION

1.   State the Problem

Using the data in the file Weather_Data.xls, find the total monthly precipitation, the total precipitation for the year, and the day on which it rained the most.

2.   Describe the Input and Output

Input

The input for this example is included in your data file called Weather_Data.xls, and consists of a two-dimensional matrix. The rows each represent a month, and the columns each represent a day.

Output

The output should be the total precipitation for each month, the total precipitation for the year, and the day on which the precipitation was at the maximum. (We have decided to present precipitation in inches since it was not specified in the problem statement.)

3.   Hand Example

For the hand example, only deal with a small subset of the data. The information included in Table 3.1 is enough. The total for January, days 1 to 4, is

$$\text{total\_1} = (0 + 0 + 272 + 0)/100 = 2.72 \text{ inches}$$

The total for February, days 1 to 4, is

$$\text{total\_2} = (61 + 103 + 0 + 2)/100 = 1.66 \text{ inches}$$

Now add the months together to get the combined total. If our sample "year" consists of just January and February, then

$$\text{total} = \text{total\_1} + \text{total\_2} = 2.72 + 1.66 = 4.38 \text{ inches}$$

To find the day on which the maximum precipitation occurred, first find the maximum in the table, then determine which row and column it is in.

Working through a hand example allows you to formulate the steps required to solve the problem in MATLAB.

4.   Develop a MATLAB Solution

First, we'll need to save the data file into MATLAB as a matrix. Because it is an Excel spreadsheet, the easiest approach is to use the import wizard as shown in Figure 3.6. Double click on the file in the current directory window to launch the import wizard.

Once the import wizard has completed the import, the variable name Weather_Data will appear in the workspace window.

Now, write the script M-file to solve the problem:

```
clc
%Example 3.3 - Weather Data
%In this example we will find the total precipitation
%for each month, and for the entire year, using a data file
%We will also find the month and day on which the precipitation
%was the maximum
%
wd=Weather_Data;
wd(2,29)=0;     %Change the -99999 values to 0
wd(2,30)=0;
wd(2,31)=0;
wd(4,31)=0;
```

```
wd(6,31)=0;
wd(9,31)=0;
wd(11,31)=0;
%Use the transpose operator to change rows to columns
wd = wd';
%Find the sum of each column, which is the sum for each month
monthly_total=sum(wd)/100
%Find the annual total
yearly_total = sum(monthly_total)
%Find the annual maximum, and the month in which it occurs
[maximum_precip,month]=max(max(wd))
%Find the annual maximum, and the day on which it occurs
[maximum_precip,day]=max(max(wd'))
```

Notice that the code did not start with our usual **clear, clc** commands, because that would clear the workspace, effectively deleting the **Weather_Data** variable. Next, we rename the **Weather_Data** to **wd**, because it is shorter to type. Because we'll be using this variable frequently, it's a good idea to make it short to minimize the chance of errors caused by mistyping.

Next, the values entered into the file for days of the month that don't exist (such as February 31) must be changed from –99999 to 0. Since the row number corresponds to the month and the column number corresponds to the day, we can define the precipitation for February 29 with the command

```
wd(2,29) = 0;
```

The semicolon suppresses the output so that we don't clutter up the command window when the program runs.

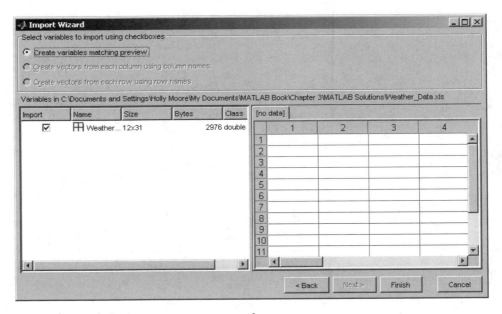

Figure 3.6. MATLAB Import Wizard.

Next, the matrix **wd** is transposed, so that the data for each month is in a column instead of a row. That allows us to use the **sum** command to add up all the precipitation values for the month.

Now, we can add up all the monthly totals to get the total for the year. An alternative syntax could have been

```
yearly_total = sum(sum(wd))
```

Finding the maximum daily precipitation is easy—what makes this example hard is determining the day and month where the maximum occurred. The command

```
[maximum_precip,month] = max(max(wd))
```

is easier to understand if we break it up into two commands. The first command is

```
[a,b] = max(wd)
```

These commands return a matrix of maximums for each column, which in this case is the maximum for each month. This value is assigned to the variable name **a**. The variable **b** becomes a matrix of index numbers, which represent the row in each column where the maximum occurred. The output is as follows:

```
a =
    Columns 1 through 9
    272  135  78  260  115  240  157  158  138
    Columns 10 through 12
    156  255  97
b =
    Columns 1 through 9
    3  18  27  1  6  25  12  24  28
    Columns 10 through 12
    5  26  14
```

When we execute the second **max** command, we determine the maximum precipitation for the entire data set, which is the maximum value in matrix **a**. We also find the index number for that maximum, from matrix **a**:

```
[c,d]=max(a)
c =
        272
d =
            1
```

These results tell us that the maximum precipitation occurred in column 1 of the **a** matrix, which means it occurred in the first month.

Similarly, transposing the **wd** matrix **(wd')** and finding the maximum twice allows us to find the day of the month on which the maximum occurred.

There are several things you should notice about the MATLAB screen in Figure 3.7. In the **workspace window**, both **Weather_Data** and **wd** are listed. **Weather_Data** is a 12×31 matrix, whereas **wd** is a 31×12 matrix. All of the variables created when the M-file was executed are now available to the command window. This makes it easy to perform additional calculations in the command window after the M-file has completed running.

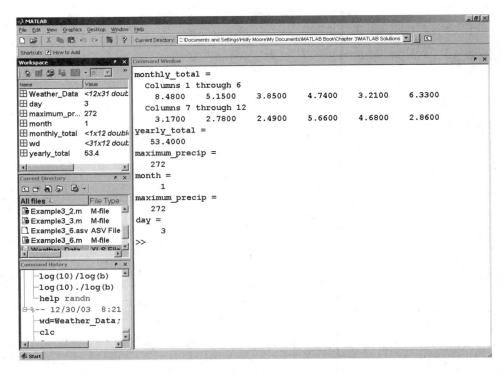

Figure 3.7. Results from the precipitation calculations.

For example, notice that we forgot to change the **maximum_precip** value from hundredths of an inch to inches. Adding the command

maximum_precip=maximum_precip/100

would correct that oversight. Also notice that the Weather_Data.xls file is still in the current directory. Finally, notice that the **command history window** only reflects commands issued from the **command window**. It does not show commands executed from an M-file.

5.   Test the Solution

Open the Weather_Data.xls file, and confirm that the maximum precipitation occurred on January 3. Once you've confirmed that your M-file program works, you can use it to analyze other data. The National Weather Service maintains similar records for all of its recording stations. ∎

Variance and Standard Deviation

Two of the most important statistical measurements of a set of data are the variance and the standard deviation. Before we give their mathematical definitions, it is useful to develop an intuitive understanding of these values. Consider the values of vectors **data_1** and **data_2**, plotted in Figures 3.8(a) and 3.8(b).

If we attempt to draw a line through the middle of the values in the plots, this line would be at approximately 3.0 in both plots. Thus, we would assume that both vectors have approximately the same mean value of 3.0. However, the data in the two vectors clearly have some distinguishing characteristics. The data values in **data_2** vary more, or deviate more, from the mean. Thus, measures of variance and deviation for the values

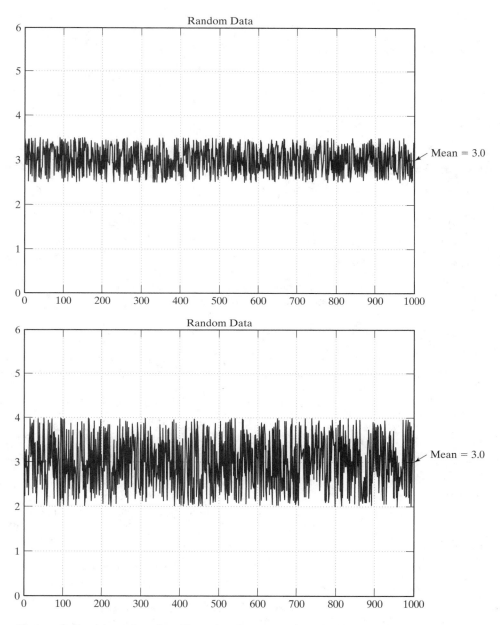

Figure 3.8. (a) Random data (data_1) with a mean of 3.0. (b) Random data (data_2) with a mean of 3.0.

in **data_2** will be greater than measures of variance and deviation for **data_1**. An intuitive understanding of variance (or deviation) relates to the variance of the values from the mean. The larger the variance, the further the values fluctuate from the mean value.

Mathematically, the variance σ^2 for a set of data values (which we will assume are stored in a vector **x**) can be computed with the following equation:

$$\sigma^2 = \frac{\sum\limits_{k=1}^{N} (x_k - \mu)^2}{N - 1}.$$

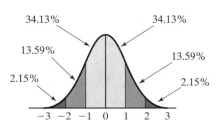

Figure 3.9. Normal distribution of data.

This equation is a bit intimidating at first, but if you look at it closely it seems much simpler. The term $x_k - \mu$ is the difference, or deviation, of x_k from the mean. This value is squared so that we will always have a positive value. We then add together the squared deviations for all of the data points. This sum is then divided by $N - 1$, which approximates an average. (The equation for variance sometimes uses a denominator of N, but the form here has statistical properties that make $N - 1$ generally more desirable.) Thus, the variance is the average squared deviation of the data from the mean.

The standard deviation is defined as the square root of the variance, or

$$\sigma = \sqrt{\sigma^2}$$

where σ is the Greek symbol sigma. In a normal (Gaussian) distribution of a large amount of data, approximately 68 percent of the data falls within one sigma variation of the mean ($+/-$ one sigma). If you extend the range to a two-sigma variation ($+/-$ two sigma), approximately 95 percent of the data should fall inside these bounds, and if you go out to three sigma, over 99 percent of the data should fall in this range. (see Figure 3.9.)

The syntax for calculating standard deviation is as follows. (MATLAB does not have a built in function for variance):

std(x)	Computes the standard deviation of the values in a vector **x**. For example, if **x** $= [1\ 5\ 3]$, the standard deviation is 2. However, standard deviations are not usually calculated for small samples of data.	**x=[1, 5, 3];** **std(x)** **ans =** **2**
	Returns a row vector containing the standard deviation calculated for each column of a matrix **x**. For example, if **x** $= \begin{bmatrix} 1 & 5 & 3 \\ 2 & 4 & 6 \end{bmatrix}$, the standard deviation in column 1 is 0.7071, the standard deviation in column 2 is 0.7071, and the standard deviation in column 3 is 2.1213.	**x=[1, 5, 3; 2, 4, 6];** **std(x)** **ans =** **0.7071 0.7071** **2.1213**

Again, standard deviations are not usually calculated for small samples of data.

3.1.5 Random Numbers

There are many engineering problems that require the use of random numbers in the development of a solution. In some cases, the random numbers are used to develop a simulation of a complex problem. The simulation can be tested over and over to analyze the results, and each test represents a repetition of the experiment. We also use random numbers to approximate noise sequences. For example, the static we hear on a radio is a noise sequence. If we are testing a program that uses an input data file that represents a radio signal, we may want to generate noise and add it to a speech signal or music signal to provide a more realistic sound.

Uniform Random Numbers

Random numbers are not defined by an equation; instead, they can be characterized by a distribution of values. For example, random numbers that are equally likely to be any value between an upper and lower limit are called uniform random numbers.

The **rand** function in MATLAB generates random numbers uniformly distributed over the interval 0 to 1. A seed value is used to initiate a random sequence of values. This seed value is initially set to zero, but it can be changed with the rand function. The **rand** function is used as follows:

rand(n)	Returns an **n** × **n** matrix. Each value in the matrix is a random number between 0 and 1.	`rand(2)`
		`ans =`
		`   0.9501 0.6068`
		`   0.2311 0.4860`

rand(m,n)	Returns an **m** × **n** matrix. Each value in the matrix is a random number between 0 and 1.	`rand(3,2)`
		`ans =`
		`   0.8913 0.0185`
		`   0.7621 0.8214`
		`   0.4565 0.4447`

rand ('seed',n)	Sets the value of the seed to the value of **n**. The value of **n** is initially set to 0. This causes MATLAB to use a different starting point in its random number calculations.	`rand('seed',3)`
		`rand(2)`
		`ans =`
		`   0.5387 0.0512`
		`   0.3815 0.2851`

rand ('seed')	Returns the current value of the random number generator.	`rand('seed')`
		`ans =`
		`   1.6147e+009`

Random sequences with values that range between values other than 0 and 1 are often needed. Suppose we want to generate values between –5 and +5. First, we generate random numbers and store them in the matrix **r** (all the values are between 0 and 1):

```
r = rand(100,1);
```

Because the difference between –5 and +5 is 10, we know that we want our random numbers to vary over a range of 10, so we'll need to multiply everything by 10:

```
r = r * 10;
```

Now our random numbers vary from 0 to 10. If we add the lower bound (–5) to our matrix, via the command

```
r = r-5;
```

the result will be random numbers varying from –5 to +5. We can generalize these results with the equation

$$x = (b - a) \cdot r + a$$

where

      a is the lower bound

      b is the upper bound

      r is a set of random numbers

Gaussian Random Numbers

When we generate a random number sequence with a uniform distribution, all values are equally likely to occur. However, we sometimes need to generate random numbers using distributions in which some values are more likely to be generated than others. For example, suppose that a random number sequence represents outdoor temperature measurements taken over a period of time. We would find that the temperature measurements have some variation, but typically are not equally likely. For example, we might find that the values vary only a few degrees, although larger changes would occasionally occur because of storms, cloud shadows, and day-to-night changes.

Random number sequences that have some values that are more likely to occur than others can often be modeled with a **Gaussian random variable** (also called a **normal random variable**). An example of a set of values with a Gaussian distribution is shown in Figure 3.9. Although a uniform random variable has specific upper and lower bounds, a Gaussian random variable is not defined in terms of upper and lower bounds; it is defined in terms of the mean value and the variance, or standard deviation, of the values. For Gaussian random numbers, approximately 68 percent of the values will fall with one standard deviation, 95 percent with two standard deviations, and 99 percent within three standard deviations from the mean.

MATLAB will generate Gaussian values with a mean of 0 and a variance of 1.0 if we specify a normal distribution. The functions for generating Gaussian values are as follows:

randn(n)	Returns an **n** × **n** matrix. Each value in the matrix is a Gaussian (or normal) random number with a mean of 0 and a variance of 1.	randn(2) ans = −0.4326 0.1253 −1.6656 0.2877

randn(m,n)	Returns an **m** × **n** matrix. Each value in the matrix is a Gaussian (or normal) random number with a mean of 0 and a variance of 1.	randn(3,2)
		ans =
		−1.1465 0.0376
		  1.1909 0.3273
		  1.1892 0.1746

randn **('seed',n)**	Sets the value of the seed to the value of **n**. The value of **n** is initially set to 0. This results in different random numbers being calculated. The **randn** function generates the same sequence of random numbers if the same seed is used.	randn('seed',3) rand(2) ans = −2.0880 0.1389 0.6262 −1.2370
randn **('seed')**	Returns the current value of the random number generator.	randn('seed') ans = 1.6147e+009

To modify Gaussian values with a mean of 0 and a variance of 1 to another Gaussian distribution, multiply the values by the standard deviation of the desired distribution, and add the mean of the desired distribution. Thus, if *r* is a random number sequence with a mean of 0 and a variance of 1.0, the following equation will generate a new random number with a standard deviation of a and a mean of b:

$$x = a \cdot r + b$$

For example, to create a sequence of 500 Gaussian random variables with a standard deviation of 2.5 and a mean of 3, use

```
x = randn(1,500)*2.5 + 3;
```

3.2   MANIPULATING MATRICES

As you solve more and more complicated problems with MATLAB, you'll find that you will need to combine small matrices into larger matrices, extract information from large matrices, create very large matrices, and use matrices with special properties.

3.2.1   Defining Matrices

We know that a matrix can be defined by typing in a list of numbers enclosed in square brackets. The numbers can be separated by spaces or commas at the user's discretion. (You can even combine the two techniques in the same matrix definition.) New rows are indicated with a semicolon:

```
A = [3.5];
B = [1.5, 3.1]; or B = [1.5    3.1];
C = [-1, 0, 0; 1, 1, 0; 0, 0, 2];
```

A matrix can also be defined by listing each row on a separate line, as in the following set of MATLAB commands:

```
C = [-1,    0, 0;
      1,    1, 0;
      1,   -1, 0;
      0,    0, 2];
```

If there are too many numbers in a row to fit on one line, you can continue the statement on the next line, but a comma and an ellipsis (...) are needed at the end of the line to indicate that the row is to be continued. You can also use the ellipsis to continue long assignment statements in MATLAB.

If we want to define F with 10 values, we could use either of the following statements:

```
F = [1,52,64,197,42,-42,55,82,22,109];
```

or

```
F = [1,52,64,197,42,-42, . . .
        55,82,22,109];
```

MATLAB also allows you to define a matrix by using another matrix that has already been defined. For example, the following statements

```
B = [1.5, 3.1];
S = [3.0, B]
```

return

```
S =
     3.0    1.5    3.1
```

Similarly,

```
T = [ 1, 2, 3; S]
```

returns

```
T=
     1      2      3
     3      1.5    3.1
```

We can also change values in a matrix, or include additional values, by using a reference to specific locations. Thus, the command

```
S(2) = -1.0;
```

changes the second value in the matrix **S** from 1.5 to –1. If you type the matrix name **S** into the command window—that is,

```
S
```

then MATLAB returns

```
S =
     3.0    -1.0    3.1
```

We can also extend a matrix by defining new elements. If we execute the command

```
S(4) = 5.5;
```

we extend the matrix **S** to four elements instead of three. If we define element **S(8)**

```
S(8) = 9.5;
```

matrix **S** will have eight values, and the values of **S(5)**, **S(6)**, and **S(7)** will be set to **0**. Thus,

```
S
```

returns

```
S =
     3.0    -1.0    3.1    5.5    0    0    0    9.5
```

3.2.2   Using the Colon Operator

The colon operator is a very powerful operator for defining new matrices and modifying existing matrices. An evenly spaced matrix can be defined with the colon operator. Thus,

```
H = 1:8
```

returns

```
H =
     1   2   3   4   5   6   7   8
```

The default spacing is 1. However, when colons are used to separate three numbers, the middle value becomes the spacing. For example,

```
time = 0.0:0.5:2.0
```

returns

```
time =
      0    0.5000   1.0000   1.5000   2.0000
```

The colon operator can also be used to extract data from matrices, which becomes very useful in data analysis. When a colon is used in a matrix reference in place of a specific subscript, the colon represents the entire row or column.

If we define

```
M = [1 2 3 4 5; 2 3 4 5 6;3 4 5 6 7];
```

then we can extract column 1 from matrix **M** with the command

```
x = M(:, 1)
```

which returns

```
x =
     1
     2
     3
```

You can extract any of the columns in a similar manner, so that

```
y = M(:, 4)
```

returns

```
y =
     4
     5
     6
```

Similarly, to extract a row, use

```
z = M(1,:)
```

which returns

```
z =
     1     2     3     4     5
```

In all of the preceding examples, read the colon as "all of the rows," or "all of the columns."

You don't have to extract an entire row or an entire column. The colon operator can also be used to mean " from row _ to row _" or "from column _ to column _." To extract the two bottom rows of the **M** matrix, type

```
w = M(2:3,:)
```

which returns

```
w =
     2     3     4     5     6
     3     4     5     6     7
```

Similarly, to extract just the four numbers in the lower right-hand corner of matrix **M**, use

```
w = M(2:3,4:5)
```

which returns

```
w =
     5     6
     6     7
```

In MATLAB it is valid to have a matrix that is empty. For example, the following statements will each generate an empty matrix:

```
a = [];
b = 4:-1:5;
```

Finally, using the matrix name with a single colon, as in

```
M(:)
```

transforms **M** into one long column matrix:

```
x =
    1
    2
    3
    2
    3
    4
    3
    4
    5
    4
    5
    6
    5
    6
    7
```

The matrix was formed by first listing column 1, then adding column 2 onto the end, then column 3, etc. Actually, the computer does not store two-dimensional arrays in a two-dimensional pattern. It "thinks" of a matrix as one long list, just like the **x** to the left. There are two ways you can extract a single value from an array, by using the row, column notation. To find the value on row 2, column 3, use the following commands:

```
M
M =
    1    2    3    4    5
    2    3    ④    5    6
    3    4    5    6    7
M(2,3)
ans =
        4
```

Alternatively, you can use a single index number. The value on row 2, column 3 of matrix **M** is element number 8. Count down column 1, then down column 2, and finally down column 3 to the correct element:

```
M(8)
ans = 4
```

EXAMPLE 3.4

CLIMATOLOGICAL DATA

Climatologists examine weather data over long periods of time, trying to find a pattern. (See Figure 3.10.) Weather data has been kept reliably in the United States since the 1850s; however, most reporting stations have only been in place since the 1930s and 1940s. Climatologists perform statistical calculations on the data they collect. Although the data in Weather_Data.xls only represents one location for one year, we can use the data to practice statistical calculations. Find the mean daily precipitation for each month, the mean daily precipitation for the year, then find the standard deviation for each month and for the year.

SOLUTION

1. State the Problem

Find the mean daily precipitation for each month, and for the year, based on the data in Weather_Data.xls. Also find the standard deviation of the data during each month and during the entire year.

Figure 3.10. A hurricane over Florida.

2.   Describe the Input and Output

Input
    Use the Weather_Data.xls file as input to the problem.

Output

Find the following:

    mean daily precipitation for each month
    mean daily precipitation for the year
    standard deviation of the daily precipitation data for each month
    standard deviation of the daily precipitation data for the year

3.   Hand Example

Just use the data for the first four days of the month:

    January average = $(0 + 0 + 272 + 0)/4 = 68$ hundredths of an inch of precipitation, or 0.68 inch.

    The standard deviation is found from the following equation:

$$\sigma = \sqrt{\frac{\sum_{k=1}^{N}(x_k - \mu)^2}{N - 1}}.$$

    Using only the first four days of January, first calculate the sum of the squares of the difference between the mean and the actual value:

$$(0 - 68)^2 + (0 - 68)^2 + (272 - 68)^2 + (0 - 68)^2 = 55,488$$

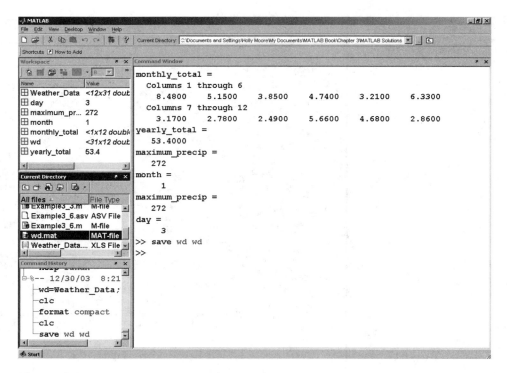

Figure 3.11. The current directory records the name of the saved file.

Divide by the number of data points minus 1:

$$55,488/(4-1) = 18,496$$

Finally, take the square root to give 136 hundredths of an inch of precipitation, or 1.36 inches.

4. Develop a MATLAB Solution

First, we need to load the Weather_Data.xls file (see Figure 3.11), and edit out the −99999 entries. Although we could do that in a similar manner to the process described in Example 3.3, there is an easier way. The data from Example 3.3 could be saved to a file, so that it is available to use later. If you want to save the entire workspace, just type

```
save  <filename>
```

where filename is a user-defined file name. If you just want to save one variable, type

```
save <filename>  <variable_name>
```

which saves a single variable or list of variables to a file. All we need to save is the variable **wd**, so the following command is sufficient:

```
save wd wd
```

This command saves the matrix **wd** into the **wd.mat** file. Check the current directory window to make sure that **wd.mat** has been stored.

Now, the M-file we create to solve this example can load the data automatically:

```
clear, clc
%  Example 3.4 Climatological Data
%  In this example we find the mean daily
%  precipitation for each month
%  and the mean daily precipitation for the year
%  We also find the standard deviation of the data
%
%  Changing the format to bank often makes the output
%  easier to read
format bank
%  By saving the variable wd from the last example, it is
%  available to use in this problem
load wd
Average_daily_precip_monthly = mean(wd)
Average_daily_precip_yearly = mean(wd(:))
%  Another way to find the average yearly precipitation
Average_daily_precip_yearly = mean(mean(wd))
% Now calculate the standard deviation
Monthly_Stdeviation = std(wd)
Yearly_Stdeviation = std(wd(:))
```

The following results are shown in the command window:

```
Average_daily_precip_monthly =
  Columns 1 through 3
        27.35          16.61          12.42
  Columns 4 through 6
        15.29          10.35          20.42
  Columns 7 through 9
        10.23           8.97           8.03
  Columns 10 through 12
        18.26          15.10           9.23
Average_daily_precip_yearly =
        14.35
Average_daily_precip_yearly =
        14.35
Monthly_Stdeviation =
  Columns 1 through 3
        63.78          35.06          20.40
  Columns 4 through 6
        48.98          26.65          50.46
  Columns 7 through 9
        30.63          30.77          27.03
  Columns 10 through 12
        42.08          53.34          21.01
Yearly_Stdeviation =
        39.62
```

The mean daily precipitation for the year was calculated in two equivalent ways. The mean of each month was found, and then the mean (average) of the monthly values was found. This works out to be the same as taking the mean of all of the data at once. Recall that

```
wd(:)
```

converts the two-dimensional matrix **wd** into a one-dimensional matrix, thus making it possible to find the mean in one step.

The situation is different for the standard deviation of daily precipitation for the year. It is necessary to perform just one calculation:

```
std(wd(:))
```

Otherwise, you would find the standard deviation of the standard deviation—not what you want at all.

5.   Test the Solution

First, check the results to make sure they make sense. For example, the first time we executed the M-file, the **wd** matrix still contained –99999 values. That resulted in mean values less than one. Since it isn't possible to have negative rainfall, checking the data for reasonability alerted us to the problem. Finally, calculating the mean daily rainfall for one month by hand would serve as an excellent check; however, it would be tedious. You can use MATLAB to help you by calculating the mean without using a predefined function. The command window is a convenient place to perform these calculations:

```
load wd
sum(wd(:,1))   %Find the sum of all of the rows in column 1 of
matrix wd
ans =
      848.00
ans/31
ans =
      27.35
```

Compare this result with the January (Month 1) results found from the M-file program. ∎

EXAMPLE 3.5

USING TEMPERATURE DATA

The data collected by the National Weather Service is extensive (see Figure 3.12), but it is not always organized in exactly the way we would like. Take for example the summary of the 1999 Asheville, North Carolina, Climatological Data presented in Table 3.2.

The numeric information can be extracted from the table, and should be saved in an Excel file, Named **Asheville_1999.xls**. Use MATLAB to confirm that the reported values on the annual row are correct for the mean maximum temperature and the mean minimum temperature, as well as for the annual high temperature and the annual low temperature. Combine these four columns of data into a new matrix, called temp_data.

SOLUTION

1.   State the Problem

Calculate the annual mean maximum temperature, the annual mean minimum temperature, the highest temperature reached during the year, and the lowest temperature reached during the year, for 1999 in Asheville, North Carolina.

2.   Describe the Input and Output

Input

   Import a matrix from the excel file, Asheville_1999.xls

Output

Find the following four values:

   annual mean maximum temperature
   annual mean minimum temperature
   highest temperature
   lowest temperature

TABLE 3.2 Annual Climatological Summary, Station: 310301/13872, Asheville, North Carolina, 1999
(Elev. 2240 ft. above sea level; Lat. 35°36'N, Lon. 82°32'W)

Temperature (°F)

1999 Month	MMXT Mean Max.	MMNT Mean Min.	MNTM Mean	DPNT Depart. from Normal	HTDD Heating Degree Days	CLDD Cooling Degree Days	EMXT Highest	High Date	EMNP Lowest	Low Date	DT90 Max >=90°	DX32 Max <=32°	DT32 Min <=32°	DT00 Min <=0°
1	51.4	31.5	41.5	5.8	725	0	78	27	9	5	0	2	16	0
2	52.6	32.1	42.4	3.5	628	0	66	8	16	14	0	2	16	0
3	52.7	32.5	42.6	-4.8	687	0	76	17	22	8	0	0	19	0
4	70.1	48.2	59.2	3.6	197	30	83	10	34	19	0	0	0	0
5	75.0	51.5	63.3	-0.1	69	25	83	29	40	2	0	0	0	0
6	80.2	60.9	70.6	0.3	4	181	90	8	50	18	1	0	0	0
7	85.7	64.9	75.3	1.6	7	336	96	31	56	13	8	0	0	0
8	86.4	63.0	74.7	1.9	0	311	94	13	54	31	7	0	0	0
9	79.1	54.6	66.9	0.2	43	106	91	2	39	23	3	0	0	0
10	67.6	45.5	56.6	0.4	255	1	78	15	28	25	0	0	2	0
11	62.2	40.7	51.5	4.0	397	0	76	9	26	30	0	0	8	0
12	53.6	30.5	42.1	2.7	706	0	69	4	15	25	0	0	20	0
Annual	68.0	46.3	57.2	1.6	3718	990	96	Jul	9	Jan	19	4	81	0

Precipitation (inches)

1999 Month	TPCP Total	DPNP Depart. from Normal	EMXP Greatest Observed Day	EMXP Date	TSNW Total Fall	MXSD Max Depth	MXSD Max Date	DP01 >=.10	DP05 >=.50	DP10 >=1.0
1	4.56	2.09	1.61	2	2.7	1	31	9	2	2
2	3.07	-0.18	0.79	17	1.2	0T	1	6	3	0
3	2.47	-1.41	0.62	3	5.3	1	26	8	1	0
4	2.10	-1.02	0.48	27	0.0T	0T	2	6	0	0
5	2.49	-1.12	0.93	7	0.0	0		5	2	0
6	2.59	-0.68	0.69	29	0.0	0		6	2	0
7	3.87	0.94	0.80	11	0.0	0		10	4	0
8	0.90	-2.86	0.29	8	0.0	0		4	0	0
9	1.72	-1.48	0.75	28	0.0	0		4	1	0
10	1.53	-1.24	0.59	4	0.0	0		3	2	0
11	3.48	0.56	1.71	25	0.3	0		5	3	1
12	1.07	-1.72	0.65	13	0.0T	0T	17	3	1	0
Annual	29.85	-8.12	1.71	Nov	9.5	1	Mar	69	21	3

Notes

(blank) Not reported.

+   Occurred on one or more previous dates during the month. The date in the Date field is the last day of occurrence. Used through December 1983 only.

A   Accumulated amount. This value is a total that may include data from a previous month or months or year (for annual value).

B   Adjusted Total. Monthly value totals based on proportional available data across the entire month.

E   An estimated monthly or annual total.

X   Monthly means or totals based on incomplete time series. 1 to 9 days are missing. Annual means or totals include one or more months which had 1 to 9 days that were missing.

M   Used to indicate data element missing.

T   Trace of precipitation, snowfall, or snowdepth. The precipitation data value will = zero.

S   Precipitation amount is continuing to be accumulated. Total will be included in a subsequent monthly or yearly value. Example: Days 1–20 had 1.35 inches of precipitation, then a period of accumulation began. The element TPCP would then be 00135S and the total accumulated amount value appears in a subsequent monthly value. If TPCP = "M" there was no precipitation measured during the month. Flag is set to "S" and the total accumulated amount appears in a subsequent monthly value.

U.S. Department of Commerce National Oceanic & Atmospheric Administration

Figure 3.12. Temperature data collected from a weather satellite were used to create this composite false-color image representing temperatures in the eastern and northeastern portions of the United States.

Create a matrix composed of the mean maximum temperature values, the mean minimum temperature values, the highest monthly temperatures, and the lowest monthly temperatures. Do not include the annual data.

3. Hand Example

Using a calculator, add the values in column 2 of the table, and divide by 12.

4. Develop a MATLAB Solution

First, import the data from Excel, then save it in the current directory as Asheville_1999. Save the variable Asheville_1999 as the file Asheville_1999.mat. This makes it available to be loaded into the workspace from our M-file program. We have

```
% Example 3.5
% In this example we extract data from a large matrix and
% use the data analysis functions to find the mean high and mean
% low temperatures for the year, and to find the high tem-
perature
% and the low temperature for the year
%
clear, clc
% load the data matrix from a file
load asheville_1999
% extract the mean high temperatures from the large matrix
mean_max = asheville_1999(1:12,2);
% extract the mean low temperatures from the large matrix
```

```
mean_min = asheville_1999(1:12,3);
%  Calculate the annual means
annual_mean_max = mean(mean_max)
annual_mean_min = mean(mean_min)
%  extract the high and low temperatures from the large matrix
high_temp = asheville_1999(1:12,8);
low_temp = asheville_1999(1:12,10);
%  Find the max and min temperature for the year
max_high = max(high_temp)
min_low = min(low_temp)
%  Create a new matrix with just the temperature information
new_table =[mean_max, mean_min, high_temp, low_temp]
```

The results are displayed in the command window:

```
annual_mean_max =
   68.0500
annual_mean_min =
   46.3250
max_high =
   96
min_low =
    9
new_table =
   51.4000   31.5000   78.0000    9.0000
   52.6000   32.1000   66.0000   16.0000
   52.7000   32.5000   76.0000   22.0000
   70.1000   48.2000   83.0000   34.0000
   75.0000   51.5000   83.0000   40.0000
   80.2000   60.9000   90.0000   50.0000
   85.7000   64.9000   96.0000   56.0000
   86.4000   63.0000   94.0000   54.0000
   79.1000   54.6000   91.0000   39.0000
   67.6000   45.5000   78.0000   28.0000
   62.2000   40.7000   76.0000   26.0000
   53.6000   30.5000   69.0000   15.0000
```

5.   Test the Solution

Compare the results to the bottom line of the table from the Asheville, North Carolina Climatological Survey. It is important to confirm that the results are accurate before you start to use any computer program to process data.   ■

EXAMPLE 3.6

FLIGHT SIMULATOR

Computer simulations are used to generate situations that model or emulate a real world situation. Some computer simulations are written to play games such as checkers, poker, and chess. To play the game, you indicate your move, and the computer will select an appropriate response. Other animated games use computer graphics to develop an interaction as you use the keys or a mouse to play the game. In more sophisticated computer simulations, such as those in a flight simulator, the computer not only responds to the input from the user, but also generates values, such as temperatures, wind speeds, and the locations of other aircraft. (See Figure 3.13.) The simulators also model emergencies that occur during the flight of an aircraft. If all of this information generated by the computer were always the same set of information, the value of the simulator would be greatly reduced. It is important that there be randomness to the generation of the data.

Figure 3.13. The wind rarely blows at a steady rate.

Simulations that use random numbers to generate values that model events are called Monte Carlo simulations.

Write a program to generate a random-number sequence to simulate one hour of wind speed data that are updated every 10 seconds. Assume that the wind speed will be modeled as a uniform distribution, random number that varies between a lower limit and an upper limit. Let the lower limit be 5 mph and the upper limit be 10 mph. Save the data to an ASCII file named windspd.dat.

SOLUTION

1. State the Problem

Generate one hour of wind speed data using a lower limit of 5 mph and an upper limit of 10 mph.

2. Describe the Input and Output

Input
    Lower limit of 5 mph
    Upper limit of 10 mph

Output
    Table of time versus wind speed
    Data file of time and corresponding wind speed

3. Hand Example

This simulation uses MATLAB's random-number generator to generate numbers between 0 and 1. We then modify these values to be between a lower limit (5) and an upper limit (10). Using the equation developed in Section 3.1.5,

$$x = (b - a) \cdot r + a$$

we first multiply the range $(10 - 5)$ times the random numbers, and then add the lower bound (5). Hence, the value 0.1 would be

$$x = (10 - 5) \cdot 0.1 + 5 = 5.5$$

4. Develop a MATLAB Solution

```
%Example 3.6
clear, clc
%These statements generate one hour of simulated
%wind speeds
%
%Enter high and low speeds
low_speed = 5;
high_speed = 10;
%Enter a seed
seed = 24;
rand('seed',seed)
%Define the time matrix
t = 0:10:3600;
%Convert time to hours
t=t/3600;
%Determine how many time values exist
num = length(t)
%Calculate the speed values
speed = (high_speed - low_speed)*rand(1,num) + low_speed;
%Create a table
table = [t',speed']
save windspd.dat table -ascii
```

We entered a seed in this solution. Although we chose 24, any seed would do just as well. Notice also that we used the length command to determine how many elements were in the **t** matrix. The length command returns the maximum dimension of a matrix, and since **t** is a 1×361 matrix, the result was 361.

5. Test the Solution

The amount of data created makes testing this solution difficult. One way to determine if the results are in the correct range is to look at every value of speed, and make sure each one is between 5 and 10. This would be tedious and error prone. However, if we create an *x-y* plot of **t** and **speed**, we can quickly check to see if the results are in the correct range.

```
plot(t,speed)
```

We can see from Figure 3.14 that the wind speed does indeed vary between 5 mph and 10 mph. ∎

3.3 COMPUTATIONAL LIMITATIONS

The variables stored in a computer can assume a wide range of values. For most computers, the range extends from 10^{-308} to 10^{308}, which should be enough to accommodate most computations. However, it is possible for the result of an expression to be outside of this range. For example, suppose that we execute the following commands:

```
x = 2.5e200;
y = 1.0e200;
z = x*y
```

MATLAB responds with

```
z =
      Inf
```

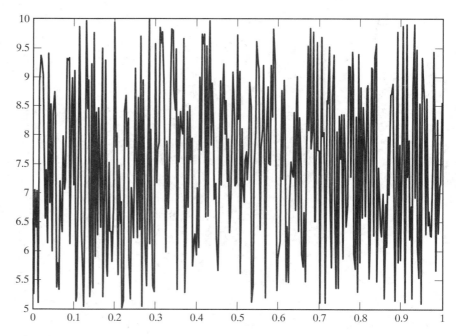

Figure 3.14. Random wind speeds.

because the answer (**2.5°e400**) is outside of the allowable range. This error is called exponent overflow, because the exponent of the result of an arithmetic operation is too large to store in the computer's memory.

Exponent underflow is a similar error, caused by the exponent of the result of an arithmetic operation being too small to store in the computer's memory. Using the same allowable range, we obtain an exponent underflow with the commands

```
x = 2.5e-200;
y = 1.0e200
z = x/y
```

which together return

```
z = 0
```

The result of an exponent underflow is zero.

We also know that the division by zero is an invalid operation. If an expression results in a division by zero, the result of the division is infinity:

```
z = y/0
z =
        Inf
```

MATLAB may also print a warning telling you that division by zero is not possible.

3.4   SPECIAL VALUES AND FUNCTIONS

MATLAB includes a number of predefined constants, special values, and special matrices that are available to the programs we write. Most of these special values and special matrices are generated by MATLAB using functions. As we learned earlier in this chapter, a MATLAB function typically requires inputs called arguments to compute a result. However, some functions don't require any input arguments. Although used as if they were scalar constants, the following functions do not require any input:

pi   Represents the mathematical constant π.

i, j   Represents an imaginary number, the $\sqrt{-1}$.

Inf   Represent infinity, which typically occurs as a result of division by zero.

NaN   Represents not-a-number and typically occurs when an expression is undefined, as in the division of zero by zero.

clock Represents the current time in a six-element row vector containing year, month, day, hour, minute, and seconds.

date   Represents the current date in a character-string format, such as 02-Jan-2004.

eps   Represents the epsilon floating-point precision for the computer being used. This epsilon precision is the smallest amount with which two values can differ in the computer.

ans   Represents a value computed by an expression, but not stored in a variable name.

MATLAB allows you to redefine these special values as variable names, which can have unexpected consequences. For example, the following MATLAB code is allowed, even though it is not wise:

```
pi = 12.8;
```

From this point on, any time the variable pi is called, the new value will be used. Similarly, you can redefine *any* function as a variable name:

```
sin = 10;
```

To restore sin to its function as a trigonometric function (or to restore the default value of pi), you must clear the workspace. Thus,

```
clear
pi
```

returns

```
pi =
    3.1416
```

SUMMARY

In this chapter, we explored the various predefined MATLAB functions. These functions included general mathematical functions, trigonometric functions, data analysis functions, and random number generation. We expanded our understanding of how to create matrices, including creating new matrices and extracting values from existing matrices. We explored the computational limits inherent to MATLAB and introduced special values, such as pi, that are built into the program.

MATLAB SUMMARY

The following MATLAB summary lists and briefly describes a number of special characters, commands, and functions:

Special Characters

eps	smallest difference recognized
i	imaginary number

Inf	infinity
j	imaginary number
Nan	Not a number
pi	mathematical constant, π

Commands and Functions

abs	computes the absolute value
asin	computes the inverse sine (arcsine)
ceil	rounds to the nearest integer toward positive infinity
cos	computes the cosine
cumprod	computes a cumulative product of the values in an array
cumsum	computes a cumulative sum of the values in an array
erf	calculates the error function
exp	computes the value of e^x
fix	rounds to the nearest integer toward zero
floor	rounds to the nearest integer toward minus infinity
help	opens the help function
length	determines the largest dimension of an array
log	computes the natural log
log10	computes the log base 10
log2	computes the log base 2
max	finds the maximum value in an array, and determines which element stores the maximum value
mean	computes the average of the elements in an array
median	finds the median of the elements in an array
min	finds the minimum value in an array, and determines which element stores the minimum value
prod	multiplies the values in an array
rand	calculates evenly distributed random numbers
randn	calculates normally distributed (Gaussian) random numbers
rem	calculates the remainder in a division problem
round	rounds to the nearest integer
sign	determines the sign (positive or negative)
sin	computes the sine
sinh	computes the hyperbolic sine
size	determines the number of rows and columns in an array
sort	sorts the elements of a vector into ascending order
sqrt	calculates the square root of a number
std	determines the standard deviation
sum	sums the values in an array
tan	computes the tangent

KEY TERMS

composition of functions
function
Monte Carlo simulation
mean
median

nesting
normal random variable
seed
simulation
standard deviation

underflow
uniform random number
variance

Problems

1. Sometimes it is convenient to have a table of sin, cos, and tan values instead of using a calculator. Create a table of all three of these trigonometric functions for angles from 0 to 2π, with a spacing of 0.1 radians. Your table should contain a column for the angle, then sin, cos, and tan.

2. The range of an object shot at an angle θ with respect to the x axis and an initial velocity v_o is given by

    $$R(\theta) = \frac{v^2}{g}\sin(2\theta) \text{ for } 0 \le \theta \le \frac{\pi}{2} \text{ and neglecting air resistance.}$$

    Use $g = 9.9$ m/s^2 and an initial velocity of 100 m/s. Show that the maximum range is obtained at $\theta = \frac{\pi}{4}$ by computing the range in increments of 0.05 from $0 \le \theta \le \frac{\pi}{2}$. Because you are using discrete angles, you will only be able to determine θ to within 0.05 radians.

    > *Hint:* Remember, **max** can be used to return not only the maximum value in an array, but also the element number where the maximum value is stored.

3. MATLAB contains functions to calculate the natural log (**log**), the log base 10 (**log10**) and the log base 2 (**log2**). However, if you want to find a logarithm to another base, for example base b, you'll have to do the math yourself:

    $$\log_b(x) = \frac{\log_e(x)}{\log_e(b)}.$$

    What is the log of 10 to the base b, when b is defined from 1 to 10 in increments of 1?

4. Populations tend to expand exponentially:

    $$P = P_0 e^{rt}$$

    where P is the current population

    P_0 is the original population
    r is the rate, expressed as a fraction
    t is the time

    If you originally have 100 rabbits that breed at a rate of 90 percent (0.9) per year, find how many rabbits you will have at the end of 10 years.

5. Chemical reaction rates are proportional to a rate constant, k, which changes with temperature according to the Arrhenius equation

    $$k = k_0 e^{-Q/RT}$$

    For a certain reaction

    $$Q = 8{,}000 \text{ cal/mole}$$
    $$R = 1.987 \text{ cal/mole K}$$
    $$k_0 = 1200 \text{ min}^{-1}$$

find the values of k for temperatures from 100K to 500K, in 50-degree increments. Create a table of your results.

6. The vector **G** represents the distribution of final grades in a statics course. Compute the mean, median, and standard deviation of G. Which better represents the "most typical grade," the mean or the median? Why?

$$\mathbf{G} = [68, 83, 61, 70, 75, 82, 57, 5, 76, 85, 62, 71, 96, 78, 76, 68, 72, 75, 83, 93]$$

Use MATLAB to determine the number of grades in the array. (Don't just count them.)

7. Generate 10,000 Gaussian random numbers with a mean of 80 and standard deviation of 23.5. Use the **mean** function to confirm that your array actually has a mean of 80. Use the **std** function to confirm that your standard deviation is actually 23.5.

8. A small rocket is being designed to make wind shear measurements in the vicinity of thunderstorms. Before testing begins, the designers are developing a simulation of the rocket's trajectory. They have derived the following equation, which they believe will predict the performance of the test rocket, where t is the elapsed time, in seconds:

$$\text{height} = 2.13t^2 - 0.0013t^4 + 0.000034t^{4.751}$$

a. Compute and print a table of time versus height, at 2-second intervals, up through 100 seconds. (The equation will actually predict negative heights. Obviously, the equation is no longer applicable once the rocket hits the ground. For now, don't worry about this physical impossibility; just do the math.)

b. Use MATLAB to find the maximum height achieved by the rocket.

c. Use MATLAB to find the time the maximum height is achieved.

9. Create the following matrix **A**:

$$\mathbf{A} = \begin{bmatrix} 3.4 & 2.1 & 0.5 & 6.5 & 4.2 \\ 4.2 & 7.7 & 3.4 & 4.5 & 3.9 \\ 8.9 & 8.3 & 1.5 & 3.4 & 3.9 \end{bmatrix}$$

a. Create a matrix **B** by extracting the first column of matrix **A**.

b. Create a matrix **C** by extracting the second row of matrix **A**.

c. Use the colon operator to create a matrix **D** by extracting the first through third columns of matrix **A**.

d. Create a single valued matrix **E** by extracting the value from the 2nd row, 3rd column ($\mathbf{A}_{2,3}$).

e. Create a matrix **F** by extracting the values of elements ($\mathbf{A}_{1,3}$) ($\mathbf{A}_{2,4}$) and ($\mathbf{A}_{3,5}$) and combining them into a single matrix.

10. **Sensor Data.**

Suppose that a file named sensor.dat contains information collected from a set of sensors. Each row contains a set of sensor readings, with the first row containing values collected at 0 seconds, the second row containing values collected at 1.0 seconds, etc.

a. Write a program to read the data file and print the number of sensors and the number of seconds of data contained in the file. (Hint: use the **size** function.)

b. Find both the maximum value and minimum value recorded on each sensor. Use MATLAB to determine at what times they occurred.

c. Find the mean and standard deviation for each sensor, and for all the data values collected. Remember, column 1 does not contain sensor data; it contains time data.

11. **Temperature Data.**

Suppose you are designing a container to ship sensitive medical materials between hospitals. The container needs to keep the contents within a specified temperature range. You have created a model predicting how the container responds to exterior temperature, and now need to run a simulation.

a. Create a normal distribution of temperatures (Gaussian distribution) with a mean of 70°F, and a standard deviation of 2 degrees, corresponding to 2 hours duration. You'll need a temperature for each time value from 0 to 120 minutes.

b. Plot the data on an x-y plot. (As we haven't learned about labels, don't worry about them. Recall that the MATLAB function for plotting is plot(x,y).)

c. Find the maximum temperature and the minimum temperature.

4

Plotting

GRAND CHALLENGE: COMPUTATIONAL ACCELERATOR PHYSICS

Particle accelerators have the potential to change radioactive waste into elements which are not radioactive. This would help with our nation's increasingly severe disposal problem for waste from nuclear power plants and from weapons production facilities. Currently, the only way to get rid of these waste products is to bury them or store them in secure areas—hardly a long-term solution. Particle accelerators could also be used to produce radioactive fuels, such as tritium. These projects benefit from high-resolution modeling techniques that allow researchers to ask "what if" questions and predict the results without doing the actual experiment. Only the most promising approaches are then tried out in the actual accelerator. The results of this kind of three-dimensional modeling are easier to interpret when presented graphically.

4.0 INTRODUCTION

Large tables of data are difficult to interpret. Engineers use graphing techniques to make the information more accessible. With a graph it is easy to identify trends, pick out highs and lows, and isolate data points that may be measurement or calculation errors. A graph can also be used as a quick check to determine whether or not a computer solution is yielding expected results.

4.1 TWO-DIMENSIONAL PLOTS

The most common plot used by engineers is the x-y plot. The data that we plot are usually read from a data file, or computed in programs and stored in vectors that we will call

OBJECTIVES

After reading this chapter, you should be able to

- create and label two-dimensional plots
- adjust the appearance of your plots
- create three-dimensional plots
- use the interactive MATLAB plotting tools

x and *y*. Generally, the *x* values represent the **independent variable** and the *y* values represent the **dependent variable**. The *y* values can be computed as a function of *x*, or the *x* and *y* values might be measured in an experiment.

4.1.1   Basic Plotting

Once the **x** and **y** vectors have been defined, MATLAB makes it easy to create plots. The data shown in the accompanying table were collected from an experiment with a remotely controlled model car. The experiment was repeated 10 times, and we have measured the distance that the car traveled for each trial, as shown in the following table, and in Figure 4.1.

Trial	Distance, ft
1	58.5
2	63.8
3	64.2
4	67.3
5	71.5
6	88.3
7	90.1
8	90.6
9	89.5
10	90.4

Assume that the trial values are stored in a vector called **x** (the user can define any convenient name), and the distance values are stored in a vector called **y**:

```
x = [1:10];
y = [ 58.5, 63.8, 64.2, 67.3, 71.5, 88.3, 90.1, 90.6, 89.5, 90.4];
```

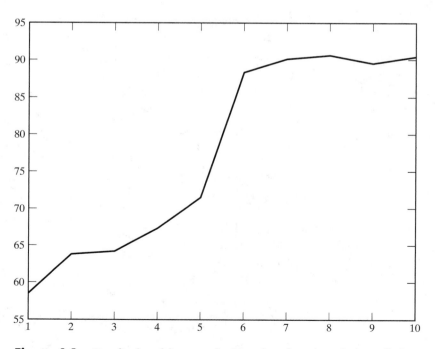

Figure 4.1.   Simple plot of distances for 10 trials with a remotely controlled model car.

To plot these points, we use the plot command, with **x** and **y** as arguments:

```
plot(x,y)
```

A graphics window automatically opens, which MATLAB calls Figure 1. The resulting plot is shown in Figure 4.1. (Slight variations in the scaling of the plot may occur, depending on the computer type and the size of the graphics window.)

Good engineering practice requires that we include units and a title in our plot. The following commands add a title, x- and y- axis labels, and a background grid:

```
plot(x,y)
title('Laboratory Experiment 1')
xlabel('Trial')
ylabel('Distance, ft')
grid on
```

These commands generated the plot in Figure 4.2. They could also be listed on a single line or two, separated by commas:

```
plot(x,y), title('Laboratory Experiment 1'),
xlabel('Trial'), ylabel('Distance, ft'), grid on
```

As you type these commands into MATLAB, notice that the type color changes to red when you enter a single quote ('). This alerts you that you are starting a string. The color changes to purple when you type the final single quote ('), indicating that you have completed the string. Paying attention to these visual aids will help you to avoid coding mistakes.

If you are working in the command window, the graphics window will open on top of the other windows. To continue working, either click in the command window or minimize the graphics window. You can also resize the graphics window to whatever size is convenient for you.

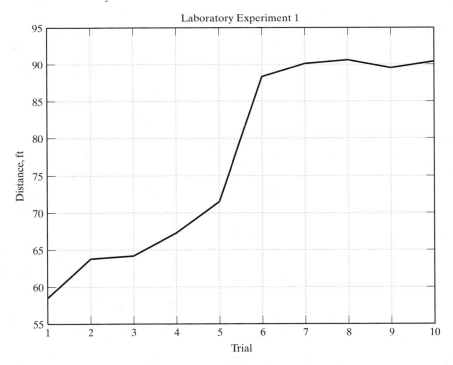

Figure 4.2. Adding a grid, a title, and labels makes a plot more usable.

If you are working in an M-file, when you request a plot and then continue on with more computations, MATLAB will generate and display the graphics window and then return immediately to execute the rest of the commands in the program. (See Figure 4.3.) If you request a second plot, the graph you created will be overwritten. There are two possible solutions to this problem: (1) use the **pause** command to temporarily halt the execution of your M-file program, or (2) create a second figure using the **figure** function.

The **pause** command stops the program execution until any key is pressed. If you want to pause for a specified number of seconds, use the **pause(n)** command, which will cause an execution pause for **n** seconds before continuing.

The **figure** command allows you to open a new figure window. The next time you request a plot, it will be displayed in this new window. For example,

```
figure(2)
```

opens a window named Figure 2, which then becomes the window used for subsequent plotting.

Creating a plot with more than one line can be accomplished in several ways. By default, the execution of a second plot statement will erase the first plot. However, you can layer plots on top of one another by using the **hold on** command. Execute the following statements to create a plot with both functions plotted on the same graph, as shown in Figure 4.4:

```
x = 0:pi/100:2*pi;
y1 = cos(x*4);
plot(x,y1)
y2 = sin(x);
hold on;
plot(x, y2)
```

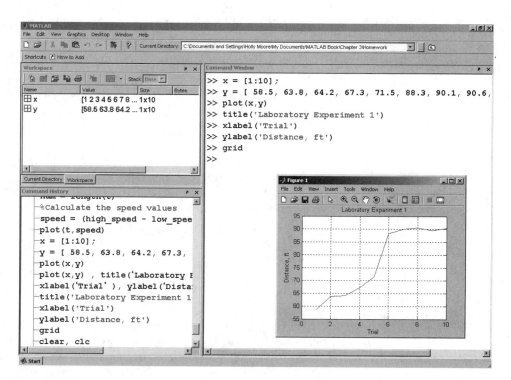

Figure 4.3. The graphics window opens on top of the command window. You can resize it to a convenient shape.

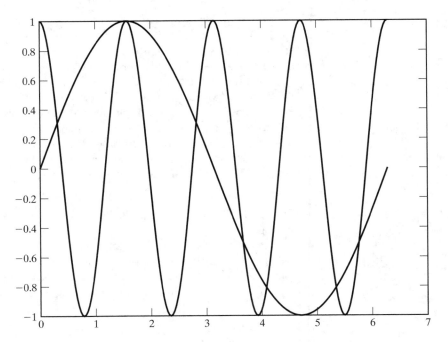

Figure 4.4. Creating multiple plots on the same graph.

Semicolons are optional on both the plot statements and the **hold on** statement.

MATLAB will continue to layer the plots until the **hold off** command is executed:

```
hold off
```

Another way to create a graph with multiple lines is to request both lines in a single **plot** command. MATLAB interprets the input to **plot** as alternating **x** and **y** vectors, as in

```
plot(X, Y, W, Z)
```

where the variables **X**, **Y** form an ordered set of values to be plotted, and **W** and **Z** form a second ordered set of values. Using the data from the previous example,

```
plot(x,y1,x,y2)
```

produces the same graph as Figure 4.4, with one exception—the two lines are different colors. MATLAB uses a default plotting color (blue) for the first line drawn in a plot command. When using the **hold on** approach, each line is drawn in a separate plot command, and thus is the same color. By requesting two lines in a single command such as **plot(x, y1, x, y2)**, the second line defaults to green, allowing the user to distinguish between the two plots.

If the **plot** function is called with a single matrix argument, MATLAB draws a separate line for each column of the matrix. The x-axis is labeled with the row index vector 1:k, where k is the number of rows in the matrix. This produces an evenly spaced plot, sometimes called a line plot. If **plot** is called with two arguments, one a vector and the other a matrix, MATLAB successively plots a line for each row in the matrix. For example, combine **y1** and **y2** into a single matrix **Y**, and plot **Y** versus **x**:

```
Y = [y1 y2]
plot(x,Y)
```

This creates the same plot as Figure 4.4, with each line a different color.
Here's another more complicated example:

```
X = 0:pi/100:2*pi;
Y1 = cos(X)*2;
Y2 = cos(X)*3;
Y3 = cos(X)*4;
Y4 = cos(X)*5;
Z = [Y1; Y2; Y3; Y4];
plot(X,Y1,X,Y2,X,Y3,X,Y4)
```

which produces the result shown in Figure 4.5. The same result is obtained with

```
plot(X, Z)
```

The **peaks** function is a function of two variables that produces sample data that are useful for demonstrating certain graphing functions. (The data are created by scaling and translating Gaussian distributions.) Calling peaks with a single argument **n** will create an $n \times n$ matrix. We can use peaks to demonstrate the power of using a matrix argument in the plot function. Hence,

```
plot(peaks(100))
```

results in the impressive graph in Figure 4.6.

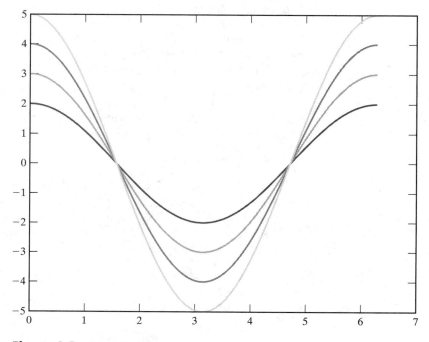

Figure 4.5.   Multiple plots on the same graph.

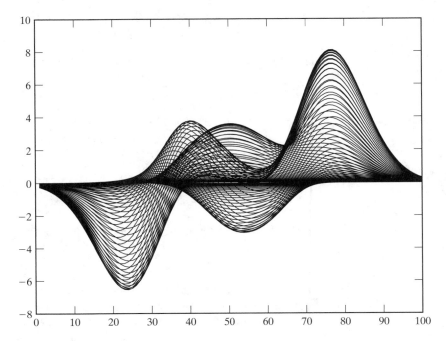

Figure 4.6. The peaks function plotted using a single argument in the plot command.

4.1.2 Line, Color, and Mark Style

The command **plot(x,y)** generates an x-y plot that connects the points represented by the vectors **x** and **y** with straight line segments. Graphs that appear to be curved are actually created by using a large number of points, but still connecting them with very short straight-line segments. In the default mode, MATLAB uses a blue line for the first set of data plotted, and changes the color for subsequent sets of data. Although the graph is created by connecting data points, those points are not shown on the graph in the default mode.

You can change the appearance of your plots by selecting user defined line styles and line colors, and by choosing to show the data points on the graph with user specified mark styles. By typing

```
help plot
```

in the command window, you can determine what choices are available to you. You can select solid (the default), dashed, dotted, and dash-dot line styles, and you can choose to show the points. The choices include plus signs, stars, circles, and x-marks, among others. There are seven different color choices. See Table 4.1 for a complete list.

The following commands illustrate the use of line, color, and mark styles.

```
x = [1:10];
y = [ 58.5, 63.8, 64.2, 67.3, 71.5, 88.3, 90.1, 90.6, 89.5, 90.4];
plot(x,y,':ok')
```

The resulting plot (see Figure 4.7) consists of a dashed line, data points marked with circles, and drawn in black. The indicators were listed inside a string, denoted with

TABLE 4.1 Line, Mark, and Color Options

Line Type	Indicator	Point Type	Indicator	Color	Indicator
solid	-	point	.	blue	b
dotted	:	circle	o	green	g
dash-dot	-.	x-mark	x	red	r
dashed	--	plus	+	cyan	c
		star	°	magenta	m
		square	s	yellow	y
		diamond	d	black	k
		triangle down	v		
		triangle up	^		
		triangle left	<		
		triangle right	>		
		pentagram	p		
		hexagram	h		

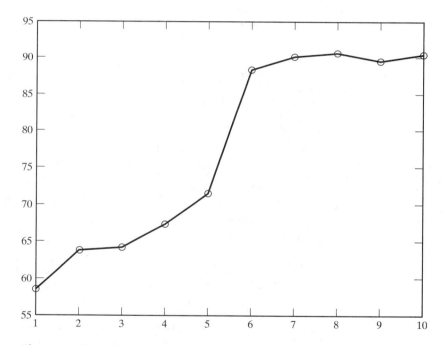

Figure 4.7. Adjusting the line, mark, and color style.

single quotes. The order in which they are entered is arbitrary, and does not affect the output.

To specify line, mark, and color styles for multiple lines, add a string containing the choices after each pair of data. If the string is not included, the defaults are used. For example,

```
plot(x,y,':ok',x,y*2,'--xr',x,y/2,'-b')
```

results in the graph shown in Figure 4.8.

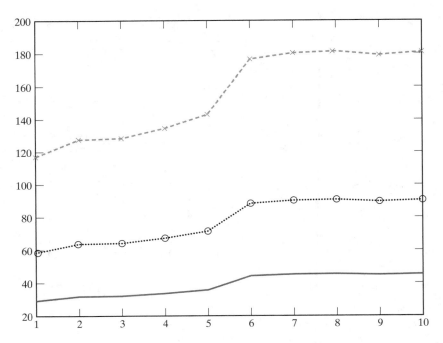

Figure 4.8. Multiple plots with varying line styles, colors, and point styles.

4.1.3 Axes Scaling

MATLAB automatically scales the axes to fit the data values. However, you can override this scaling with the axis command. There are several forms of the axis command:

axis   Freezes the current axis scaling for subsequent plots. A second execution of the command returns the system to automatic scaling.

axis(v)   Specifies that the axis being used is a four-element vector **v** that contains the scaling values **[xmin,xmax,ymin,ymax]**.

4.1.4 Annotating Plots

MATLAB offers several additional functions that allow you to annotate your plots:

legend('string1', 'string 2', etc) allows you to add a legend to your graph. The legend shows a sample of the line, and lists the string you have specified.

text(x_coordinate, y_coordinate, 'string',) allows you to add a text box to the graph. The box is placed at the specified x and y coordinates, and contains the string value specified.

The following code modifies the graph from Figure 4.8 with both a **legend** and a **text box**.

```
legend('line 1', 'line 2', 'line3')
text(1,100,'Label plots with the text command')
```

In addition, we added a title and x and y labels:

```
xlabel('My x label'), ylabel('My y label')
title('Example graph for Chapter 4')
```

The results are shown in Figure 4.9.

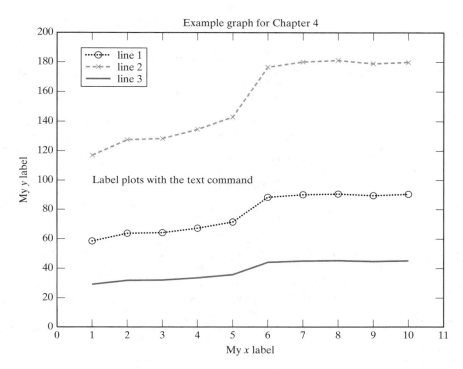

Figure 4.9. Final version of the sample graph, annotated with a legend, a text box, title, and x and y labels.

EXAMPLE 4.1

USING THE CLAUSIUS–CLAPEYRON EQUATION

In Example 3.1, the Clausius–Clapeyron equation was applied to find the saturation vapor pressure of water in the atmosphere, for different temperatures. The saturation water vapor pressure is useful to meteorologists because it can be used to calculate relative humidity, an important component of weather prediction, when the actual partial pressure of water in the air is known.

The results of our calculations were presented as a table. However, it is usually useful to also present calculational results graphically. Redo the calculations from Example 3.1, but this time present the results graphically.

The Clausius–Clapeyron equation is

$$\ln(P^{\circ}/6.11) = \left(\frac{\Delta H_v}{R_{\text{air}}}\right)\left(\frac{1}{273} - \frac{1}{T}\right)$$

where

P° is the saturation vapor pressure for water, in mbar, at temperature T
ΔH_v is the latent heat of vaporization for water, 2.453×10^6 J/kg
R_v is the gas constant for moist air, 461 J/kg
T is the temperature in degrees K

SOLUTION

1.   State the Problem

Find the saturation vapor pressure at temperatures from –60°F to 120°F, using the Clausius–Clapeyron equation.

2.   Describe the Input and Output

Input

$$\Delta H_v = 2.453 \times 10^6 \text{ J/kg}$$
$$R_{air} = 461 \text{ J/kg}$$
$$T = -60°\text{F to } 120°\text{F}$$

Since the number of temperature values was not specified, we'll choose to recalculate every 10°F.

Output

Table of temperature versus saturation vapor pressures
Graph of temperature versus saturation vapor pressures

3.   Hand Example

Change the temperatures from Fahrenheit to Kelvin:

$$T_k = (T_f + 459.6)/1.8$$

Solve the Clausius–Clapeyron equation for the saturation vapor pressure $(P°)$:

$$\ln(P°/6.11) = \left(\frac{\Delta H_v}{R_{air}}\right)\left(\frac{1}{273} - \frac{1}{T}\right)$$

$$P° = 6.11 \exp\left(\left(\frac{\Delta H_v}{R_{air}}\right)\left(\frac{1}{273} - \frac{1}{T}\right)\right)$$

Notice that the expression for the saturation vapor pressure, $P°$, is an exponential equation. We would expect the graph to have the following shape:

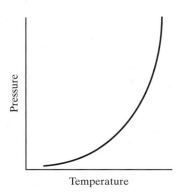

4.   Develop a MATLAB Solution

```
%Example 4.1
%Using the Clausius-Clapeyron Equation, find the
%saturation vapor pressure for water at different temperatures
%
TF=[-60:10:120];          %Define temp matrix in F
TK=(TF + 459.6)/1.8;      %Convert temp to K
Delta_H=2.45e6;           %Define latent heat of vaporization
R_air = 461;              %Define ideal gas constant for air
```

```
%
% Calculate the Vapor Pressures
Vapor_Pressure = 6.11*exp((Delta_H/R_air)*(1/273 - 1./TK));
% Display the results in a table
my_results = [TF',Vapor_Pressure']
%
% Create an x-y plot
plot(TF,Vapor_Pressure)
title('Clausius-Clapeyron Behavior')
xlabel('Temperature, F')
ylabel('Saturation Vapor Pressure, mbar')
```

The resulting table is

```
my_results =
        -60.0000      0.0698
        -50.0000      0.1252
        -40.0000      0.2184
        -30.0000      0.3714
        -20.0000      0.6163
        -10.0000      1.0000
              0       1.5888
         10.0000      2.4749
         20.0000      3.7847
         30.0000      5.6880
         40.0000      8.4102
         50.0000     12.2458
         60.0000     17.5747
         70.0000     24.8807
         80.0000     34.7729
         90.0000     48.0098
        100.0000     65.5257
        110.0000     88.4608
        120.0000    118.1931
```

A figure window opens to display the graphical results. (See Figure 4.10.)

5.   Test the Solution

The plot follows the expected trend. It is almost always easier to determine if computational results make sense when a graph is produced. Tabular data is extremely difficult to absorb.   ■

EXAMPLE 4.2

BALLISTICS

The range of an object shot at an angle θ with respect to the x-axis and an initial velocity v_o (see Figure 4.11) is given by

$$R(\theta) = \frac{v^2}{g}\sin(2\theta) \text{ for } 0 \le \theta \le \frac{\pi}{2} \text{ and neglecting air resistance.}$$

Use $g = 9.9$ m/s^2 and an initial velocity of 100 m/s. Show that the maximum range is obtained at $\theta = \frac{\pi}{4}$ by computing and plotting the range in increments of 0.05 from

$$0 \le \theta \le \frac{\pi}{2}$$

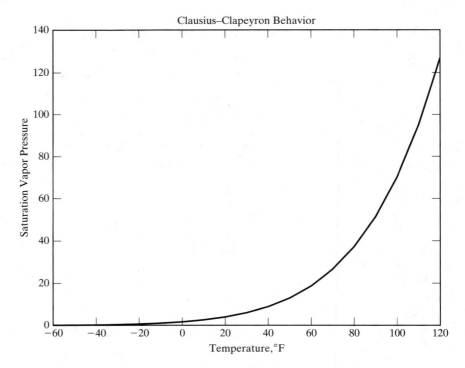

Figure 4.10. A plot of the Clausius–Clapeyron equation.

Figure 4.11.   Ballistic motion.

Repeat your calculations with an initial velocity of 50 m/s, and plot both sets of results on a single graph.

SOLUTION

1.   State the Problem

Calculate the range as a function of launch angle.

2.   Describe the Input and Output

Input

g = 9.9 m/s^2
θ = 0 to $\pi/2$, incremented by 0.05
v_0 = 50 m/s and 100 m/s

Output

Range, R
Present the results as a plot

3.   Hand Example

If the cannon is pointed straight up, we know that the range is zero, and if the cannon is horizontal, the range is also zero. (See Figure 4.12.) That means that the range must increase with the cannon angle, up to some maximum, and then decrease. A sample calculation at 45 degrees ($\pi/4$ radians) shows

$$R(\theta) = \frac{v^2}{g}\sin(2\theta)$$

$$R\left(\frac{\pi}{4}\right) = \frac{100^2}{9.9}\sin\left(\frac{2\cdot\pi}{4}\right) = 1010 \text{ meters when the initial velocity is 100 m/sec.}$$

4.   Develop a MATLAB Solution

```
%Example 4.3
%The program calculates the range of a ballistic projectile
%
% Define the constants
g = 9.9;
v1 = 50;
v2 = 100;
% Define the angle vector
angle = 0:0.05:pi/2;
% Calculate the range
R1 = v1^2/g*sin(2*angle);
R2 = v2^2/g*sin(2*angle);
%Plot the results
plot(angle,R1,angle,R2,':')
title('Cannon Range')
xlabel('Cannon Angle')
ylabel('Range, meters')
legend('Initial Velocity = 50 m/s', 'Initial Velocity = 100 m/s')
```

Notice that the plot command requested MATLAB to print the second set of data as a dashed line. A title, labels, and legend were also added. (See Figure 4.13.)

Figure 4.12.   The range is zero if the cannon is perfectly vertical or perfectly horizontal.

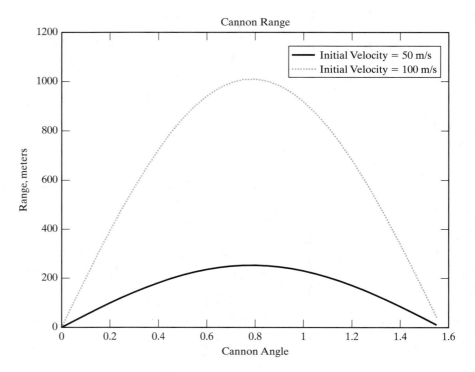

Figure 4.13. The predicted range of a projectile.

5. Test the Solution

Compare the MATLAB results to the hand example results, shown in Figure 4.13. Both graphs start and end at zero. The maximum range for an initial velocity of 100 m/sec is approximately 1000 m, which corresponds well to the calculated value of 1010 m. Notice that both solutions peak at the same angle, approximately 0.8 radians. The numerical value for $\pi/4$ is 0.785 radians, confirming the hypothesis presented in the problem statement, that the maximum range is achieved by pointing the cannon at an angle of $\pi/4$ radians (45 degrees). ∎

4.1.5 Other Types of Two-dimensional Plots

Although simple x-y plots are the most common type of engineering plot, there are many other ways to represent data. Depending on the situation, these techniques may be more appropriate that an x-y plot.

Polar Plots

MATLAB provides plotting capability with polar coordinates:

polar(theta, rho) Generates a polar plot of angle theta (in radians) and radial distance, rho.

For example,

```
x=0:pi/100:pi;
y=sin(x);
polar(x,y)
```

generates the plot in Figure 4.14. A title was added in the usual way:

title('The sine function plotted in polar coordinates is a circle.')

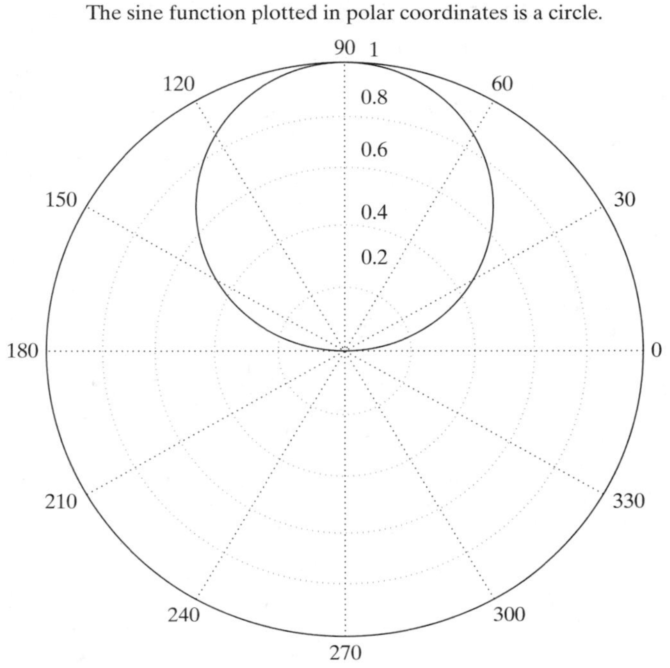

The sine function plotted in polar coordinates is a circle.

Figure 4.14.   A polar plot of the sine function.

Logarithmic Plots

For most plots that we generate, the x- and y-axes are divided into equally spaced intervals. These plots are called linear plots. Occasionally, we may want to use a logarithmic scale on one or both of the axes. A logarithmic scale (base 10) is convenient when a variable ranges over many orders of magnitude, because the wide range of values can be graphed without compressing the smaller values. Logarithmic plots are also useful for representing data that varies exponentially.

The MATLAB commands for generating linear and logarithmic plots of the vectors **x** and **y** are the following:

`plot(x,y)`	Generates a linear plot of the vectors **x** and **y**.
`semilogx(x,y)`	Generates a plot of the values of **x** and **y** using a logarithmic scale for **x** and a linear scale for **y**.
`semilogy(x,y)`	Generates a plot of the values of **x** and **y** using a linear scale for **x** and a logarithmic scale for **y**.
`loglog(x,y)`	Generates a plot of the vectors **x** and **y**, using a logarithmic scale for both **x** and **y**.

It is important to recognize that the logarithms of a negative value and of zero do not exist. Therefore, if the data to be plotted in a semilog plot or a log–log plot contain negative or zero values, a warning message will be printed by MATLAB informing you that these data points have been omitted from the data plotted.

Each of the commands for logarithmic plotting can be executed with one argument, as we saw in **plot(y)** for a linear plot. In these cases, the plots are generated with the values of the indices of the vector **y** used as **x** values.

Bar Graphs and Pie Charts

Bar graphs, histograms, and pie charts are popular techniques for reporting data:

bar(x)	When **x** is a vector, bar generates a vertical bar graph. When **x** is a two-dimensional matrix, bar groups the data by row.
barh(x)	When **x** is a vector, barh generates a horizontal bar graph. When **x** is a two-dimensional matrix, barh groups the data by row.
bar3(x)	Generates a three-dimensional bar chart.
barh3(x)	Generates a three-dimensional horizontal bar chart.
pie(x)	Generates a pie chart. Each element in the matrix is represented as a slice of the pie.
pie3(x)	Generates a three-dimensional pie chart. Each element in the matrix is represented as a slice of the pie.

Examples of some of these graphs were generated for Figure 4.15. The subplot command (described in Section 4.1.6), makes it possible to display all four plots in one figure:

```
clear, clc
x=[1,2,5,4,8];
y=[x;1:5];
subplot(2,2,1)
bar(x),title('A bargraph of vector x')
subplot(2,2,2)
bar(y),title('A bargraph of matrix y')
```

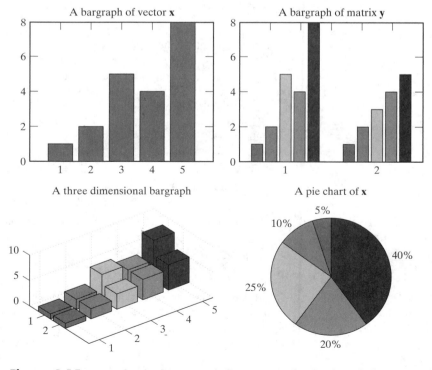

Figure 4.15. Sample two-dimensional plots presented using the subplot command to divide the window into quadrants.

```
subplot(2,2,3)
bar3(y),title('A three dimensional bargraph')
subplot(2,2,4)
pie(x),title('A pie chart of x')
```

Histograms

A histogram is a special type of graph particularly relevant to statistics. A histogram is a plot showing the distribution of a set of values. In MATLAB, the histogram computes the number of values falling in 10 bins that are equally spaced between the minimum and maximum values, from the set of values. For example, if we define a matrix **x**, with the grades from the Introduction to Engineering final exam (see Figure 4.16), the scores could be represented in a histogram:

```
x=[100,95,74,87,22,78,34,35,93,88,86,42,55,48];
hist(x)
```

The default number of bins is 10, but if we have a large data set we may want to divide up the data into more categories (bins). For example, to create a histogram with 25 bins, the command would be

```
hist(x, 25)
```

4.1.6   Subplots

The subplot command allows you to split the graphing window into subwindows. Two subwindows can be arranged either top-and-bottom or left-to-right. A four-window split has two subwindows on the top and two subwindows on the bottom. The arguments to the subplot command are three integers, m, n, and p. The digits m and n specify that the graph

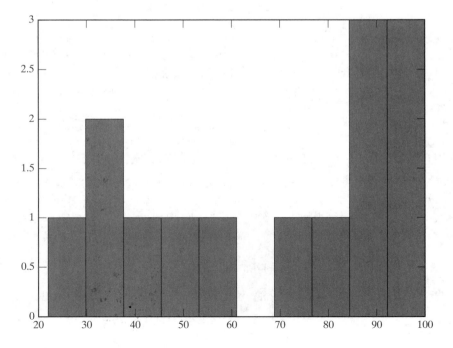

Figure 4.16.   A histogram of final-exam grade data.

window is to be split into an *m*-by-*n* grid of smaller windows, and the digit *p* specifies the *p*th window for the current plot. The windows are numbered from left to right, top to bottom. Therefore, the following commands specify that the graph window is to be split into a top plot and a bottom plot, and the current plot is to be placed in the top subwindow:

```
subplot(2,1,1)
plot(x,y)
```

Figure 4.17 contains four plots that illustrate the subplot command, along with the linear and logarithmic plot commands. This figure was generated with the following statements run from an M-file:

```
clear, clc
% Generate plots of a polynomial
%
x = 0:0.5:50;
y = 5*x.^2;
subplot(2,2,1)
plot(x,y)
    title('Polynomial - linear/linear')
    ylabel('y'), grid
subplot(2,2,2)
semilogx(x,y)
    title('Polynomial - log/linear')
    ylabel('y'), grid
subplot(2,2,3)
semilogy(x,y)
    title('Polynomial - linear/log')
    xlabel('x'), ylabel('y'), grid
subplot(2,2,4)
loglog(x,y)
    title('Polynomial - log/log')
    xlabel('x'), ylabel('y'), grid
```

The indenting is intended to make the code easier to read—MATLAB ignores white space. As a matter of style, notice that only the bottom two subplots have *x*-axis labels.

EXAMPLE 4.3

UDF ENGINE PERFORMANCE

Use the following equations to calculate the velocity and acceleration of the advanced turboprop engine called an unducted fan (UDF), and display the results as a table of time, velocity, and acceleration:

$$\text{velocity} = 0.00001 \text{ time}^3 - 0.00488 \text{ time}^2 + 0.75795 \text{ time} + 181.3566$$

$$\text{acceleration} = 3 - 0.000062 \text{ velocity}^2$$

In addition create an *x-y* plot with two lines, one for velocity and one for acceleration.

SOLUTION

1. State the Problem

Calculate the velocity and acceleration, using a script M-file.

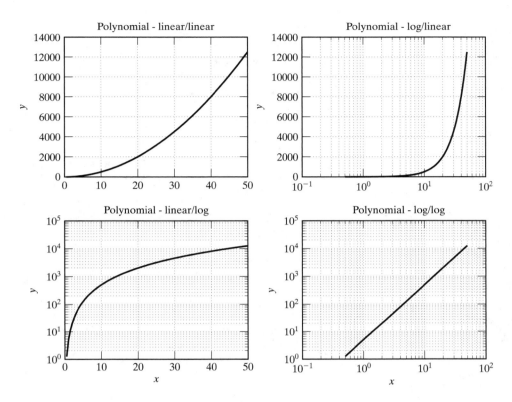

Figure 4.17. Linear and logarithmic plots.

2. Describe the Input and Output

Input

Start time is	0 seconds
Final time is	120 seconds
Time increment is	10 seconds

Output

Velocity
Acceleration

Present the results both as a table and as a plot.

3. Hand Example

Solve the equations stated in the problem for time = 10 seconds and 100 seconds:

$$\text{velocity} = 0.00001\ \text{time}^3 - 0.00488\ \text{time}^2 + 0.75795\ \text{time} + 181.3566$$
$$= 188.46\ \text{m/sec}$$
$$= 218.35\ \text{m/sec}$$
$$\text{acceleration} = 3 - 0.000062\ \text{velocity}^2$$
$$= .798\ \text{m/sec}^2$$
$$= 0.04404\ \text{m/sec}^2$$

4. Develop a MATLAB Solution

```
clear, clc
%Example 4.2
%These commands generate velocity and acceleration
%values for a UDF aircraft test
%
%Define the time matrix
time = 0:10:120;
%
%Calculate the velocity matrix
velocity = 0.00001*time.^3 - 0.00488*time.^2 ...
                  + 0.75795*time + 181.3566;
%
%Use the calculated velocities to find the acceleration
acceleration = 3 - 6.2e-5*velocity.^2;
%
%Present the results in a table
[time', velocity', acceleration']
%
%Create individual x-y plots
plot(time,velocity)
title('Velocity of a UDF Aircraft')
xlabel('time, seconds')
ylabel('velocity, meters/sec')
grid on
%
figure(2)
plot(time, acceleration)
title('Acceleration of a UDF Aircraft')
xlabel('time, seconds')
ylabel('acceleration, meters/sec^2')
grid on
%
%Use plotyy to create a scale on each side of the plot
figure(3)
plotyy(time, velocity,time,acceleration)
title('UDF Aircraft Performance')
xlabel('time, seconds')
ylabel('velocity, meters/sec')
grid on
```

The results are returned to the command window:

```
ans =
         0      181.3566      0.9608
   10.0000      188.4581      0.7980
   20.0000      194.6436      0.6511
   30.0000      199.9731      0.5207
   40.0000      204.5066      0.4070
   50.0000      208.3041      0.3098

   60.0000      211.4256      0.2286
   70.0000      213.9311      0.1625
   80.0000      215.8806      0.1105
   90.0000      217.3341      0.0715
  100.0000      218.3516      0.0440
  110.0000      218.9931      0.0266
  120.0000      219.3186      0.0178
```

Three graphics windows open. (See Figures 4.18, 4.19, and 4.20.)

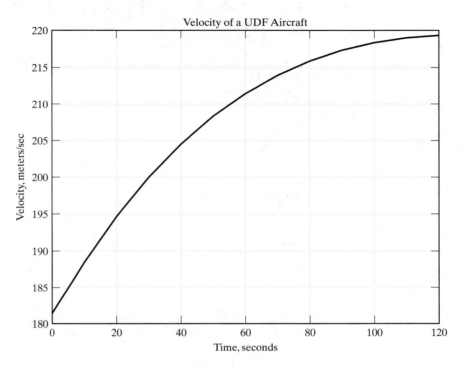

Figure 4.18.   Velocity of an unducted fan aircraft.

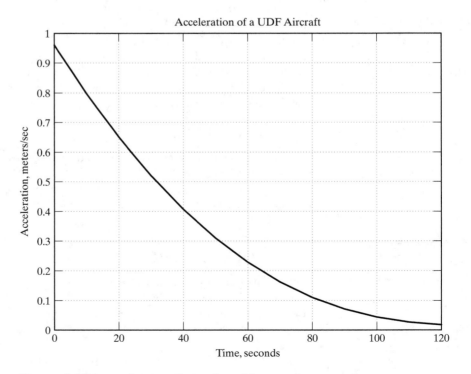

Figure 4.19.   Acceleration of an unducted fan aircraft.

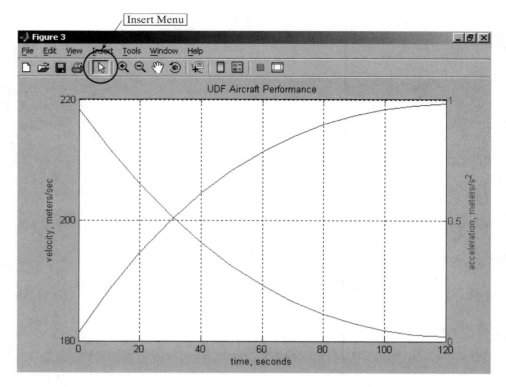

Figure 4.20. Plot using two y axes.

The third plot (Figure 4.20) is a bit more complicated. We used the **plotyy** function instead of the **plot** function to force the addition of a second scale on the right-hand side of the plot. We needed this because velocity and acceleration have different units—otherwise we could have just used the same syntax in plot. It's possible to add the right hand y-axis label from the command line, but it's difficult. Instead, use the **Insert** option from the menu bar. Just remember, if you rerun your program, you'll lose the right-hand label.

5. Test the Solution

Compare the MATLAB results to the hand example results. Notice that the velocity and acceleration calculated from the hand example and the MATLAB solution match. MATLAB automatically scales your graphs using the data plotted. Sometimes it is preferable to use a standard scale, in which case you could use the axis command to control the graphing area. ∎

EXAMPLE 4.4

RATES OF DIFFUSION

Metals are often treated to make them stronger and therefore to wear longer. One problem with making a piece of metal strong is that it becomes difficult to form it into a desired shape. One strategy to get around this problem is to form a soft metal into the shape you desire, and then to harden the surface. This makes the metal wear well, without making it brittle.

A common hardening process is called carburizing. The metal part is exposed to carbon, which diffuses into the part, making it harder. This is a very slow process if performed at low temperatures, but can be accelerated by heating the part. The diffusivity is a measure of how fast diffusion occurs, and can be modeled as

$$D = D_0 \exp\left(\frac{-Q}{RT}\right)$$

where

D is the diffusivity, cm^2/s
D_0 is the diffusion coefficient, cm^2/s
Q is the activation energy, J/mole, 8.314 J/mole K
R is the ideal gas constant, J/mole K
T is the temperature, K

As iron is heated, it changes structure, and its diffusion characteristics change. The values of D_0 and Q are shown in the table for carbon diffusing through each of iron's structures:

Metal Type	D_0 (cm²/s)	Q (J/mole K)
alpha Fe (BCC)	.0062	80,000
gamma Fe (FCC)	0.23	148,000

Create a plot of diffusivity versus inverse temperature (1/T) using the data provided. Try the rectangular, semilog, and log–log plots to see which you think might represent the results best. Let the temperature vary from room temperature (25°C) to 1200°C.

SOLUTION

1.   State the Problem

Calculate the diffusivity for carbon in iron.

2.   Describe the Input and Output

Input

For C in alpha iron, $D_0 = 0.0062$ cm²/s and $Q = 80,000$ J/mole K
For C in gamma iron, $D_0 = 0.23$ cm²/s and $Q = 148,000$ J/mole K
$R = 8.314$ J/mole K
T varies from 25°C to 1200°C

Output

Calculate the diffusivity, and plot it.

3.   Hand Example

$$D = D_0 \exp\left(\frac{-Q}{RT}\right)$$

At room temperature, the diffusivity for carbon in alpha iron is

$$D = .0062\exp\left(\frac{-80000}{8.314 \cdot (25 + 273)}\right)$$

$$D = 5.9 \times 10^{-17}$$

(Notice that temperature had to be changed from Celsius to Kelvin.)

4.   Develop a MATLAB Solution

```
% Example 4.4
% Calculate the Diffusivity of Carbon in Iron
clear, clc
% Define the constants
D0alpha = .0062;
D0gamma = 0.23;
Qalpha = 80000;
Qgamma = 148000;
R = 8.314;
T = 25:5:1200;
% Change T from C to K
T = T+273;
% Calculate the Diffusivity
Dalpha = D0alpha*exp(-Qalpha./(R*T));
Dgamma = D0gamma*exp(-Qgamma./(R*T));
% Plot the Results
subplot(2,2,1)
plot(1./T,Dalpha, 1./T,Dgamma)
title('Diffusivity of C in Fe')
xlabel('Inverse Temperature, K^-1'),ylabel('Diffusivity, cm^2/s')
grid on
subplot(2,2,2)
semilogx(1./T,Dalpha, 1./T,Dgamma)
title('Diffusivity of C in Fe')
xlabel('Inverse Temperature, K^-1'),ylabel('Diffusivity, cm^2/s')
grid on
subplot(2,2,3)
semilogy(1./T,Dalpha, 1./T,Dgamma)
title('Diffusivity of C in Fe')
xlabel('Inverse Temperature, K^-1'),ylabel('Diffusivity, cm^2/s')
grid on
subplot(2,2,4)
loglog(1./T,Dalpha, 1./T,Dgamma)
title('Diffusivity of C in Fe')
xlabel('Inverse Temperature, K^-1'),ylabel('Diffusivity, cm^2/s')
grid on
```

Subplots were used in Figure 4.21 so that all four variations of the plot are in the same figure. Notice that x-labels were added only to the bottom two graphs (to reduce clutter), and that a legend was added only to the first plot. The semilogy plot resulted in straight lines, and allows a user to read values from the graph easily over a wide range of both temperatures and diffusivities. This is the plotting scheme usually performed to present diffusivity values in textbooks and handbooks.

5.   Test the Solution

Compare the MATLAB results to the hand example results.
        We calculated that the diffusivity was

$$5.9 \times 10^{-17} \text{ cm}^2/\text{sec at } 25°\text{C}$$

for carbon in alpha iron. To check our answer, we'll need to change 25°C to Kelvin, and take the inverse:

$$1/(25 + 273) = 3.36 \times 10^{-3}$$

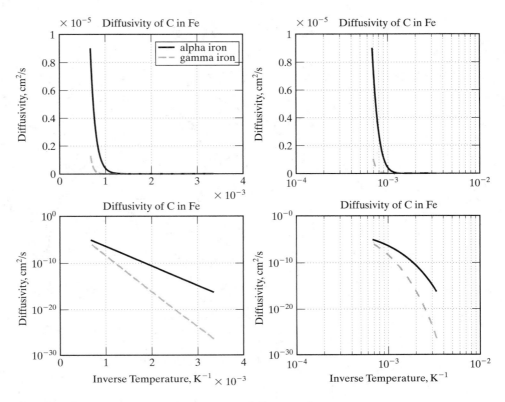

Figure 4.21. Diffusivity data plotted using different scales.

From the **semilogy** graph (lower left-hand corner), we can see that the diffusivity for alpha iron is approximately 10^{-17} cm²/sec. ∎

4.2   THREE-DIMENSIONAL PLOTTING

MATLAB offers a variety of three-dimensional plotting commands. Several of these formats are discussed in this section.

4.2.1   Three-Dimensional Line Plot

The **plot3** function is similar to the **plot** function, except that it accepts data in three dimensions. (See Figure 4.22.) Instead of just providing **x** and **y** vectors, the user must also provide a **z** vector. These ordered "triples" are then plotted in three-spaces and connected with straight lines. For example,

```
clear, clc
x = linspace(0,10*pi,100);
y = cos(x);
z = sin(x);
plot3(x,y,z)
grid
xlabel('angle')
ylabel('cos(x)')
zlabel('sin(x)')
title('A Spring')
```

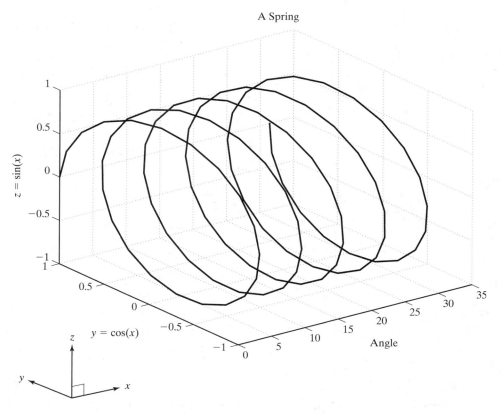

Figure 4.22. A three-dimensional plot of a spring.

The title, labels, and grid are added in the usual way, with the addition of **zlabel** for the z-axis.

The coordinate system used with **plot3** is oriented using the right-handed coordinate system familiar to engineers:

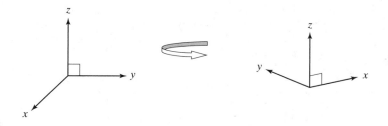

4.2.2 Surface Plots

Surface plots allow us to represent data as a surface. We will be experimenting with **mesh** plots and with **surf** plots.

Mesh Plots

There are several ways to use mesh plots. They can be used to good effect with a single two-dimensional ($n \times m$) matrix. In this application, the value in the matrix represents the **z** value in the plot. The **x** and **y** values are based on the matrix dimensions. For example, the following matrix

```
z = [1, 2, 3, 4,  5,  6,  7,  8,  9, 10;
     2, 4, 6, 8, 10, 12, 14, 16, 18, 20;
     3, 4, 5, 6,  7,  8,  9, 10, 11, 12]

    mesh(z)
    xlabel('x-axis')
    ylabel('y-axis')
    zlabel('z-axis')
```

generates the graph shown in Figure 4.23.

The graph is a "mesh" created by connecting the points defined in **z** into a rectilinear grid. Notice that the *x*-axis goes from 0 to 10, with each point coordinate corresponding to a row; and y goes from 0 to 3, with each point corresponding to a column.

The mesh function can also be used with three arguments, **mesh(x,y,z)**, where each is a two-dimensional matrix. In this case, **x** is a list of *x*-coordinates, **y** is a list of *y*-coordinates, etc. All three matrices must be the same size, since together they represent a list of ordered triples defining the plotting points:

```
z = [1, 2, 3, 4,  5,  6,  7,  8,  9, 10;
     2, 4, 6, 8, 10, 12, 14, 16, 18, 20;
     3, 4, 5, 6,  7,  8,  9, 10, 11, 12]

x = linspace(1,50,10)
y = linspace(500,1000,3)
```

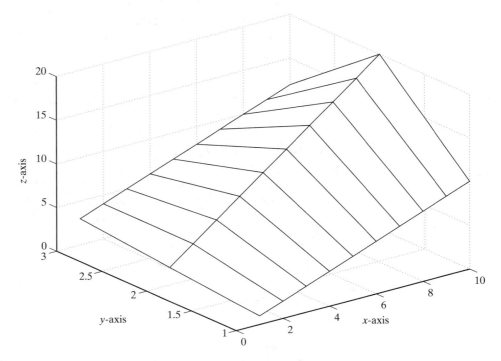

Figure 4.23. Simple mesh created with a single two-dimensional matrix.

This creates a two-dimensional **z** matrix, with 10 rows and 3 columns, but it only creates one-dimensional **x** and **y** matrices. The **x** matrix is one row by 10 columns, and the **y** matrix is one row by three columns. We can then use the **meshgrid** function to create two matrices that are the same size, three rows by 10 columns. The command

```
[new_x, new_y] = meshgrid(x,y)
```

returns

```
new_x =
Columns 1 through 6
        1.00        6.44       11.89       17.33       22.78       28.22
        1.00        6.44       11.89       17.33       22.78       28.22
        1.00        6.44       11.89       17.33       22.78       28.22
Columns 7 through 10
       33.67       39.11       44.56       50.00
       33.67       39.11       44.56       50.00
       33.67       39.11       44.56       50.00
new_y =
Columns 1 through 6
      500.00      500.00      500.00      500.00      500.00      500.00
      750.00      750.00      750.00      750.00      750.00      750.00
     1000.00     1000.00     1000.00     1000.00     1000.00     1000.00
Columns 7 through 10
      500.00      500.00      500.00      500.00
      750.00      750.00      750.00      750.00
     1000.00     1000.00     1000.00     1000.00
```

Notice that in the case of **new_x** all the rows are the same, whereas in the case of **new_y** all the columns are the same. The creation of these new matrices provides us with appropriate input to the **mesh** function

```
mesh(new_x, new_y, z)
```

which then generates the plot represented in Figure 4.24(a).

The **meshgrid** function is also useful in calculations with multiple variables.

Surf Plots

Surf plots are similar to **mesh** plots, but **surf** creates a three-dimensional colored surface instead of a mesh. The colors vary depending on the value of **z**.

The **surf** command expects the same input as **mesh**: either a single input such as **surf(z)**, in which case it uses the row and column indices as *x*- and *y*-coordinates; or three two-dimensional matrices. Figure 4.24(b) was generated using the same commands as those used to generate Figure 4.24(a), except that **surf** replaced **mesh**.

The shading scheme for surface plots is controlled with the shading command. The default, shown in Figure 4.24(b) is "faceted flat." Interpolated shading can create interesting effects. The plot shown in Figure 4.24(c) was created by adding

```
shading interp
```

to the previous list of commands. Flat shading without the grid is generated when

```
shading flat
```

is used, as shown in Figure 4.24(d).

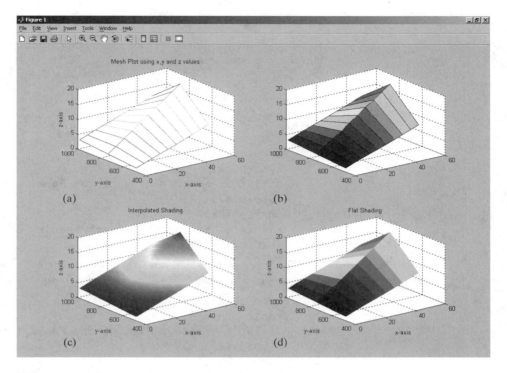

Figure 4.24.   Mesh and surf plots created using three input arguments.

The color scheme used in surface plots can be controlled using the **colormap** function. For example,

```
colormap(gray)
```

forces a gray-scale representation for surface plots. This may be more appropriate if you'll be making black and white copies of your plots. Other **colormaps** available are

```
autumn
spring
summer
winter
jet (default)
bone
colorcube
cool
copper
flag
hot
hsv
pink
prism
white
```

Use the **help** command to see a description of these options:

```
help colormap
```

Contour Plots

Contour plots are two-dimensional representations of three-dimensional surfaces. Maps often represent elevations with contours. MATLAB offers an example function called

peaks

that generates an interesting three-dimensional shape, as seen in Figure 4.25.

Figure 4.25(a) and 4.25(b) were generated as in the previous example:

```
figure(2)
subplot(2,2,1)
surf(peaks)
title('a. Surface Plot of the Peaks function')
subplot(2,2,2)
surf(peaks)
title('b. Surface Plot with Shading of the Peaks function')
shading interp
```

The contour command was used to create Figure 4.25(c), and the surfc command was used to create Figure 4.25(d):

```
subplot(2,2,3)
contour(peaks)
title('c. Contour Plot of the Peaks function')
subplot(2,2,4)
surfc(peaks)
title('d. Combination Surface and Contour Plot')
```

Additional options for using all of the three-dimensional plotting functions are included in the Help window.

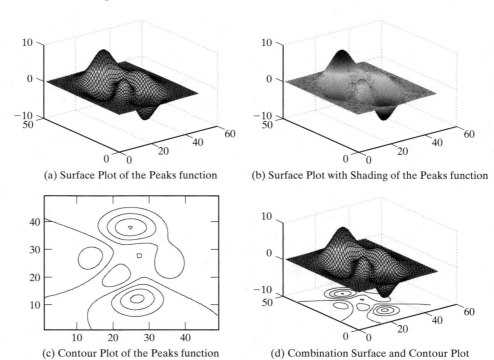

(a) Surface Plot of the Peaks function

(b) Surface Plot with Shading of the Peaks function

(c) Contour Plot of the Peaks function

(d) Combination Surface and Contour Plot

Figure 4.25. Surface and contour plots of the peaks function.

4.3   EDITING PLOTS FROM THE MENU BAR

In addition to controlling the way your plots look by using MATLAB commands, you can also edit a plot once you've created it. The plot in Figure 4.26 was created using the sphere command, which is one of several example functions, like **peaks**, used for demonstrating plotting.

To annotate the graph, select the insert menu. Notice that you can insert labels, titles, legends, text boxes, etc., all by using this menu. The **Tools menu** allows you to change the way the plot looks by zooming in or out, changing the aspect ratio, etc. The figure toolbar underneath the menu tool bar offers icons that allow you to do the same thing.

The plot in Figure 4.26 doesn't really look like a sphere; it's missing labels and a title, and it may not be clear what the colors mean. We edited this plot by first adjusting the shape:

Select **Edit → Axis Properties** from the menu tool bar.

From the **Property Editor – Axis window**,

select **Inspector → Data Aspect Ratio Mode**

Set the mode to manual.

(See Figure 4.27.)

Similarly, labels, a title, and a color bar were added (Figure 4.28) using the **Insert menu** option on the menu bar. Editing your plot in this manner is more interactive and allows you to fine-tune its appearance. Once you have the plot looking the

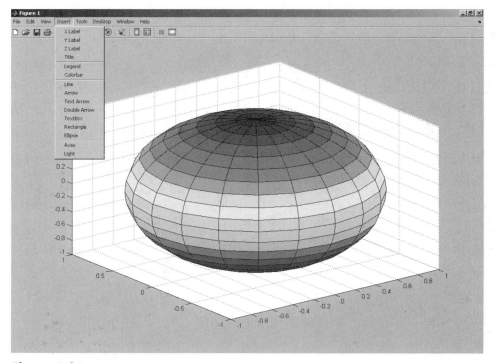

Figure 4.26.   A plot of a sphere.

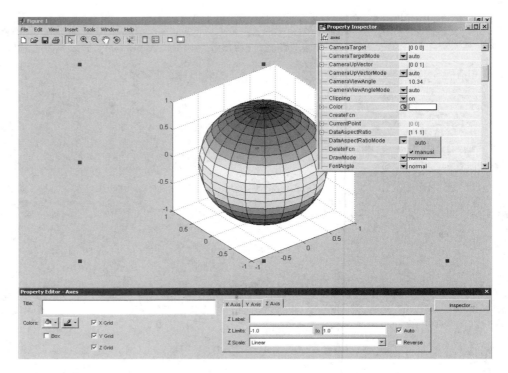

Figure 4.27. MATLAB allows you to edit plots using commands from the toolbar.

way you'd like it to, simply go to the **Edit menu** and select **Copy Figure**. This will allow you to paste your results into a word processing document. Most of the plot figures in this book were created using this technique. The only problem with editing a figure interactively is that, if you run your MATLAB program again, you will lose all of your improvements.

4.4 CREATING PLOTS FROM THE WORKSPACE WINDOW

A great feature of MATLAB 7 is the ability to interactively create plots from the workspace window. In the workspace window, select a variable, then select the drop-down menu on the **plotting icon** (shown in Figure 4.29). MATLAB will list the plotting options it thinks are reasonable for the data stored in your variable. Simply select the appropriate option, and your plot is created in the current **figure window**. If you don't like any of the suggested plot types, choose **More plots . . .** from the drop-down menu, and a new window will open with the complete list of available plotting options. This is especially useful, as it may suggest options that had not occurred to you. For example, Figure 4.30 shows a stem plot of the **x** matrix highlighted in the figure.

If you want to plot more than one variable, highlight the first, then hold down the **Ctrl** key and select the additional variables. (To annotate your plots, use the interactive editing process.) The interactive environment is a rich resource. You'll get the most out of it by exploring and experimenting. (See Figure 4.30.)

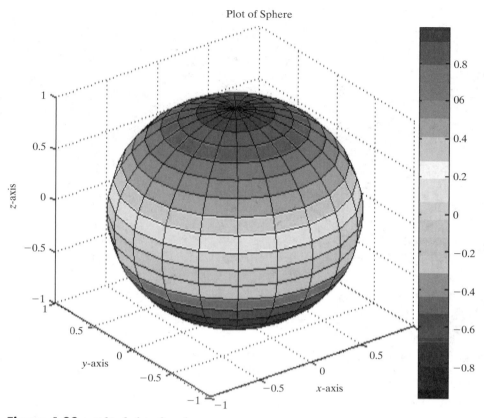

Figure 4.28.   Edited plot of a sphere.

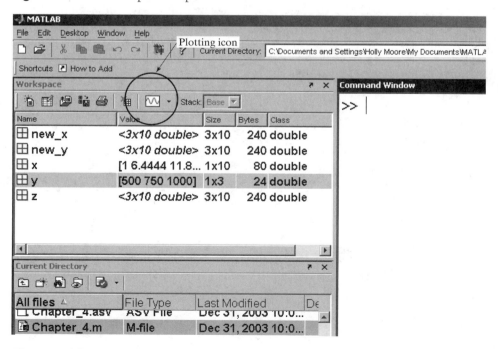

Figure 4.29.   Plotting from the workspace window.

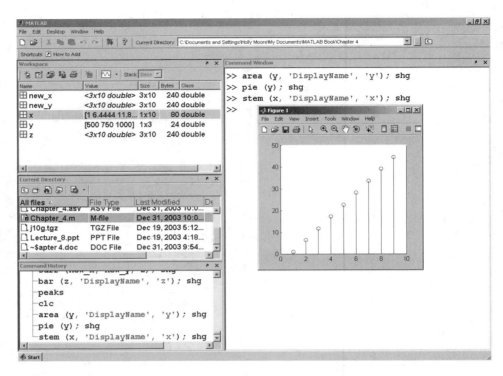

Figure 4.30. A stem plot created interactively from the workspace window.

SUMMARY

A wide variety of plotting options are available in MATLAB, many of which are not covered here. Use the Help function to find out more about graphing options, or use the interactive graphing capability accessible from the workspace window. Graphs are useful in engineering to display results, identify trends, and pinpoint errors. No engineering graph should ever be presented without a title and axis labels. Although extremely complicated graphics are possible in MATLAB, the simple x-y plot is the one most commonly used by engineers.

MATLAB SUMMARY

This MATLAB summary lists all of the special characters, commands, and functions that were defined in this chapter:

Special Characters

Line Type	Indicator	Point Type	Indicator	Color	Indicator
solid	-	point	.	blue	b
dotted	:	circle	o	green	g
dash-dot	-.	x-mark	x	red	r
dashed	--	plus	+	cyan	c
		star	°	magenta	m
		square	s	yellow	y
		diamond	d	black	k

Line Type	Indicator	Point Type	Indicator	Color	Indicator
		triangle down	v		
		triangle up	^		
		triangle left	<		
		triangle right	>		
		pentagram	p		
		hexagram	h		

Commands and Functions

autumn	optional colormap used in surface plots
axis	freezes the current axis scaling for subsequent plots or specifies the axis dimensions
bar	generates a bar graph
bar3	generates a three-dimensional bar graph
barh	generates a horizontal bar graph
barh3	generates a horizontal three-dimensional bar graph
bone	optional colormap used in surface plots
colorcube	optional colormap used in surface plots
colormap	color scheme used in surface plots
cool	optional colormap used in surface plots
copper	optional colormap used in surface plots
figure	opens a new figure window
flag	optional colormap used in surface plots
grid off	turns the grid off
grid on	adds a grid to the current and all subsequent graphs in the current figure
hist	generates a histogram
hold off	instructs MATLAB to erase figure contents before adding new information
hold on	instructs MATLAB not to erase figure contents before adding new information
hot	optional colormap used in surface plots
hsv	optional colormap used in surface plots
jet	default colormap used in surface plots
legend	adds a legend to a graph
loglog	generates an x-y plot, with both axes scaled logarithmically
mesh	generates a mesh plot of a surface
meshgrid	divides each of two vectors into separate two-dimensional matrices, the size of which is determined by the source vectors
pause	pauses the execution of a program until any key is hit
peaks	creates a sample matrix used to demonstrate graphing functions
pie	generates a pie chart
pie3	generates a three-dimensional pie chart
pink	optional colormap used in surface plots
plot	creates an x-y plot
plot3	generates a three-dimensional line plot
polar	creates a polar plot

prism	optional colormap used in surface plots
semilogx	generates an x-y plot, with the x-axis scaled logarithmically
semilogy	generates an x-y plot, with the y-axis scaled logarithmically
shading flat	shades a surface plot with one color per grid section
shading interp	shades a surface plot by interpolation
sphere	example function used to demonstrate graphing
spring	optional colormap used in surface plots
subplot	divides the graphics window into sections available for plotting
summer	optional colormap used in surface plots
surf	generates a surface plot
surfc	generates a combination surface and contour plot
text	adds a textbox to a graph
title	adds a title to a plot
white	optional colormap used in surface plots
winter	optional colormap used in surface plots
xlabel	adds a label to the x-axis
ylabel	adds a label to the y-axis

Problems

Projectiles Use the following information in Problems 1 through 4.

The distance a projectile travels when fired at an angle θ is a function of time and can be divided into horizontal and vertical distances.

$$\text{Horizontal } (t) = t \cdot V_0 \cdot \cos(\theta)$$

$$\text{Vertical } (t) = t \cdot V_0 \cdot \sin(\theta) - \tfrac{1}{2}gt^2$$

where

Horizontal	is the distance traveled in the x direction
Vertical	is the distance traveled in the y direction
V_0	is the initial velocity
g	is the acceleration due to gravity, 9.8 m/s^2
t	is time

1.   For the projectile just described and fired at an initial velocity of 100 m/s and a launch angle of $\pi/4$ (45°), find the distance traveled both horizontally and vertically (in the x and y directions) for times from 0 to 20 seconds. Graph horizontal distance versus time on one plot, and in a new figure window plot vertical distance versus time (time on the x-axis). Don't forget a title and labels.

2.   In a new figure window, plot horizontal distance on the x-axis and vertical distance on the y-axis.

3.   Calculate new vectors for the vertical (v_1, v_2, and v_3) and horizontal (h_1, h_2, and h_3) distance traveled, assuming launch angles of $\pi/2$, $\pi/4$, $\pi/6$. In a new figure window, graph horizontal distance on the x-axis and vertical distance on the y-axis, for all three cases. (You'll have three lines.) Make one line solid, one dashed, and one dotted. Add a legend to identify which line is which.

4.   In Problems 1 through 3, you created four plots. Combine these into one figure, using the **subplot** function of MATLAB.

5. When interest is compounded continuously, the following equation represents the growth of your savings:

$$P = P_0 e^{rt}$$

where

   P is the current balance
   P_0 is the initial balance
   r is the growth rate, expressed as a decimal fraction
   t is the time invested

Determine the amount in your account at the end of each year if you invest $1000 at 8 percent (0.08) for 30 years. Plot time on the x-axis and current balance on the y-axis.

6. Create a plot with four subplots, using the information from Problem 5.
   a. In the first quadrant plot t versus P on a rectangular coordinate system.
   b. In the second quadrant plot t versus P, scaling the x-axis logarithmically.
   c. In the third quadrant plot t versus P, scaling the y-axis logarithmically.
   d. In the fourth quadrant plot t versus P, scaling both axes logarithmically.

   Which of the four plotting techniques do you think displays the data best?

7. The vector **G** represents the distribution of final grades in a statics course:

   G = [68, 83, 61, 70, 75, 82, 57, 5, 76, 85, 62, 71, 96, 78, 76, 68, 72, 75, 83, 93]

   a. Use MATLAB to sort the data and create a bar graph of the scores.
   b. Create a histogram of the scores.

8. In the statics class just described, above there are

   2 A's
   4 B's
   8 C's
   4 D's
   2 E's

   a. Create a pie chart of this distribution. Add a legend of the grade names (A, B, C, etc.)
   b. Use the menu text option to add a text box to each pie slice (instead of a legend).
   c. Create a three-dimensional pie chart of the same data.

9. Create a vector of x values from 0 to 20π, with a spacing of $\pi/100$, where
   $$y = x \cdot \sin(x)$$
   $$z = x \cdot \cos(x)$$

   a. Create an x-y plot of x and y.
   b. Create a polar plot of x and y.
   c. Create a three-dimensional line plot of x, y, and z. Don't forget a title and labels.

10. Figure out how to adjust your input to **plot3** in Problem 7, to create a graph that looks like a tornado.

Peaks   Use the following information for Problems 11 through 15. The equation used in the peaks function is

```
z = 3*(1-x).^2.*exp(-(x.^2) - (y+1).^2) ...
  - 10*(x/5 - x.^3 - y.^5).*exp(-x.^2-y.^2) ...
  - 1/3*exp(-(x+1).^2 - y.^2)
```

z is a two-dimensional matrix determined by the values of **x** and **y**. Because **z** is a two-dimensional matrix, both **x** and **y** must be two-dimensional matrices. Create a vector **x**, from −3 to +3 with 100 values. Create a vector **y**, from −3 to +3 with 100 values.

Use the **meshgrid** function to map **x** and **y** into two-dimensional matrices, and then use them to calculate **z**.

11.   Use the **mesh** plotting function to create a three-dimensional plot of **z.**

12.   Use the **surf** plotting function to create a three-dimensional plot of **z**. Compare the results you generate using a single input (**z**), or inputs for all three dimensions (**x,y,z**).

13.   Modify your surface plot with interpolated shading. Try using different colormaps.

14.   Generate a contour plot of **z**.

15.   Generate a combination surface, contour plot of **z**.

16.   Redo Problem 3. However, this time create a matrix **theta** of the three angles. Use the **meshgrid** function to create a mesh of **theta** and the time vector (**t**), then use the two new meshed variables you create to recalculate vertical distance (**v**) and horizontal distance (**h**) traveled. Each of your results should be a 20 × 3 matrix. Use the plot command to plot **h** on the x-axis and **v** on the y-axis.

5

Programming in MATLAB

GRAND CHALLENGE: SPEECH RECOGNITION

The modern jet cockpit has literally hundreds of switches and gauges. Several research programs have been looking at the feasibility of using a speech recognition system in the cockpit to serve as a pilot's assistant. The system would respond to verbal requests from the pilot for information such as fuel status or altitude. The pilot would use words from a small vocabulary that the computer had been trained to understand. In addition to understanding a selected set of words, the system would also have to be trained to understand the speech of the particular pilot who would be using the system. This training information could be stored on a diskette and inserted into the computer at the beginning of a flight so that the system could recognize the current pilot. The computer system would also use speech synthesis to respond to the pilot's request for information.

INTRODUCTION

So far, we have used MATLAB in two modes: as a scratch pad in the command window and to write simple programs in the editing window. In both cases we have assumed that the programmer was the user. In this chapter we'll move on to more complicated programs, written in the editing window, assuming that the programmer and the user may be different people. That will make it necessary to communicate with the user through input and output commands, instead of rewriting the actual code to solve similar problems. We'll also write programs where the logic is included to allow the computer to make choices depending on the input.

SECTIONS

OBJECTIVES

After reading this chapter, you should be able to

- perform matrix calculations with two variables
- write programs that interact with the user through input statements and formatted output commands
- create user defined functions
- understand the use of logical operators, logical functions, and control structures in MATLAB

5.1   PROBLEMS WITH TWO VARIABLES

Calculations for many simpler MATLAB applications use only one variable. Of course, most physical phenomena can vary with many different factors. In this section, we consider how to perform these calculations when the variables are represented by vectors.

Consider the following MATLAB statements:

```
x = 3
y = 5
A = x * y
```

Since **x** and **y** are scalars, it's an easy calculation, $x \cdot y = 15$. Thus,

```
A =
      15
```

Now let's see what happens if **x** is a matrix and **y** is still a scalar:

```
x = 1:5;
```

returns five values of **x**. Because **y** is still a scalar with only one value (5)

```
A = x * y
```

returns

```
A =
      5    10    15    20    25
```

But what happens if **y** is also a vector? Then

```
y = 1:3;
A = x * y
```

returns an error statement

```
??? Error using ==> *
Inner matrix dimensions must agree.
```

This error statement reminds us that the asterisk is the operator for matrix multiplication, which is not what we want. We want the dot-asterisk operator (. *), which will perform an element-by-element multiplication. However, the two vectors **x** and **y** will need to be the same length for this to work:

```
y = linspace(1,3,5)
```

creates a new **y** with five evenly spaced elements:

```
y =
      1.0000    1.5000    2.0000    2.5000    3.0000
A = x .* y
A =
      1    3    6    10    15
```

However, although this solution works, the result is probably not what you really want. You can think of the results as the diagonal on a matrix, as shown in Figure 5.1.

What if you want to know the result for element 3 of vector **x**, and element 5 of vector **y**? This approach obviously doesn't give us all the possible answers. We want a two-dimensional matrix of answers that corresponds to all of the combinations of **x** and **y**. In order for your answer, **A**, to be a two-dimensional matrix, the input vectors have to be two-dimensional matrices. MATLAB has a built-in function called **meshgrid** that will help you accomplish this—and **x** and **y** don't even have to be the same size.

	1	2	3	4	5
1.0	1				
1.5		3			
2.0			6		
2.5				10	
3.0			?		15

x is the column header above the numbers 1–5; *y* is the row header beside the values 1.0–3.0.

Figure 5.1.   Results of an element-by-element calculation.

First let's change **y** back to a three-element vector:

```
y = 1:3;
```

Then we'll use **meshgrid** to create a new two-dimensional version of both **x** and **y** that we'll call **new_x** and **new_y**:

```
[new_x, new_y]=meshgrid(x,y)
```

The **meshgrid** command takes the two input vectors and creates two 2-D matrices. Each of the resulting matrices has the same number of rows and columns. The number of columns is determined by the number of elements in the **x** vector, and the number of rows is determined by the number of elements in the **y** vector.

```
new_x =
        1    2    3    4    5
        1    2    3    4    5
        1    2    3    4    5
new_y =
        1    1    1    1    1
        2    2    2    2    2
        3    3    3    3    3
```

Notice that all the rows in **new_x** are the same, and all the columns in **new_y** are the same. Now it's possible to multiply **new_x** times **new_y**, and get the 2-D grid of results we really want:

```
A = new_x.*new_y
A =
        1    2    3    4    5
        2    4    6    8   10
        3    6    9   12   15
```

EXAMPLE 5.1

FREE FALL

The general equation for the distance that a free-falling body has traveled (neglecting air friction) is

$$d = \tfrac{1}{2}gt^2$$

where

d is distance
g is the acceleration due to gravity
t is time

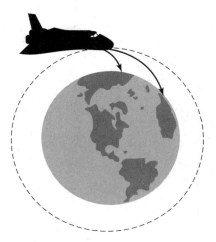

Figure 5.2. The space shuttle is constantly falling toward the earth.

TABLE 5.1 Acceleration Due to Gravity in Our Solar System

Mercury	$g = 3.7$ m/s^2
Venus	$g = 8.87$ m/s^2
Earth	$g = 9.8$ m/s^2
Earth's Moon	$g = 1.6$ m/s^2
Mars	$g = 3.7$ m/s^2
Jupiter	$g = 23.12$ m/s^2
Saturn	$g = 8.96$ m/s^2
Uranus	$g = 8.69$ m/s^2
Neptune	$g = 11.0$ m/s^2
Pluto	$g = .58$ m/s^2

When a satellite orbits a planet, it is in free fall. Many people believe that when the space shuttle enters orbit it leaves gravity behind; but gravity is what keeps the shuttle in orbit. The shuttle (or any satellite) is actually falling toward the earth. If it is going fast enough horizontally, it stays in orbit—if it's going too slowly, it hits the ground. (See Figure 5.2.)

The value of the constant, g, acceleration due to gravity depends on the mass of the planet. On different planets, g has different values. Find how far an object would fall at times from 0 to 100 seconds on each of the planets in our solar system and on our moon. (Refer to Table 5.1.) Plot the results, both on a rectangular plot and on a log–log plot.

SOLUTION

1. State the Problem

Find the distance traveled by a free-falling object.

2. Describe the Input and Output

Input

Value of g, the acceleration due to gravity, on each of the planets and the moon. Time = 0 to 100 seconds

Output

Distances calculated for each planet and the moon

3. Hand Example

$$d = \tfrac{1}{2} g\, t^2, \text{ so on Mercury at 100 seconds:}$$
$$d = \tfrac{1}{2} \times 3.7 \text{ m/s}^2 \times 100^2 \text{ s}^2$$
$$d = 18{,}500 \text{ meters}$$

4. Develop a MATLAB Solution

```
%Example 5.1
%Free fall
clear, clc
%Try the problem first with only two planets, and a course grid

figure(1)
%Define constants
G = [3.7, 8.87];
T=0:10:100;

%Map g and t into 2D matrices
[g,t]=meshgrid(G,T);

%Calculate the distances
d=1/2*g.*t.^2;

%Generate the plots
subplot(2,1,1)
plot(T,d)
title('Distance Traveled on the Planets during Free fall')
xlabel('time, sec')
ylabel('distance, m')
subplot(2,1,2)
loglog(T,d)
xlabel('time, sec')
ylabel('distance, m')
```

This program produces the plot in Figure 5.3.

5. Test the Solution

Compare the MATLAB solution to the hand solution. From Figure 5.3, we can see that the distance traveled on Mercury at 100 seconds is approximately, 20,000—which corresponds to the hand calculation.

Figure 5.3 represents the calculations for just the first two planets, and was performed first to work out any programming difficulties. Notice that the log–log plot is a straight line. This occurs because distance is calculated using a power function:

$$\log(d) = \log\!\left(\tfrac{1}{2}g\right) + \log(t^2),$$

which can be rearranged to

$$\log(d) = \log\!\left(\tfrac{1}{2}g\right) + 2\log(t).$$

Since we are using a log–log plot, we can see that this equation represents a straight line, if we replace $\log(d)$ with y, and $\log(t)$ with x:

$$y = \log\!\left(\tfrac{1}{2}g\right) + 2x$$

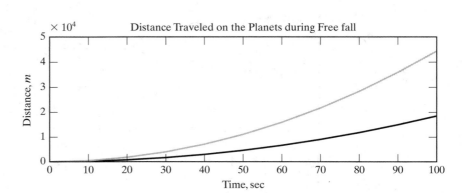

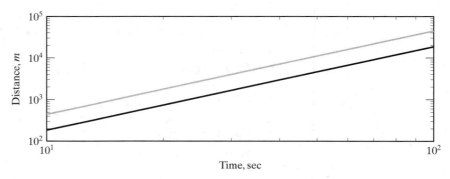

Figure 5.3. Distance traveled on Mercury and Venus.

The slope is 2, and the intercept is $\log\left(\frac{1}{2}g\right)$:

```
%Redo the problem with all the data
%Define constants
G = [3.7, 8.87, 9.8, 1.6, 3.7, 23.12,8.96, 8.69,11.0, 0.58];
T=0:100;
%Map g and t into 2D matrices
[g,t]=meshgrid(G,T);
%Calculate the distances
d=1/2*g.*t.^2;
%Generate the plots
figure(2)
subplot(2,1,1)
plot(T,d)
%legend('Mercury','Venus','Earth','Moon','Mars','Jupiter',
'Saturn', % 'Uranus','Neptune','Pluto')
title('Distance Traveled on the Planets during free fall')
xlabel('time, sec')
ylabel('distance, m')
subplot(2,1,2)
loglog(T,d)
xlabel('time, sec')
ylabel('distance, m')
%
%Try some different graphing approaches
figure(3)
mesh(g,t,d)
xlabel('acceleration due to gravity')
```

```
ylabel('time, sec')
zlabel('distance, m')
title('A surface plot of the distance traveled on the
planets')

figure(4)
bar(max(d))
title('Distance traveled in 100 seconds on the planets and
the moon')
xlabel('planet')
ylabel('distance, meters')
```

The second plot (Figure 5.4) is similar to Figure 5.3, except that it includes all 9 planets and the moon. Because there is so much data, the graph is difficult to interpret. We tried some different plotting approaches to try and make the meaning of the calculations clearer. Figure 5.5 is a mesh plot of the results, which illustrates that, as the acceleration due to gravity (g) goes up, the distance traveled goes up. Figure 5.6 probably illustrates the results the best. It is a bar graph of the distance traveled at 100 seconds on each planet.

Once you've decided how best to present the data, you could add text boxes labeling each bar with the appropriate planet name.

Hint: As you create a MATLAB program in the editing window, you may want to comment out parts of the code that you know work, then uncomment them later. Although you can do this by adding one % at a time to each line, it's easier to select **text** from the menu bar. Just highlight the part of the code you want to comment out, then choose **comment** from the **text** drop-down menu. To uncomment, highlight and select **uncomment** from the **text** drop-down menu. You can also access the capability by right-clicking your mouse.

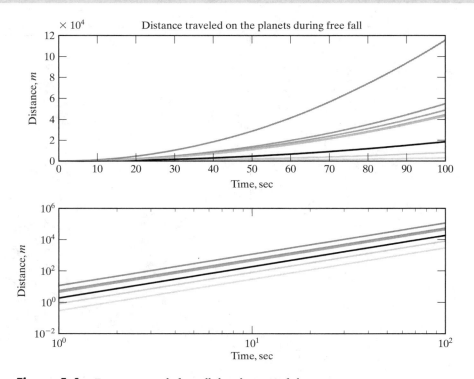

Figure 5.4. Distance traveled on all the planets and the moon.

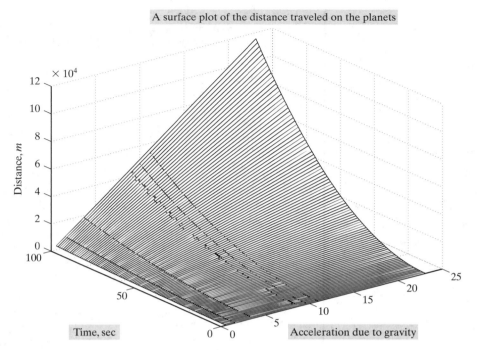

Figure 5.5. Distance traveled presented on a surface plot.

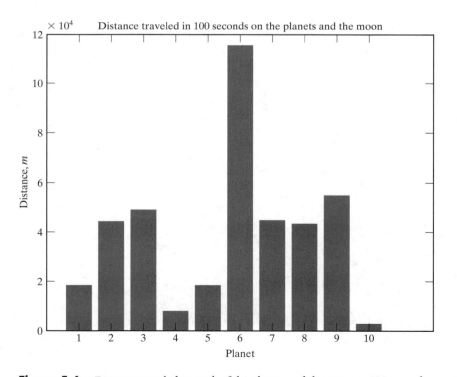

Figure 5.6. Distance traveled on each of the planets and the moon in 100 seconds. ∎

5.2   INPUT/OUTPUT

MATLAB offers built-in functions to allow a user to communicate with a program as it executes. The **input** command pauses the program and prompts the user for input, while the **disp** and **fprintf** commands provide output to the command window. The **pause** command stops the program execution until any key is typed. This allows the user to look at intermediate results and then continue running the program.

5.2.1   User Defined Input

Although we have written programs in script M-files, we have assumed the programmer (you) and the user are the same person. To run the program with different input values, we actually changed some of the code. We can create more general programs by allowing the user to input values of a matrix from the keyboard while the program is running. The **input** function allows us to do this. It displays a text string in the command window, then waits for the user to provide the requested input. For example,

```
z = input('Enter a value')
```

displays

```
Enter a value
```

in the command window. If the user enters a value such as

```
5
```

the program assigns the value of 5 to the variable **z**. If the input command does not end with a semicolon, the value entered is displayed on the screen:

```
z =
   5
```

The same approach can be used to enter a one- or two-dimensional matrix. The user must provide the appropriate brackets and delimiters (commas and semicolons). For example,

```
z = input('Enter values for z in brackets ')
```

requests the user to input a matrix such as

```
[ 1, 2, 3; 4, 5, 6]
```

and responds

```
z =
   1   2   3
   4   5   6
```

This user input value of **z** can then be used in subsequent calculations by the script M-file.

EXAMPLE 5.2   USER DEFINED INPUT

Let's rewrite Example 5.1, but ask the user for the value of g (acceleration due to gravity) instead of hard wiring in values for each planet. Also, let's request the user to provide the initial, final, and increment values for the time vector.

SOLUTION

1. State the Problem

Find the distance traveled by a free-falling object.

2. Describe the Input and Output

Input

Value of g, the acceleration due to gravity, provided by the user
Time, provided by the user

Output

Distances calculated for each planet and the moon

3. Hand Example

$$d = \tfrac{1}{2}gt^2, \text{ so on the moon at 100 seconds,}$$
$$d = \tfrac{1}{2} \times 1.6 \text{ m/s}^2 \times 100^2 \text{ s}^2$$
$$d = 8000$$

4. Develop a MATLAB Solution

```
%Example 5.2
%Free fall
clear, clc
%Request input from the user
  g = input('What is the value of acceleration due to gravity?')
  start=input('What starting time would you like?')
  finish = input('What ending time would you like?')
  incr = input('What time increments would you like calculated?')
t=start:incr:finish;
%Calculate the distance
d=1/2*g*t.^2;
%plot the results
loglog(t,d)
title('Distance traveled in free fall')
xlabel('time,s'),ylabel('distance, m')
%Find the maximum distance traveled
final_distance = max(d)
```

This solution is much shorter because the user controls the input, and the programmer does not need to program in every solution. The interaction in the command window is shown as follows:

```
What is the value of acceleration due to gravity?1.6
g =
    1.6000

What starting time would you like?0
start =
    0

What ending time would you like?100
finish =
    100
```

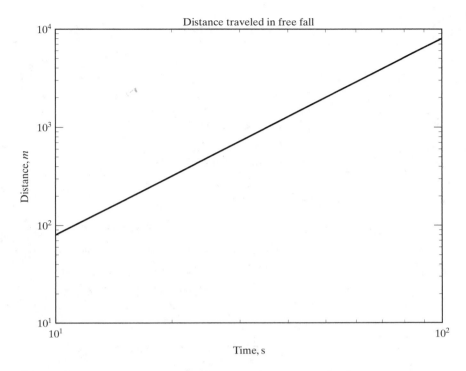

Figure 5.7. Distance traveled when the acceleration is 1.6 m/s^2.

```
What time increments would you like calculated?10
incr =
        10

    final_distance =
        8000
```

Only one plot was created, because there is so much less data calculated. (See Figure 5.7.)

5. Test the Solution

Compare the MATLAB solution to the hand solution. Since the user can control the input, we entered the data used in the hand solution. MATLAB tells us that the final distance traveled is 8000, which, since we entered 100 seconds as the final time, corresponds to the distance traveled at 100 seconds. ∎

5.2.2   Output Options

There are several ways to display the contents of a matrix. The simplest way is to enter the name of the matrix, without a semicolon. The name of the matrix will be repeated and the values of the matrix will be displayed, starting on the next line. For example, first define a matrix **x**:

```
x = 1:5;
```

Because there is a semicolon at the end of the assignment statement, the values in **x** are not repeated in the command window. However, if later in your program you want to display **x**, simply type in the variable name:

```
x
```

which returns

```
x =
     1     2     3     4     5
```

MATLAB offers two other approaches to displaying results: the **disp** function and the **fprintf** function.

Display *Function*

The display (**disp**) function can be used to display the contents of a matrix without printing the matrix's name:

```
disp(x)
```

returns

```
     1     2     3     4     5
```

The display command can also be used to display a string (text enclosed in single quote marks):

```
disp('The values in the x matrix are:');
disp(x);
```

returns

```
The values in the x matrix are:
     1   2   3   4   5
```

The semicolon at the end of the **disp** function is optional. Notice that the two **disp** functions are displayed on separate lines. You can get around this by creating a matrix of your two outputs, using the **num2str** function:

```
disp(['The values in the x array are: ' num2str(x)])
```

which returns

```
The values in the x array are:  1 2 3 4 5
```

The **disp** function requires a matrix as input. It can be a string, a variable that represents a matrix, or the programmer can define the matrix inside square brackets, using the standard matrix definition rules. The matrix can be composed of numeric information, or strings. The **num2str** function changes an array of numbers into a string. In the example above, we used **num2str** to transform the **x** matrix into a string. You can see the resulting matrix by typing

```
A = ['The values in the x array are:  ' num2str(x)]
```

which returns

```
A =
     The values in the x array are:  1 2 3 4 5
```

Checking in the workspace window, we see that **A** is a 1×45 matrix. The workspace window also tells us that the matrix contains character data, instead of numeric information, both from the icon in front of **A** and in the class column:

Name	Size	Bytes	Class
abc A	1×45	90	char array

Formatted Output

The **fprintf** function gives you even more control over the output than you have with the **disp** function. In addition to displaying both text and matrix values, you can specify the format to be used in displaying the values, and you can specify when to skip to a new line. If you are a C programmer, you will be familiar with the syntax of this function. With few exceptions, the MATLAB **fprintf** functions use the same formatting specifications as the C **fprintf** function. This is hardly surprising, since MATLAB was written in C.

The general form of this command contains two arguments—a string and a list of matrices:

```
fprintf(format-string, var,…)
```

Consider the following example:

```
temp = 98.6;
fprintf('The temperature is %f degrees F ', temp)
```

The string, which is the first argument inside the **fprintf** function, contains a place holder (**%**) where the value of the variable (in this case **temp**) will be inserted. This place holder also contains formatting information. In this example, the **%f** tells MATLAB to display the temperature in a default fixed-point format:

```
The temperature is 98.600000 degrees F
```

Note that the default precision is six digits after the decimal point. In addition to floating-point format, MATLAB allows you to specify an exponential format, **%e**, or lets you allow MATLAB to choose whichever is shorter, fixed point or exponential (**%g**). (See Table 5.2.)

MATLAB does not automatically start a new line after an **fprintf** function is executed, so if the following new commands are issued:

```
ftemp = 100.1;
fprintf('The temperature is %f degrees F',temp);
```

MATLAB continues the command window display on the same line:

```
The temperature is 98.600000 degrees FThe temperature is
100.100000 degrees F
```

To cause MATLAB to start a new line, you'll need to use **\n**, called a linefeed, at the end of the string:

```
temp = 98.6;
fprintf('The temperature is %f degrees F \n', temp);
ftemp = 100.1;
fprintf('The temperature is %f degrees F \n',temp);
```

TABLE 5.2 Type Field Format

Type Field	Result
%f	fixed point, or decimal notation
%e	exponential notation
%g	whichever is shorter, %f or %e

TABLE 5.3 Special Format Commands

Format Command	Resulting Action
\n	linefeed
\r	carriage return (similar to linefeed)
\t	tab
\b	backspace

which returns the output

```
The temperature is 98.600000 degrees F
The temperature is 100.100000 degrees F
```

Other special format commands are listed in Table 5.3.

You can further control how the variables are displayed by using the optional **width field** and **precision field** with the format command. The **width field** controls the minimum number of characters to be printed. It must be a positive decimal integer. The **precision field** is preceded by a period (.) and specifies the number of decimal places after the decimal point for exponential and fixed-point types. For example, **%8.2f** specifies that the minimum total width available to display your result is 8 digits, two of which are after the decimal point:

```
fprintf('The temperature is %8.2f degrees F\n',temp);
```

returns

```
The temperature is   100.10 degrees F
```

Many times when you use the **fprintf** function, your variable will be a matrix. For example,

```
temp = [98.6, 100.1, 99.2];
```

MATLAB will repeat the string in the **fprintf** command until it uses all of the values in the matrix:

```
fprintf('The temperature is %8.2f degrees F\n',temp);
```

returns

```
The temperature is    98.60 degrees F
The temperature is   100.10 degrees F
The temperature is    99.20 degrees F
```

If the variable is a two-dimensional matrix, MATLAB uses the values one column at a time, going down the first column, then the second, etc. Here's a more complicated example:

```
patient = 1:3;
temp = [98.6, 100.1, 99.2];
```

Combine these two matrices:

```
history = [patient;temp]
```

returns

```
history =
        1.0000      2.0000      3.0000
       98.6000    100.1000     99.2000
```

Now we can use the **fprintf** function to create a table that is easier to interpret:

fprintf('Patient %4f had a temperature of %7.2f \n',history)

sends the following output to the command window:

```
Patient     1 had a temperature of    98.60
Patient     2 had a temperature of   100.10
Patient     3 had a temperature of    99.20
```

As you can see, the **fprintf** function allows you to have a great deal of control over the form of the output.

EXAMPLE 5.3

FORMATTING OUTPUT

Let's redo Example 5.2, but this time let's create a table of results instead of a plot, and use the **disp** and **fprintf** commands to control the appearance of the output.

SOLUTION

1. State the Problem

Find the distance traveled by a free-falling object.

2. Describe the Input and Output

Input

Value of g, the acceleration due to gravity, provided by the user.
Time

Output

Distances calculated for each planet and the moon

3. Hand Example

$$d = \frac{1}{2}gt^2, \text{ so on the moon at 100 seconds,}$$

$$d = \frac{1}{2} \times 1.6 \text{ m/s}^2 \times 100^2 \text{ s}^2$$

$$d = 8000$$

4. Develop a MATLAB Solution

```
%Example 5.3
%Free fall
clear, clc
%Request input from the user
g = input('What is the value of acceleration due to gravity?')
start=input('What starting time would you like?')
finish = input('What ending time would you like?')
incr = input('What time increments would you like calculated?')
t=start:incr:finish;
%Calculate the distance
d=1/2*g*t.^2;
%Create a matrix of the output data
table=[t;d];
%Send the output to the command window
fprintf('For g of  %5.1f ft/second^2...
\n the following data was calculated \n', g)
```

```
disp('Distance Traveled in free fall')
disp('time,sec      distance, m')
fprintf('%8.0f  %10.2f\n',table)
```

This M-file produces the following interaction in the command window:

```
What is the value of acceleration due to gravity?1.6
g =
    1.6000

What starting time would you like?0
start =
    0

What ending time would you like?100
finish =
    100

What time increments would you like calculated?10
incr =
    10

For g of 1.6 ft/second^2
 the following data was calculated:

Distance traveled in free fall
time,sec      distance, m
    0           0.00
   10          80.00
   20         320.00
   30         720.00
   40        1280.00
   50        2000.00
   60        2880.00
   70        3920.00
   80        5120.00
   90        6480.00
  100        8000.00
```

5. Test the Solution

Compare the MATLAB solution to the hand solution. Since the output is a table, it is easy to see that the distance traveled at 100 seconds is 8000 m. Try using other data as input, and compare your results to the graphs produced in Examples 5.1 and 5.2. ∎

5.3   FUNCTIONS

The MATLAB programming language is built around functions. A function is simply a piece of computer code that accepts an input argument from the user and provides output to the program. Functions allow us to program efficiently, since we don't need to rewrite the computer code for calculations that are performed frequently. For example, most computer programs contain a function that calculates the sine of a number. In MATLAB, **sin** is the function name used to call up a series of commands that perform the necessary calculations. The user needs to provide an angle, and MATLAB returns a result. It isn't necessary for the user to even know that MATLAB uses an approximation to an infinite series to find the value of **sin**.

We have already explored many of MATLAB's built-in functions, but you may wish to define your own functions that are used commonly in your programming. User defined functions are stored as M-files, and can be accessed by MATLAB if they are in the **current directory**.

5.3.1 Syntax

User defined MATLAB functions are written in M-files. Access a new function M-file the same way a script M-file is created: select **File → New → m-file** from the menu bar. To explain how function M-files work, we'll use several examples.

Here's a really simple function to get started with:

```
function s=f(x)
% A function that adds 3 to every member of an array x
s=x+3;
```

These lines of code define a function called **f**. Notice that the first line starts with the word **function**. This is a requirement for all user defined functions. Next, an output variable that we've named **s** is set equal to the function name, with the input arguments enclosed in parentheses (**x**). A comment line follows that will be displayed if a user types:

```
help f
```

once the function has been saved in the current directory. The file name must be the same as the function name, so in this case it must be stored as **f**, which is the default suggestion when the save icon is selected from the menu bar.

Finally, the output, **s**, is defined as **x + 3**.

From the **command window**, or inside a **script M-file**, the **f** function is now available. Now type

```
f(3)
```

and the program returns

```
ans =
    6
```

More complicated functions can be written that require more than one input argument. For example, these lines of code define a function called **g**, with two inputs, **x** and **y**:

```
function output=g(x,y)
%This function multiplies x and y together
%Be sure that x and y are the same size matrices
a = x .*y;
output=a;
```

You can use the comment lines to let users know what kind of input is required and to describe the function. In this example an intermediate calculation (for **a**) was performed, but the only output from this function is the variable we've named **output** this time. This output can be a matrix containing a variety of numbers, but it's still only one variable.

You can also create functions that return more than one output variable. Many of the predefined MATLAB functions return more than one result. For example, **max** returns both the maximum value in a matrix and the element number where the maximum occurs. To achieve the same result in a user-defined function, make the output a matrix of answers, instead of a single variable. For example,

```
function   [dist, vel, accel] = motion(t)
% This function calculates the distance, velocity and
acceleration of a car
accel = 0.5 .*t;
vel = accel .* t;
dist = vel.*t;
```

Once saved as **motion** in the current directory, you can use the function to find values of **distance**, **velocity**, and **acceleration** at specified times:

```
[distance, velocity, acceleration] = motion(10)

distance =
        500
velocity =
        50
acceleration =
        5
```

If you call the **motion** function without specifying all three outputs, only the first output will be returned:

```
motion(10)

ans =
      500
```

Remember, all variables in MATLAB are matrices, so it's important in the example above to use the **.*** operator, which specifies element-by-element multiplication:

```
time = 0:10;
[distance, velocity, acceleration] = motion(time);
results = [time',distance',velocity',acceleration']
```

returns

```
results =
     0            0            0            0
     1.0000       0.5000       0.5000       0.5000
     2.0000       4.0000       2.0000       1.0000
     3.0000      13.5000       4.5000       1.5000
     4.0000      32.0000       8.0000       2.0000
     5.0000      62.5000      12.5000       2.5000
     6.0000     108.0000      18.0000       3.0000
     7.0000     171.5000      24.5000       3.5000
     8.0000     256.0000      32.0000       4.0000
     9.0000     364.5000      40.5000       4.5000
    10.0000     500.0000      50.0000       5.0000
```

The results were collected into the table called results to make the output easier to read. Because **time, distance, velocity**, and **acceleration** were row vectors, the transpose operator was used to make them into columns.

5.3.2   Local Variables

The variables used in function M-files are known as local variables. The only way that a function can communicate with the workspace is through input arguments and the output returned. Any variables defined within the function only exist for the function to use. For example, consider the **g** function previously described:

```
function output=g(x,y)
% This function multiplies x and y together
% Be sure that x and y are the same size matrices
a = x .*y;
output=a;
```

The variable **a** is a local variable. It can be used for additional calculations inside the **g** function, but it is not stored in the workspace. To confirm this, clear the workspace and the command window, then call the **g** function:

```
clear, clc
g(10,20)
```

returns

```
g(10,20)
ans =
        200
```

Notice that the only variable stored in the workspace window is **ans**. Not only is **a** not there, but neither is **output**, which is also a local variable:

Name	Size	Bytes	Class
⊞ ans	1:1	8	double array

Just as calculations performed in the command window, or from a script M-file, cannot access variables defined in functions, functions cannot access the variables defined in the workspace. That means that functions must be completely self-contained. The only way they can get information from your program is through the input arguments, and the only way they can deliver information is through the function output.

5.3.3   Naming Function M-files

A function M-file must have the same **file name** as its **function name** defined in the first line. For example,

```
function  my_results = velocity(t)
```

might be the first line of a user-defined function. The function's name is **velocity**, and it must be stored in the current directory as **velocity**. Function names need to conform to the same naming conventions as variable names: They must start with a letter; they may only contain letters, numbers and the underscore; and they must not be reserved names. It is possible to give a function the same name as a predefined MATLAB function, in which case the user-defined function will become the default until it is removed from the current directory or the current directory is changed. The MATLAB predefined function is not overwritten. MATLAB just looks in the current directory first for function definitions before it looks into the predefined function files. In general, it is not a good idea to use the same name for a user-defined function as for an existing MATLAB function.

5.3.4 Rules for Writing and Using Function M-files

Writing and using a function M-file requires the user to follow very specific rules, and a format when writing it. These rules are summarized as follows:

a. The function must begin with a line containing the word **function**, which is followed by the output argument, an equals sign, and the name of the function. The input arguments to the function follow the name of the function and are enclosed in parentheses. This line distinguishes the function file from a script M-file:

function output_name = function_name(input)

b. The first few lines of the function should be comments because they will be displayed if help is requested for the function name:

% Comment your function so users will know how to use it

c. The only information returned from the function is contained in the output arguments, which are, of course, matrices. Always check to be sure that the function includes a statement that assigns a value to the output argument.

d. A function that has multiple input arguments must list the arguments in the function statement, as shown in the following example, which has two input arguments:

function error = mse(w,d)

e. A function that is going to return more than one value should show all values to be returned as a vector in the function statement, as in

function   [dist, vel, accel] = motion(x)

All output values need to be computed within the function.

f. The same matrix names can be used in both a function and the program that references it. No confusion occurs as to which matrix is referenced, because the function and the program are completely separate. However, any values computed in the function, other than the output arguments, are not accessible from the program.

g. The special functions **nargin** and **nargout** can be used to determine the number of input arguments and the number of output arguments for a function. Both require a string containing the function name as input. For the motion function described earlier,

nargin('motion')

returns

ans =
        1

and

nargout('motion')

returns

ans = 3

EXAMPLE 5.4

A DEGREES TO RADIANS FUNCTION

Engineers usually measure angles in degrees, yet most computer programs and many calculators require that the input to trigonometric functions be in radians. (See Figure 5.8.) Write and test a function **DR** to change degrees to radians, and another function **RD** to change radians to degrees. Your functions should be able to accept both scalar and matrix input.

SOLUTION

1.   State the Problem

Create and test two functions, **DR** and **RD**, to change degrees to radian and radians to degrees.

2.   Describe the Input and Output

Input

    A vector of degree values
    A vector of radian values

Output

    A table of degrees to radians and
    A table of radians to degrees

3.   Hand Example

    degrees = radians $\times$ 180/π
    radians = degrees $\times$ π/180

Degrees to Radians	
Degrees	**Radians**
0	0
30	$30 \times \pi/180 = \pi/6 = 0.524$
60	$60 \times \pi/180 = \pi/3 = 1.047$
90	$90 \times \pi/180 = \pi/2 = 1.571$

Figure 5.8. Trigonometric functions require angles to be expressed in radians.

4.   Develop a MATLAB Solution

```
%Example 5.3
%
clear, clc
%Define a vector of degree values
degrees = 0:15:180;
%Call the DR function, and use it to find radians
radians = DR(degrees);
%Create a table to use in the output
degrees_radians =[degrees;radians];
%Generate an output table
disp('A table of degrees to radians')
disp('degrees   radians')
fprintf('%6.0f    %8.3f\n',degrees_radians)
%Put a blank line in the output to separate the tables
disp(' ')
%Define a vector of radian values
radians = 0:pi/12:pi;
%Call the RD function, and use it to find degrees
degrees = RD(radians);
%Generate an output table
disp('A table of radians to degrees')
disp('radians     degrees')
fprintf('%9.3f    %10.3f \n',[radians;degrees])
```

The functions called by the program are:

```
function output=DR(x)
%This function changes degrees to radians
output=x*pi/180;
```

and

```
function output=RD(x)
%This function changes radians to degrees
output=x*180/pi;
```

Remember that, in order for the script M-file to find the functions, the functions must be in the current directory and must be named **DR.m** and **RD.m**. The program generates the following results in the command window:

```
A table of degrees to radians
degrees     radians
      0       0.000
     15       0.262
     30       0.524
     45       0.785
     60       1.047
     75       1.309
     90       1.571
    105       1.833
    120       2.094
    135       2.356
    150       2.618
    165       2.880
    180       3.142
```

```
A table of radians to degrees
radians           degrees
  0.000             0.000
  0.262            15.000
  0.524            30.000
  0.785            45.000
  1.047            60.000
  1.309            75.000
  1.571            90.000
  1.833           105.000
  2.094           120.000
  2.356           135.000
  2.618           150.000
  2.880           165.000
  3.142           180.000
```

5. Test the Solution

Compare the MATLAB solution to the hand solution. Since the output is a table, it is easy to see that the conversions generated by MATLAB correspond to those calculated by hand. Notice that the titles and column headings were generated with the **disp** function. We could have used the **fprintf** function:

```
fprintf('A table of radians to degrees \n')
```

A common error is to forget the **\n**, in which case there would be no carriage return! Also notice that a blank line was inserted into the output by using the **disp** function with a blank space as input: ∎

```
disp(' ')
```

5.4   STATEMENT LEVEL CONTROL STRUCTURES

One way to think of computer programs (not just MATLAB) is to consider how the statements that compose the program are organized (Figure 5.9). Usually, sections of computer code can be categorized into one of three structures: **sequences**, **selection structures**,

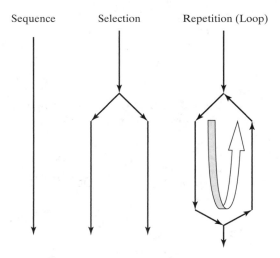

Figure 5.9. Programming structures used in MATLAB.

and **repetition structures**. This section deals mainly with writing code that contains selection structures and repetition structures.

- Sequences are lists of commands that are executed one after another.
- A selection structure allows the programmer to execute one command (or group of commands) if some criteria is true, and a second set of commands if the criteria is false. A selection statement provides the means of choosing between these paths based on a **logical condition**. The conditions that are evaluated often contain **relational** and **logical** operators or functions.
- A repetition structure, or loop, causes a group of statements to be executed zero, one, or more times. The number of times a loop is executed depends on either a counter or the evaluation of a logical condition.

5.4.1 Relational and Logical Operators

MATLAB has six relational operators for comparing two matrices of equal size, as shown in Table 5.4.

Comparisons are either true or false, and most computer programs (including MATLAB) use the number 1 for true and 0 for false. If we define two scalars

```
x = 5;
y = 1;
```

and use a relational operator such as $<$,

```
x<y
```

the result is either true or false. In this case, **x** is not less than **y**, so MATLAB responds

```
ans =
    0
```

indicating the comparison was not true. MATLAB uses this answer in selection statements and in repetition structures to make decisions.

Of course, variables in MATLAB usually represent entire matrices. If we redefine **x** and **y**, we can see how MATLAB handles comparisons between matrices:

```
x = 1:5;
y = x -4;
x<y
```

returns

```
ans =
    0   0   0   0   0
```

MATLAB compares corresponding elements and creates an answer matrix of zeros and ones. In the previous example, **x** was greater than **y** for every element comparison, so

TABLE 5.4 Relational Operators

Relational Operator	Interpretation
<	less than
< =	less than or equal to
>	greater than
> =	greater than or equal to
==	equal to
~ =	not equal to

every comparison was false, and the answer was a string of zeros. If instead,

```
x = [ 1, 2, 3, 4, 5];
y = [-2, 0, 2, 4, 6];
x<y
ans =
       0   0   0   0   1
```

which tells us that the comparison was false for the first four elements, but true for the last. *In order for MATLAB to decide that a comparison is true for an entire matrix, it must be true for every element in the matrix. In other words, all of the results must be one.*

MATLAB also allows us to combine comparisons with logical operators; **and, not**, and **or**.

Logical Operator	Interpretation
&	and
~	not
|	or

Consider the following:

```
x = [ 1, 2, 3, 4, 5];
y = [-2, 0, 2, 4, 6];
z = [ 8, 8, 8, 8, 8];
z>x & z>y
```

returns

```
ans =
       1    1    1    1    1
```

because **z** is greater than both **x** and **y** for every element. The statement

```
x>y | x>z
```

is read as "**x** is greater than **y** or **x** is greater than **z**" and returns

```
ans =
       1    1    1    0    0
```

This result is interpreted to mean that the condition is true for the first three elements and false for the last two.

These relational and logical operators are used in both selection structures and loops to determine what commands should be executed.

5.4.2   Selection Structures

MATLAB offers two kinds of selection structures: **find** and a family of **if** structures.

Find

The **find** command is unique to MATLAB, and can often be used instead of both **if** and **loop** structures. It returns a vector composed of the indices of the nonzero elements of a vector **x**. Those indices can then be used in subsequent commands. The usefulness of the **find** command is best described with examples.

Assume that you have a list of temperatures measured in a manufacturing process. If the temperature is less than 95°F, the widgets produced will be faulty:

```
temp = [100, 98, 94, 101, 93];
```

Use the **find** function to determine which widgets are faulty:

```
find(temp<95)
```

returns a vector of element numbers:

```
ans =
     3     5
```

which tells us that items 3 and 5 will be faulty. MATLAB first evaluated **temp < 95**, which resulted in a vector of zeros and ones. We can see this by just typing the comparison into MATLAB:

```
temp<95
```

which returns a vector indicating when the comparison was true (1) and when it was false (0):

```
ans =
     0     0     1     0     1
```

The **find** command looked at this vector and reported the elements for which the comparison was true (where the **ans** vector reported ones).

It's also sometimes useful to name these element lists. For example,

```
faulty = find(temp<95);
pass = find(temp>=95);
```

makes it possible to create a results table:

```
failtable=[faulty',temp(faulty)']
```

which returns a table of elements and the corresponding temperatures:

```
failtable =
     3    94
     5    93
```

When the **find** command is used with a two-dimensional matrix, a single element number is returned. As discussed before, MATLAB is a column dominant language and "thinks" of even two-dimensional matrices as one long list of numbers. Just as **fprintf** works down one column at a time, so **find** uses an element numbering scheme that works down each column one at a time. For example, consider a 10-by-3 matrix. The element numbers are shown in Figure 5.10.

An alternate way to use **find** returns the row and column designation of an element:

```
[row, column] = find(expression)
```

For example, consider the following two-dimensional matrix, and use **find** to determine the location of all elements greater than 9:

```
x=[1,2,3; 10, 5,1; 12,3,2;8, 3,1]
element = find(x>9)
[row,column]=find(x>9)
```

returns

```
x =
     1     2     3
    10     5     1
     3    12     2
     8     3     1
```

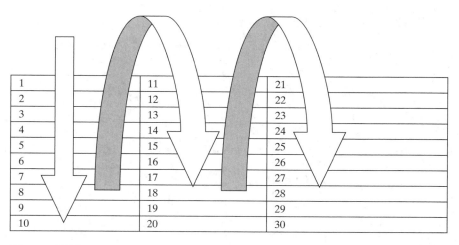

Figure 5.10. Element numbering sequence for a 10 × 3 matrix.

```
element =
     2
     7
row =
     2
     3
column =
     1
     2
```

Notice that the numbers 10 and 12 are the only two values greater than 9. By counting down the columns, we see that they are elements 2 and 7 respectively. Using the alternative designation, 10 is in row 2, column 1, and 12 is in row 3, column 2.

EXAMPLE 5.5

SIGNAL PROCESSING USING THE SINC FUNCTION

The **sinc** function is a function used in many engineering applications, but especially in signal processing applications. Unfortunately, there are two widely accepted definitions for this function:

$$f_1(x) = \frac{\sin(\pi x)}{\pi x} \quad \text{and} \quad f_2(x) = \frac{\sin x}{x}$$

Both of these functions have an indeterminate form of 0/0 when x is equal to 0. In this case, l'Hôpital's theorem from calculus can be used to prove that both functions are equal to 1 when x is equal to 0. For values of x not equal to 0, these two functions have a similar form. The first function, $f_1(x)$, crosses the x-axis when x is an integer; the second function crosses the x-axis when x is a multiple of π.

MATLAB includes a **sinc** function that uses the first definition. Assume that you would like to define another function called **sinc_x** that uses the second definition. Test your function by calculating values of **sinc_x** for x from -5π to $+5\pi$, and plotting the results.

SOLUTION

1. **State the Problem**

    Create and test a function called **sinc_x**, using the second definition:

    $$f_2(x) = \frac{\sin x}{x}$$

2. **Describe the Input and Output**

    Input

    Let x vary from -5π to $+5\pi$

    Output

    Create a plot of **sinc_x** versus **x**.

3. **Hand Example**

	Calculating the sinc function	
x	sin(x)	sinc_x(x) = sin(x)/x
0	0	0/0 = 1
$\pi/2$	1	$1/(\pi/2) = 0.637$
π	0	0
$-\pi/2$	-1	$-1/(\pi/2) = -0.637$

4. **Develop a MATLAB Solution**

    First, create the function **sinc_x**:

    ```
    function output = sinc_x(x)
    %This function calculates the value of sinc,
    %using the second definition
    % sin(x)/x

    %Determine which elements in the x array are close to 0
    set1 = find(abs(x)<0.0001);
    %Set those elements in the output array equal to 1
    output(set1) = 1;
    %Determine which elements in the x array are not close to 0
    set2 = find(abs(x)>=0.0001);
    %Calculate sin(x)/x for the elements that are not close to
    0
    % and assign the results to the corresponding output array
    elements
    output(set2) = sin(x(set2))./x(set2);
    ```

    Once we've created the function, we should test it in the command window:

    ```
    sinc_x(0)
    ans =
         1
    sinc_x(pi/2)
    ans =
         0.6366
    ```

```
sinc_x(pi)
ans =
      3.8982e-017
sinc_x(-pi/2)
ans =
    0.6366
```

Notice that **sinc_x(pi/2)** equals a very small number, but not zero. That is because MATLAB treats pi as a floating-point number and uses an approximation of its real value.

5.   Test the Solution

When we compare the results with the hand example, we see that the answers match. Now, we can use the function in our problem with confidence. We have

```
%Example 5.5
clear, clc
%Define an array of angles
x=-5*pi:pi/100:5*pi;
%Calculate sinc_x
y=sinc_x(x);
%Create the plot
plot(x,y)
title('Sinc Function'), xlabel('angle'),ylabel('sinc')
```

which generates the plot shown in Figure 5.11.

The plot also supports our belief that the function is working properly. Testing **sinc_x** with one value at a time validated its answers for a scalar input; however, the program that generated the plot sent a vector argument to the function. The plot confirms that it also performs properly with vector input.

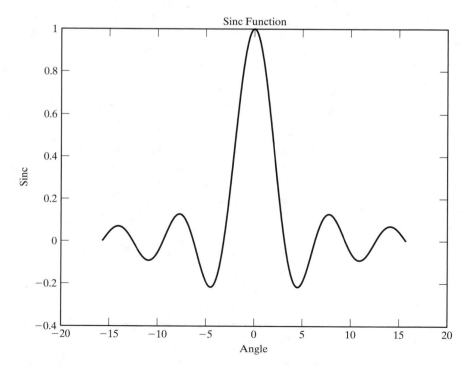

Figure 5.11.   The **sinc** function is used in electrical engineering problems.

If you have trouble understanding how this function works, remove the semi-colons that are suppressing the output, and run the program. Understanding the output from each line will help you understand the program logic better. ∎

If, else, and elseif

Most of the time, the **find** command can and should be used instead of an **if**. However, there are situations where the **if** statement is required. This section describes the syntax used in **if** statements.

If A simple **if** statement has the following form:

```
if comparison
    statements
end
```

If the logical expression (the comparison) is true, the statements between the **if** statement and the **end** statement are executed. If the logical expression is false, program control jumps immediately to the statement following the **end** statement. It is good programming practice to indent the statements within an **if** structure for readability.

For example,

```
if G<50
    count = count +1;
    disp(G);
end
```

This statement (from **if** to **end**) is easy to interpret if **G** is a scalar. For example, if **G** has a value of 25, then **count** is incremented by 1 and **G** is displayed on the screen. However, if **G** is not a scalar, then the **if** statement considers the comparison true, *only if it is true for every element*. If **G** is defined from 0 to 80,

```
G = 0:10:80;
```

then the comparison is false, and the statements inside the **if** statement are not executed! In general, **if** statements work best when dealing with scalars.

Else The simple **if** allows us to execute a series of statements if a condition is true, and to skip those steps if the condition is false. The **else** clause allows us to execute one set of statements if the comparison is true, and a different set of statements if the comparison is false. To illustrate this feature, assume that we have a variable **interval**. If the value of **interval** is less than 1, we set the value of **x_increment** to **interveral/10**; otherwise, we set the value of **x_increment** to 0.1. The following statement performs these steps:

```
if interval < 1
    x_increment = interval/10;
else
    x_increment = 0.1;
end
```

When **interval** is a scalar, this is easy to interpret. However, when **interval** is a matrix, the comparison is only true if it is true for every element in the matrix. So, if

```
interval = 0:0.5:2;
```

the elements in the matrix are not all less than 1. Therefore, MATLAB skips to the **else** portion of the statement, and all values in the **x_increment** vector are set equal to 0.1. Again, if/else statements are probably best confined to use with scalars, although you may find limited use with vectors.

Elseif   When we nest several levels of **if-else** statements, it may be difficult to determine which logical expressions must be true (or false) to execute each set of statements. In these cases, the **elseif** clause is often used to clarify the program logic, as illustrated in the following statement:

```
if temperature >100
    disp('Too hot-equipment malfunctioning')
elseif temperature >90
    disp('Normal operating temperature')
elseif temperature>50
    disp('Temperature below desired operating range')
else
    disp('Too cold-turn off equipment')
end
```

In this example, temperatures above 90 and below or equal to 100 are in the normal operating range. Temperatures outside of this range generate an appropriate message. Notice that a temperature of 101 does not trigger all of the responses. Also notice that the final **else** does not require a comparison. In order for the computation to reach the final **else**, the temperature must be less than or equal to 50.

Again, this structure is easy to interpret if **temperature** is a scalar. If it is a matrix, the comparison must be true for every element in the matrix. If you had a temperature matrix

```
temperature = [90,95,101]
```

the first comparison (**if temperature > 100**) would be false. The second comparison (**elseif temperature > 90**) would also be false. Finally, the third comparison (**elseif temperature > 50**) would be true, since all of the temperatures are above 50.

As before, **elseif** structures work well for scalars, but **find** is probably a better choice for matrices. Here's an example with an array of temperatures that generates a table of results in each category:

```
temperature = [90,45,68,84,92,95,101];
set1 = find(temperature>100);
set2 = find(temperature>90 & temperature <=100);
set3 = find(temperature>50 & temperature <=90);
set4 = find(temperature<=50);

disp('Too Hot-Equipment Malfunctioning')
disp('Element    Temperature')
table1=[set1; temperature(set1)];
fprintf('%3.0f  %8.0f \n',table1)

disp('Normal Operating Temperature')
disp('Element    Temperature')
table2=[set2; temperature(set2)];
fprintf('F%3.0f  %8.0f \n',table2)

disp('Temperature Below Desired Operating Range')
disp('Element    Temperature')
table3=[set3; temperature(set3)];
fprintf('%3.0f  %8.0f \n',table3)

disp('Too Cold-Turn Off Equipment')
disp('Element    Temperature')
table4=[set4; temperature(set4)];
fprintf('%3.0f  %8.0f \n',table4)
```

returns

```
Too Hot-Equipment Malfunctioning
Element    Temperature
   7          101
Normal Operating Temperature
Element    Temperature
   5          92
   6          95
Temperature Below Desired Operating Range
Element    Temperature
   1          90
   3          68
   4          84
Too Cold-Turn Off Equipment
Element    Temperature
   2          45
```

EXAMPLE 5.6

ASSIGNING GRADES

The **if** statement is used most effectively when the input is a scalar. Create a function to determine test grades based on the score, assuming a single input to the function. The grades should be based on the following criteria:

Grade	Score
A	90 to 100
B	80 to 90
C	70 to 80
D	60 to 70
E	<60

SOLUTION

1. State the Problem

Determine the grade earned on a test.

2. Describe the Input and Output

Input

Single score, not an array

Output

Letter grade

3. Hand Example

We determine that 85 should be a B.

But should 90 be an A or a B? We need to create more exact criteria:

Grade	Score
A	>=90 to 100
B	>=80 and < 90
C	>=70 and < 80
D	>=60 and < 70
E	<60

4.   Develop a MATLAB Solution

First, create the function:

```
function results = grade(x)
%This function requires a scalar input
if(x>=90)
    results = 'A';
elseif(x>=80)
    results = 'B';
elseif(x>=70)
    results = 'C';
elseif(x>=60)
    results = 'D';
else
    results = 'E';
end
```

5.   Test the Solution

Now test the function in the command window:

```
grade(25)
ans =
E
grade(80)
ans =
B
grade(-52)
ans =
E
grade(108)
ans =
A
```

Notice that, although the function seems to work properly, it returns grades for values over 100 and less than 0. You can now go back and add the logic to exclude those values:

```
function results = grade(x)
%This function requires a scalar input
if(x>=0 & x<=100)
if(x>=90)
    results = 'A';
elseif(x>=80)
    results = 'B';
elseif(x>=70)
    results = 'C';
elseif(x>=60)
    results = 'D';
else
    results = 'E';
end
else
    results = 'Illegal Input';
end
```

In the command window, we can test the function again:

```
grade(-10)
ans =
Illegal Input

grade(108)
ans =
Illegal Input
```

This function will work well for scalars, but if you send a vector to the function, you may get some unexpected results:

```
score = [95,42,83,77];
grade(score)
ans =
E
```

■

5.4.3 Loops

A loop is a structure that allows you to repeat a set of statements. In general, you should avoid loops in MATLAB because they are seldom needed, and they can significantly increase the execution time of a program. If you have previous programming experience, you may be tempted to use loops extensively. Try instead to formulate a solution using **find**. However, there are occasions when loops are needed, so we give a brief introduction to **for** loops and **while** loops.

For *Loops*

In general, it is possible to use either a **for** or a **while** loop in any situation that requires a repetition structure. However, **for** loops are the easier choice when you know how many times you want to repeat a set of instructions. The general format is

```
for  index = expression
    statements
end
```

Usually the expression is a vector, and the statements are repeated as many times as there are columns in the expression matrix. For example, to find 5 raised to the 100th power, first initialize a running total:

```
total = 1;
for k=1:100
    total = total * 5;
end
```

The first time through the loop, total $= 1$, so total $\times 5$ equals 5. The next time through the loop, the value of total is updated to 5×5 equals 25. After 100 times through the loop, the final value is found, and corresponds to 5^{100}. Notice that the value of **total** was suppressed, so it won't print out each time through the loop. To recall the final value of **total**, type

```
total
```

which returns

```
total =
    7.8886e+069
```

Each time through the **for** loop, the index has the value of one of the elements in the expression matrix. This can be demonstrated with another simple **for** loop:

```
for k=1:5
    k
end
```

returns

```
k =
    1
k =
    2
k =
    3
k =
    4
k =
    5
```

The rules for writing and using a **for** loop are the following:

a. The index of a **for** loop must be a variable. Although **k** is often used as the symbol for the index, any variable name can be used. The use of **k** is strictly a style issue.

b. If the expression matrix is the empty matrix, the loop will not be executed. Control will pass to the statement following the end statement.

c. If the expression matrix is a scalar, the loop will be executed one time, with the index containing the value of the scalar.

d. If the expression is a row vector, each time through the loop the index will contain the next column in the matrix.

e. If the expression matrix is a matrix, each time through the loop the index will contain the next column in the matrix. This means that the index will be a column vector!

f. Upon completion of a **for** loop, the index contains the last value used.

g. The colon operator can be used to define the expression matrix using the following format:

```
for k = initial:increment:limit
```

EXAMPLE 5.7

CALCULATING FACTORIALS USING A FOR LOOP

A factorial is the product of all of the integers from 1 to N. For example, 5 factorial is

$$1 \cdot 2 \cdot 3 \cdot 4 \cdot 5$$

In mathematics texts, a factorial is usually indicated with an exclamation point:

5! is five factorial.

MATLAB contains a built-in function for calculating factorials called **factorial**. However, suppose you would like to program your own factorial function called **fact**.

SOLUTION

1. State the Problem

Create a function called **fact** to calculate the factorial of any number. Assume you have scalar input.

2. Describe the Input and Output

Input

A scalar value, N

Output

The value of $N!$

3. Hand Example

$5! = 1 \cdot 2 \cdot 3 \cdot 4 \cdot 5 = 120$

4. Develop a MATLAB Solution

```
function output = fact(x)
%This function accepts a scalar input and calculates its
factorial
% initialize a
a = 1;
%Use a loop to calculate the factorial
for k=1:x
    a=a*k;
end
output = a;
```

5. Test the Solution

Test the function in the command window:

```
fact(5)
ans =
    120
```

This function only works if the input is a scalar. If an array is entered, the **for** loop does not execute, and the function returns a value of 1:

```
x=1:10;
>>fact(x)

ans =

    1
```

You can add an **if** statement to confirm that the input is a nonnegative integer:

```
function output = fact(x)
%This function accepts a scalar input and calculates its
factorial
%Check to confirm x is a single value array
if(length(x)>1 | x<0)
    output = 'Input must be a nonnegative integer';
else
% initialize a
a = 1;
%Use a loop to calculate the factorial
for k=1:x
```

```
        a=a*k;
    end
    output = a;
end
```

Check the new function in the command window:

```
fact(-4)
ans =
Input must be a nonnegative integer

fact(x)
ans =
Input must be a nonnegative integer
```
■

While **Loops**

The **while** loop is a structure used for repeating a set of statements as long as a specified condition is true. The general format for this control structure is:

```
while expression
    statements
end
```

The statements in the **while** loop are executed as long as the real part of the expression has all nonzero elements. The expression is usually a comparison using relational and logical operators. When the result of a comparison is true, the result is 1, and therefore "nonzero." The loop will continue repeating as long as the comparison is still true. When the expression is evaluated as false, control skips to the statement following the end statement. Consider the following example:

First initialize **a**:

```
a = 0;
```

Then find the smallest multiple of 3 that is less than 100:

```
while( a<100)
    a = a + 3;
end;
```

The last time through the loop **a** will start out as 99, then will become 102 when 3 is added to 99. The smallest multiple then becomes

```
a - 3
```

which returns

```
ans =
    99
```

The variables modified in the statements inside the loop should include the variables in the expression, or else the value of the expression will never change. If the expression is always true, then the loop will execute an infinite number of times (or until you stop the program by typing **Ctrl c**).

The break statement can be used to terminate a loop prematurely (while the comparison in the first line is still true). A break statement will cause termination of the smallest enclosing **while** or **for** loop. Here's an example:

```
n=11;
while(n>10)
```

```
                    n=input('Enter a value greater than 10: ');
                    if(n>100)
                    disp('You entered a really big number'
                    break
                    end
                    disp('You entered the number')
                    disp(n)
               end
```

EXAMPLE 5.8   CALCULATING FACTORIALS USING A WHILE LOOP

Most problems that require a loop can be solved with either a **for** loop or a **while** loop. Create a new function called **fact2** that uses a **while** loop to find $N!$. Include an **if** statement to check for negative numbers and to confirm that the input is a scalar.

SOLUTION

1. State the Problem

Create a function called **fact2** to calculate the factorial of any number.

2. Describe the Input and Output

Input

A scalar value, N

Output

The value of $N!$

3. Hand Example

$5! = 1 \cdot 2 \cdot 3 \cdot 4 \cdot 5 = 120$

4. Develop a MATLAB Solution

```
function output = fact2(x)
%This function uses a while loop to find x!
%The input must be a positive integer
if(length(x)>1 | x<0)
   output = 'The input must be a positive integer';
else
   %Initialize the running product
   a = 1;
   %Initialize the counter
   k = 1;
   while k<x
      %Increment the counter
      k = k + 1;
      %Calculate the running product
      a = a*k;

   end
   output = a;
end
```

5.   Test the Solution

Test the function in the command window:

```
fact2(5)
ans =
    120

fact2(-10)
ans =
The input must be a positive integer

fact2([1:10])
ans =
The input must be a positive integer
```

■

Improving the Efficiency of Loops

In general, using a **for** loop (or a **while** loop) is less efficient in MATLAB than using array operations. We can test this assertion by timing a long array multiplication. First, we create a matrix **A** containing 40,000 ones. The **ones** command creates an $n \times n$ matrix of ones:

```
ones(200);
```

The result is a 200×200 matrix, and all the element values are 1. Now we can compare the results of multiplying each element by π using a **for** loop and performing array multiplication. You can time the results by using the clock function and the function **etime**, which measures elapsed time. If you have a fast computer, you may need to use a larger array:

```
t0 = clock;
...
code to be timed
...
etime (clock, t0)
```

for our problem,

```
clear, clc
A=ones(200);
t0=clock;
B=A*pi;
time = etime(clock, t0);
```

giving a result of

```
time =
      0
```

The array calculation took 0 seconds, simply meaning it happened very quickly. Every time you run these lines of code you should get a different answer. The **clock** and **etime** functions used here measure how long the CPU worked between receiving the original and final timing requests. However, the CPU is doing other things besides our problem: at a minimum it is performing system tasks, and may be running other programs in the background.

To measure the time required to perform the same calculation with a loop, first we need to clear the memory and recreate the array of ones:

```
clear
A=ones(200);
```

This ensures that we are comparing calculations from the same starting point:

```
t0=clock;
for k=1:length(A(:))
    B(k)=A(k)*pi;
end
time = etime(clock, t0)
```

gives the result

```
time =
    69.6200
```

It took almost 70 seconds to perform the same calculation! The number of iterations through the **for** loop was determined by finding how many elements are in **A**. This was accomplished using the **length** command. Length returns the largest array dimension, which for our array is 200, and isn't what we want. To find the total number of elements, we used the colon operator (**:**) to represent **A** as a single list, 40,000 elements long, then used **length**, which returned 40,000. Each time through the **for** loop a new element was added to the **B** matrix—this is the step that took all the time. We can reduce the time required for this calculation by creating the **B** matrix first, and then replacing the values one at a time:

```
clear
A=ones(200);
t0=clock;
B = A;                      %Create a B matrix of ones
for k=1:length(A(:))
    B(k)=A(k)*pi;
end
time = etime(clock, t0)
```

which results in

```
time =
     0.0200
```

This is obviously a huge improvement. You could see a bigger difference between the first example (a simple array multiplication) and the last example if you created a bigger matrix. However, the intermediate example where we did not initialize **B** would take a prohibitive amount of time to execute. When a calculation is taking a long time to complete, you can confirm that the computer is really working on it by checking the lower left-hand corner for the "busy" indicator. If you want to exit the calculation manually, type **ctrl c**.

Hint: Many computer texts and manuals indicate the control key with the $^\wedge$ symbol. This is confusing at best. The command $^\wedge$c usually means to strike the ctrl key and the c key at the same time.

SUMMARY

In this chapter, we expanded our set of programming tools. We enhanced our understanding of using matrices in calculations, and in particular we explored the use of the **meshgrid** function. We learned how to communicate with users through the input command and by formatting output. We also learned how to create user defined functions. Finally, we introduced selection and loop structures. We emphasized the **find** command, but also discussed **if** structures and **for** and **while** loops.

MATLAB SUMMARY

This MATLAB summary lists and briefly describes all of the special characters, commands, and functions that were defined in this chapter:

Special Characters

<	less than
< =	less than or equal to
>	greater than
> =	greater than or equal to
==	equal to
~ =	not equal to
&	and
|	or
~	not
%f	fixed point, or decimal notation
%e	exponential notation
%g	either fixed point or exponential notation
\n	linefeed
\r	carriage return
\t	tab
\b	backspace

Commands and Functions

clock	determines the current time on the CPU clock
disp	displays matrix or text
else	defines the path if the result of an **if** statement is false
elseif	defines the path if the result of an **if** statement is false, and specifies a new logical test
end	identifies the end of a control structure
etime	finds elapsed time
find	determines which elements in a matrix meet the input criteria
for	generates a loop structure
fprintf	prints formatted information
function	identifies an M-file as a function
if	tests a logical expression
input	prompts the user to enter a value
meshgrid	maps two input vectors onto two 2-D matrices
nargin	determines the number of input arguments in a function
nargout	determines the number of output arguments from a function
num2string	converts an array into a string

ones	creates a matrix of ones
tic	starts a timing sequence
toc	stops a timing sequence
while	generates a loop structure
zeros	creates a matrix of zeros

KEY TERMS

carriage return
control structure
delimiters
file name
function
function name

index
linefeed
local variable
logical condition
logical operator
loop

relational operator
repetition
selection
sequence
user defined input

Problems

1. The distance to the horizon increases as you climb a mountain (or a hill). The expression

$$d = \sqrt{2rh + h^2}$$

where

d = distance to the horizon
r = radius of the earth
h = height of the hill

can be used to calculate that distance. The distance depends on how high the hill is and the radius of the earth. Of course, on other planets the radius is different. For example,

- Earth's diameter = 7,926 miles
- Mars' diameter = 4,217 miles

Create a MATLAB program to find the distance in miles to the horizon both on Earth and on Mars for hills from 0 to 10,000 feet. Remember to use consistent units in your calculations. You'll need to use the **meshgrid** function to solve this problem. Report your results in a table. Each column should represent a different planet, and each row should represent a different hill height. Be sure to provide a title for your table and column headings. [*Hint*: Use **disp** for the title and headings; use **fprintf** for the table values.]

2. Create a function called **distance** to find the distance to the horizon. Your function should accept two input vectors, radius and height, and should return a table similar to the one in Problem 1. Use the results of Problem 1 to validate your calculations.

3. Use your favorite Internet search engine and World Wide Web browser to identify recent currency conversions for British pounds sterling, Japanese yen, and the European euro to U.S. dollars. Use the conversion tables to create

the following tables. Use the **disp** and **fprintf** commands in your solution, which should include a title, column labels, and formatted output.

    a.   Generate a table of conversions from yen to dollars. Start the yen column at 5 and increment by 5 yen. Print 25 lines in the table.

    b.   Generate a table of conversions from the euro to dollars. Start the euro column at 1 euro and increment by 2 euros. Print 30 lines in the table.

    c.   Generate a table with four columns. The first should contain dollars, the second the equivalent number of euros, the third the equivalent number of pounds, and the fourth the equivalent number of yen.

4.   This set of problems requires you to generate temperature conversion tables. Use the following equations, which describe the relationships between temperatures in degrees Fahrenheit (T_F), degrees Celsius (T_C), degrees Kelvin (T_K), and degrees Rankine (T_R), respectively:

$$T_F = T_R - 459.67°R$$
$$T_F = \frac{9}{5}T_C + 32°F$$
$$T_R = \frac{9}{5}T_K$$

You will need to rearrange these expressions to solve some of the problems.

    a.   Generate a table with the conversions from Fahrenheit to Kelvin for values from 0°F to 200°F. Allow the user to enter the increments in degrees F between lines.

    b.   Generate a table with the conversions from Celsius to Rankine. Allow the user to enter the starting temperature and increment between lines. Print 25 lines in the table.

    c.   Generate a table with the conversions from Celsius to Fahrenheit. Allow the user to enter the starting temperature, the increment between lines, and the number of lines for the table.

5.   ***Rocket Trajectory.*** Suppose a small rocket is being designed to make wind sheer measurements in the vicinity of thunderstorms. The height of the rocket can be represented by the following equation:

$$\text{height} = 2.13t^2 - 0.0013t^4 + 0.000034t^{4.751}$$

    a.   Create a function called **height** that accepts time as an input and returns the height of the rocket. Use your function in your solutions to parts (b) and (c).

    b.   Compute, print, and plot the time and height of the rocket from the time it launches until it hits the ground, in increments of 2 seconds. If the rocket has not hit the ground within 100 seconds, print values only up through 100 seconds.

    c.   Modify the steps in part (a) so that, instead of a table, the program prints the time at which the rocket begins to fall back to the ground and the time at which it hits the ground (when the elevation becomes negative).

6.   ***Suture Packaging.*** Sutures are strands or fibers used to sew living tissue together after an injury or an operation. Packages of sutures must be sealed

carefully before they are shipped to hospitals so that contaminants cannot enter the packages. The substance that seals the package is referred to as the sealing die. Generally, sealing dies are heated with an electric heater. For the sealing process to be a success, the sealing die is maintained at an established temperature and must contact the package with a predetermined pressure for an established period of time. The period of time during which the sealing die contacts the package is called the dwell time. Assume that the range of parameters for an acceptable seal are the following:

Temperature :	**150–170°C**
Pressure:	**60–70 psi**
Dwell Time:	**2.0–2.5 sec**

a. A data file named **suture.dat** contains information on batches of sutures that have been rejected during a one-week period. Each line in the data file contains the batch number, the temperature, the pressure, and the dwell time for a rejected batch. A quality-control engineer would like to analyze this information to determine

- the percent of the batches rejected due to temperature,
- the percent rejected due to pressure and
- the percent rejected due to dwell time.

If a specific batch is rejected for more than one reason, it should be counted in all applicable totals. Give the MATLAB statements to compute and print these three percentages. Use the following data to create **suture.dat** (Don't just type in a matrix of this data—that would be cheating!)

Batch Number	Temperature	Pressure	Dwell Time
24551	145.5	62.3	2.23
24582	153.7	63.2	2.52
26553	160.3	58.9	2.51
26623	159.5	58.9	2.01
26642	160.3	61.2	1.98

b. Modify the solution developed in part (a) so that it also prints the number of batches in each rejection category and the total number of batches rejected. (Remember that a rejected batch should appear only once in the total, but could appear in more than one rejection category.)

c. Confirm that the data in **suture.dat** relates only to batches that should have been rejected. If any batch should not be in the data file, print an appropriate message with the batch information.

7. ***Timber Regrowth.*** A problem in timber management is to determine how much of an area to leave uncut so that the harvested area is reforested in a certain period of time. It is assumed that reforestation takes place at a known rate per year, depending on climate and soil conditions. A reforestation equation expresses this growth as a function of the amount of timber standing and the reforestation rate. For example, if 100 acres are left standing after harvesting and the reforestation rate is 0.05, then 105 acres are forested at the end of the first year. At the end of the second year, the number of acres forested is 110.25

acres. If year0 is the acreage forested, then

```
year1 = year0 + rate*year0 = year0*(1+rate)
year2 = year1 + rate*year1 = year1*(1+rate)
      = year0*(1+rate)*(1+rate)= year0*(1+rate)^2
year3 = year2 + rate*year2  =year2*(1+rate)
      = year0*(1+rate)^3
yearn = year0*(1+rate)^n
```

a. Assume that there are 14,000 acres total, with 2500 uncut acres and that the reforestation rate is 0.02. Print a table showing the number of acres reforested at the end of each year for a total of 20 years. You should also present your results in a bar graph, labeled appropriately.

b. Modify the program developed in part (a) so that the user can enter the number of years to be used for the table.

c. Modify the program developed in part (a) so that the user can enter a number of acres, and the program will determine how many years are required for the number of acres to be forested. (You'll need a loop for this one.)

8. **Sensor Data.**   Suppose that a file named **sensor.dat** contains information collected from a set of sensors. Each row contains a set of sensor readings, with the first row containing values collected at 0 seconds, the second row containing values collected at 1.0 seconds, etc.

Write a program to print the subscripts of sensor data values with an absolute value greater than 20.0. [*Hint*: You'll need to use the **find** command.]

9. **Power Plant Output.**   The power output in megawatts from a power plant over a period of 8 weeks has been stored in a data file named **plant.dat**. Each line in the file represents data for one week and contains the output for day 1, day 2, through day 7.

a. Write a program that uses the power-plant output data and prints a report that lists the number of days with greater-than-average power output. The report should give the week number and the day number for each of these days, in addition to printing the average power output for the plant during the 8-week period.

b. Write a program that uses the power-plant output data and prints the day and week during which the maximum and minimum power output occurred. If the maximum or minimum power output occurred on more than one day, the program should print all the days involved.

c. Write a program that uses the power-plant output data to print the average power output for each week. Also print the average power output for day 1, day 2, and so on.

10. **Faster Loops.**   When possible, it is better to avoid using **for** loops, because they are slow to execute.

a. Generate a 100,000-item vector of random digits, square this vector as an array, and use the command **tic** and **toc** to time the operation:

```
tic
...
code to be timed
...
toc
```

b. Next, perform the same peration element by element in a **for** loop. Again, time the operation using **tic** and **toc**.

c. Now, convince yourself that suppressing the printing of intermediate answers will speed execution of the code by allowing these same operations to run, and print the answers as they are calculated.

d. If you are going to be using a constant value several times in a **for** loop, calculate it once and store it, rather than calculating it each time through the loop. Demonstrate the speed increase of this process by adding **sin(0.3)** to every value in the long vector in a **for** loop.

e. As discussed in this chapter, if MATLAB must increase the size of a vector every time through a loop, the process will take more time than if the vector were already the appropriate size. Demonstrate this fact by storing the value of the foregoing addition into a new vector. Speed execution of the code by making the vector that will store the values equal to a zero vector of the appropriate size before the loop is entered:

```
zeros(1,100000);
```

6

Matrix Computations

GRAND CHALLENGE: MAPPING THE HUMAN GENOME

Some of the goals of the Human Genome Project are to

- *identify* all the genes in human DNA
- *determine* the sequences of the chemical base pairs that make up human DNA
- *store* this information in databases
- *improve* tools for data analysis
- *transfer* related technologies to the private sector
- *address* the ethical, legal, and social issues that may arise from the project

The three billion base pairs in the human genome were completely sequenced in the year 2003. (See Figure 6.1.) One of the surprises from the results was the smaller-than-expected number of genes. Early estimates of the number of genes ranged from 50,000 to 100,000, but the deciphering of the human genome resulted in mapping roughly 30,000 genes. Only about 2 percent of the base pairs make up genes; the rest of the instructions are for making proteins. Another interesting result occurred when the human genome was matched to a mouse genome. When scientists compared the human and mouse genomes, they discovered that more than 90 percent of the mouse genome could be lined up with a region on the human genome. Over 99.9 percent of the human genome is shared by all humans. The differences between individuals occur in less than 0.1 percent of the base pairs!

Sequencing the human genome was not an end unto itself. Much is still unknown. For example, the function of only one-half of the identified genes is understood. The nongene

OBJECTIVES

After reading this chapter, you should be able to

- perform operations that apply to an entire matrix as a unit
- solve simultaneous equations using MATLAB matrix operations
- use some of MATLAB's special matrices

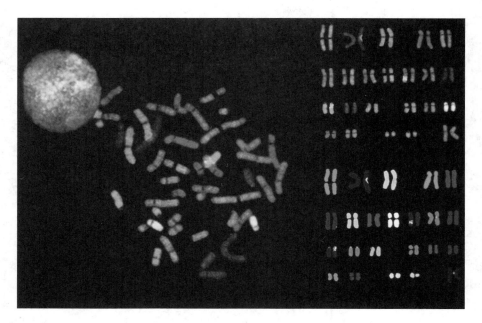

Figure 6.1. The Human Genome project.

portion of DNA is even more of a puzzle. Although the Human Genome project has successfully sequenced the human genome, the research continues in the U.S. Department of Energy's Genomes to Life program, and in a multitude of related research projects in universities, national research laboratories, and private laboratories. When large quantities of data such as that from the Human Genome project are used in calculations, it is often useful to store the information in matrices. You can learn more about the Human Genome project at http://www.doegenomes.org/.

6.1   MATRIX OPERATIONS AND FUNCTIONS

Many engineering computations use a matrix as a convenient way to represent a set of data. Here, we are generally concerned with matrices that have more than one row and more than one column. Scalar multiplication and matrix addition and subtraction are performed element by element. Matrix multiplication is covered in this section.

6.1.1   Transpose

The **transpose** of a matrix is a new matrix in which the rows of the original matrix are the columns of the new matrix. We use a superscript **T** after the name of a matrix to refer to the transpose of the matrix. For example, consider the following matrix and its transpose:

$$\mathbf{A} = \begin{bmatrix} 2 & 5 & 1 \\ 7 & 3 & 8 \\ 4 & 5 & 21 \\ 16 & 13 & 0 \end{bmatrix} \qquad \mathbf{A^T} = \begin{bmatrix} 2 & 7 & 4 & 16 \\ 5 & 3 & 5 & 13 \\ 1 & 8 & 21 & 0 \end{bmatrix}$$

If we consider a couple of the elements, we see that the value in position (3,1) of $\mathbf{A}$ has now moved to position (1,3) of $\mathbf{A}^T$, and the value in position (4,2) of $\mathbf{A}$ has now moved to position (2,4) of $\mathbf{A}^T$. In general, the row and column subscripts are interchanged to form the transpose; hence, the value in position (i, j) is moved to position (j, i).

In MATLAB, the transpose of the matrix $\mathbf{A}$ is denoted by $\mathbf{A}'$. Observe that the transpose will have a different size than the original matrix if the original matrix is not a square matrix. We frequently use the transpose operation to convert a row vector to a column vector or a column vector to a row vector.

6.1.2 Dot Product

The **dot product** is a scalar computed from two vectors of the same size. This scalar is the sum of the products of the values in corresponding positions in the vectors, as shown in the following summation equation, which assumes that there are n elements in the vectors $\mathbf{A}$ and $\mathbf{B}$:

$$\text{dot product} = \mathbf{A} \cdot \mathbf{B} = \sum_{i=1}^{n} a_i b_i$$

In MATLAB, we can compute the dot product with the following statement:

```
dot_product = sum(A.*B);
```

Recall that $\mathbf{A}.*\mathbf{B}$ contains the results of an element-by-element multiplication of $\mathbf{A}$ and $\mathbf{B}$. When $\mathbf{A}$ and $\mathbf{B}$ are both row vectors or are both column vectors, $\mathbf{A}.*\mathbf{B}$ is also a vector. We then sum the elements in this vector, thus yielding the dot product. The **dot** function may also be used to compute the dot product:

```
dot (A,B);
```

To illustrate, assume that $\mathbf{A}$ and $\mathbf{B}$ are the following vectors:

$$\mathbf{A} = [4 \quad -1 \quad 3] \quad \mathbf{B} = [-2 \quad 5 \quad 2]$$

The dot product is then

$$\begin{aligned} \mathbf{A} \cdot \mathbf{B} &= 4 \cdot (-2) + (-1) \cdot 5 + 3 \cdot 2 \\ &= (-8) + (-5) + 6 \\ &= -7 \end{aligned}$$

You can test this result by typing

```
dot (A,B);
```

EXAMPLE 6.1

CALCULATING MASS

The mass of space vehicles is extremely important. Whole groups of people in the design process keep track of the location and mass of every nut and bolt. This information is used to determine the center of gravity of the vehicle in addition to its total mass. One reason the center of gravity is important is that rockets tumble if the center of gravity is forward of the center of pressure. You can demonstrate this with a paper airplane. Put a paperclip on the nose of the paper airplane and observe how the flight pattern changes.

Although finding the center of gravity is a fairly straightforward calculation, it becomes more complex when you realize that the mass of the vehicle and the distribution of mass changes as the fuel is burned.

Figure 6.2. The center of gravity needs to be behind the center of pressure.

In this example, we will only find the total mass of some of the components used in a complex space vehicle:

Item	Amount	Mass
Bolt	3	3.50 gram
Screw	5	1.50 gram
Nut	2	0.79 gram
Bracket	1	1.75 gram

The total mass is really a dot product. You need to multiply each amount times the corresponding mass, then add them up. Write a MATLAB program to find the mass of this list of components, using matrix math.

SOLUTION

1.   State the Problem

Find the total mass

2.   Describe the Input and Output

Input

Number of each item
Mass of each item

Output

Total cost

3.   Hand Example

Item	Amount		Mass	Totals
Bolt	3	×	3.50 gram	= 10.50 gram
Screw	5	×	1.50 gram	= 7.50 gram
Nut	2	×	0.79 gram	= 1.58 gram
Bracket	1	×	1.75 gram	= 1.75 gram
				21.33 gram

4.   Develop a MATLAB Solution

```
%Example 6.1
%Determining mass
clear, clc
% Define the item vector
item = [3, 5, 2, 1];
%Define the mass vector
mass = [3.5, 1.5, .79, 1.75];
% Multiply the number of items times the cost
totals = item.*mass
% Add up the mass for each item group
total = sum(totals)
%Perform the same calculations with the dot product
total = dot(item,mass)
```

returns the following result:

```
totals =
   10.5000    7.5000    1.5800    1.7500
total =
   21.3300
total =
   21.3300
```

5.   Test the Solution

Compare the MATLAB solution to the hand solution. Both approaches give the same result and agree with the hand example. Now that we know the program works, we can use it for any number of items. For example,

```
item    = [3, 5, 2, 1, 5, 8, 9, 12, 10];
mass    = [3.5, 1.5, .79, 1.75, 5, 3, 7.5, 3, 1.5];
totals = item.*mass
total  = sum(totals)
total  = dot(item,mass)
```

gives us the total mass for nine different components.   ∎

6.1.3   Matrix Multiplication

Matrix multiplication is not accomplished by multiplying corresponding elements of the matrices. In matrix multiplication, the value in position $c(i,j)$ of the product $\mathbf{C}$ of two matrices $\mathbf{A}$ and $\mathbf{B}$ is the dot product of row i of the first matrix and column j of the second matrix, as shown in the following summation equation:

$$c_{i,j} = \sum_{k=1}^{N} a_{ik}b_{kj}$$

Because the dot product requires that the vectors have the same number of elements, the first matrix $\mathbf{A}$ must have the same number of elements N in each row as there are in each column of the second matrix $\mathbf{B}$. Thus, if $\mathbf{A}$ and $\mathbf{B}$ both have five rows and five columns, their product has five rows and five columns. Furthermore, for these matrices, we can compute both $\mathbf{AB}$ and $\mathbf{BA}$, but in general they will not be equal.

If $\mathbf{A}$ has two rows and three columns and $\mathbf{B}$ has three rows and three columns, the product $\mathbf{AB}$ will have two rows and three columns. To illustrate, consider the following matrices:

$$\mathbf{A} = \begin{bmatrix} 2 & 5 & 1 \\ 0 & 3 & -1 \end{bmatrix} \quad \mathbf{B} = \begin{bmatrix} 1 & 0 & 2 \\ -1 & 4 & -2 \\ 5 & 2 & 1 \end{bmatrix}$$

The first element in the product $\mathbf{C} = \mathbf{AB}$ is

$$\begin{aligned} c_{1,1} &= \sum_{k=1}^{3} a_{1k}b_{k1} \\ &= a_{1,1}b_{1,1} + a_{1,2}b_{2,1} + a_{1,3}b_{3,1} \\ &= 2\cdot 1 + 5\cdot(-1) + 1\cdot 5 \\ &= 2 \end{aligned}$$

Similarly, we can compute the rest of the elements in the product of $\mathbf{A}$ and $\mathbf{B}$:

$$\mathbf{AB} = \mathbf{C} = \begin{bmatrix} 2 & 22 & -5 \\ -8 & 10 & -7 \end{bmatrix}$$

In this example, we cannot compute $\mathbf{BA}$, because $\mathbf{B}$ does not have the same number of elements in each row as $\mathbf{A}$ has in each column.

An easy way to decide if a matrix product exists is to write the sizes of the two matrices side by side. Then, if the two inside numbers are the same, the product exists, and the size of the product is determined by the two outside numbers. To illustrate, in the previous example, the size of $\mathbf{A}$ is 2×3, and the size of $\mathbf{B}$ is 3×3. Therefore, if we want to compute $\mathbf{AB}$, we write the sizes side by side:

$$2 \times 3, 3 \times 3$$

The two inner numbers are both the value 3, so $\mathbf{AB}$ exists, and its size is determined by the two outer numbers, 2×3. If we want to compute $\mathbf{BA}$, we again write the sizes side by side:

$$3 \times 3, 2 \times 3$$

The two inner numbers are not the same, so $\mathbf{BA}$ does not exist. If the two inner numbers are the same, then $\mathbf{A}$ is said to be *conformable for multiplication* to $\mathbf{B}$.

In MATLAB, matrix multiplication is denoted by an asterisk. Thus, the command to perform matrix multiplication of matrices $\mathbf{A}$ and $\mathbf{B}$ is

```
A * B;
```

For example, generate the matrices in our previous example, and then compute the matrix product:

```
A = [2,5,1;0,3,-1 ];
B = [1,0,2;-1,4,-2; 5,2,1 ];
C = A * B;
```

The results are as follows:

```
C =
      2   22   -5
     -8   10   -7
```

Note that **B** * **A** does not exist, because the number of columns of **B** does not equal the number of rows of **A**. In other words, **B** is not conformable for multiplication with **A**. Execute the MATLAB command

```
C = B*A;
```

You will get the following warning message:

```
??? Error using ==> *
Inner matrix dimensions must agree.
```

EXAMPLE 6.2

FINDING MASS

Suppose you would like to know which vendor offers the best overall mass total for the items you'll use. Your list of items stays the same, but the mass of each item is different because they are purchased from different vendors.

Item	Amount	Mass vendor A	Mass vendor B	Mass vendor C
Bolt	3	3.50 g	2.98 g	2.50 g
Screw	5	1.50 g	1.75 g	1.60 g
Nut	2	0.79 g	1.25 g	0.99 g
Bracket	1	1.75 g	0.95 g	1.25 g

The total mass for each vendor is a dot product. You need to multiply each amount times the corresponding mass, then add them up. But it would be nice to do just one calculation. Matrix multiplication is the answer. We'll need to define the amount vector as a row, but the mass matrix will be a 4 × 3 matrix.

SOLUTION

1.   State the Problem

Find the total mass for each vendor

2.   Describe the Input and Output

Input

Number of each item
Mass of each item, for each vendor

Output

Total mass

3. Hand Example

Item	Amount		Mass	Totals
Bolt	3	×	3.50	= 10.50
Screw	5	×	1.50	= 7.50
Nut	2	×	0.79	= 1.58
Bracket	1	×	1.75	= 1.75
				21.33

4. Develop a MATLAB Solution

```
%Example 6.2
clear, clc
item = [3, 5, 2, 1]
mass =[  3.50  2.98  2.50;
         1.50  1.75  1.60;
         0.79  1.25  0.99;
         1.75  0.95  1.25]

item * mass
```

returns the following result:

```
item =
   3   5   2   1

mass =
   3.5000    2.9800    2.5000
   1.5000    1.7500    1.6000
   0.7900    1.2500    0.9900
   1.7500    0.9500    1.2500
ans =
   21.3300   21.1400   18.7300
```

5. Test the Solution

Based on this solution, it appears that vendor C is the best choice. Notice that the item array is a 1 × 4 matrix, and the mass array is a 4 × 3 matrix. The "inner dimensions" match, confirming that matrix multiplication is possible for these two arrays. ∎

EXAMPLE 6.3

COMPARING DESIGNS

Let's suppose two engineers are promoting competing designs:

Item	Amount Design A	Amount Design B	Mass Vendor A	Mass Vendor B	Mass Vendor C
Bolt	3	5	3.50 g	2.98 g	2.50 g
Screw	5	2	1.50 g	1.75 g	1.60 g
Nut	2	3	0.79 g	1.25 g	0.99 g
Bracket	1	2	1.75 g	0.95 g	1.25 g

Now, we not only need to multiply each amount times the corresponding mass, then add them up, but we need to do it for each design. Yet again, matrix multiplication is the answer. We'll need to define the amounts as a 2 × 4 matrix, but the mass matrix will still be a 4 × 3 matrix.

SOLUTION

1. State the Problem

Find the total mass for each vendor, for each design

2. Describe the Input and Output

Input

Number of each item, for each design
Mass of each item, for each vendor

Output

Total mass

3. Hand Example

Item	Amount		Mass	Totals
Bolt	3	×	3.50	= 10.50
Screw	5	×	1.50	= 7.50
Nut	2	×	0.79	= 1.58
Bracket	1	×	1.75	= 1.75
				21.33

4. Develop a MATLAB Solution

```
%Example 6.3
clear, clc
%Define the item matrix
item = [3,5,2,1;5,2,3,2]
%Define the mass matrix
mass = [3.5000  2.9800  2.5000;
   1.5000   1.7500   1.6000;
   0.7900   1.2500   0.9900;
   1.7500   0.9500   1.2500]
%Calculate the total mass
item * mass
```

returns the following result:

```
item =
   3   5   2   1
   5   2   3   2
mass =
   3.5000    2.9800    2.5000
   1.5000    1.7500    1.6000
   0.7900    1.2500    0.9900
   1.7500    0.9500    1.2500
ans =
   21.3300   21.1400   18.7300
   26.3700   24.0500   21.1700
```

5. Test the Solution

Based on this solution, it appears that design A, vendor C is the best choice. Notice that the item array is a 2×4 matrix, and the mass array is a 4×3 matrix. The "inner dimensions" match, confirming that matrix multiplication is possible for these two arrays.

Compare the MATLAB solution with the hand solution, and with the results from Examples 6.1 and 6.2, to confirm that we are getting consistent results. ∎

6.1.4 Matrix Powers

Recall that if **A** is a matrix, then the operation $\mathbf{A}.^{\wedge}2$ squares each element in **A**. If we want to square the matrix—that is, compute **A**°**A**—we use the operation **A^2**. **A^4** is equivalent to **A**°**A**°**A**°**A**. To perform a matrix multiplication between two matrices, the number of rows in the first matrix must be the same value as the number of columns in the second matrix. Therefore, to raise a matrix to a power, the number of rows must equal the number of columns, and thus the matrix must be a square matrix—for example,

Create the matrix **A** = [1, 2; 3, 4]. Raise the matrix to the second power:

```
C = A^2;
```

The results will be as follows:

```
C =
        7       10
       15       22
```

Note that raising **A** to the **matrix power** of two is different from raising **A** to the **array power** of two:

```
C = A.^2;
```

Raising **A** to the array power of two produces the following results:

```
C =
        1        4
        9       16
```

6.1.5 Matrix Inverse

By definition, the **inverse** of a square matrix **A** is the matrix $\mathbf{A}^{-1}$ such that the matrix products $\mathbf{AA}^{-1}$ and $\mathbf{A}^{-1}\mathbf{A}$ are both equal to the identity matrix. For example, consider the following two matrices **A** and **B**:

$$\mathbf{A} = \begin{bmatrix} 2 & 1 \\ 4 & 3 \end{bmatrix} \qquad \mathbf{B} = \begin{bmatrix} 1.5 & -0.5 \\ -2 & 1 \end{bmatrix}$$

If we compute the products **AB** and **BA**, we obtain the following matrices (do the matrix multiplications by hand to be sure you follow the steps):

$$\mathbf{AB} = \begin{bmatrix} 1 & 0 \\ 0 & 1 \end{bmatrix} \qquad \mathbf{BA} = \begin{bmatrix} 1 & 0 \\ 0 & 1 \end{bmatrix}$$

Therefore, **A** and **B** are inverses of each other, or $\mathbf{A} = \mathbf{B}^{-1}$ and $\mathbf{B} = \mathbf{A}^{-1}$.

Computing the inverse of a matrix is a tedious process; fortunately, MATLAB contains an **inv** function that performs the computations for us. (We do not present the steps for computing an inverse in this text. Refer to a linear algebra text if you are interested in the techniques for computing an inverse.) Thus, if we execute **inv(A)** using the matrix **A** defined previously, the result will be the matrix **B**. Similarly, if we execute **inv(B)**, the result should be the matrix **A**. Try this yourself.

There are matrices for which an inverse does not exist; these matrices are called **singular**, or **ill-conditioned matrices**. When you attempt to compute the inverse of an ill-conditioned matrix in MATLAB, an error message is printed.

6.1.6   Determinants

A **determinant** is a scalar computed from the entries in a square matrix. Determinants have various applications in engineering, including computing inverses and solving systems of simultaneous equations. For a 2×2 matrix **A**, the determinant is

$$|\mathbf{A}| = a_{1,1}a_{2,2} - a_{2,1}a_{1,2}$$

Therefore, the determinant of **A**, or $|\mathbf{A}|$, is equal to 8 for the following matrix:

$$\mathbf{A} = \begin{bmatrix} 1 & 3 \\ -1 & 5 \end{bmatrix}$$

For a 3×3 matrix **A**, the determinant is

$$\begin{aligned} |\mathbf{A}| = {} & a_{1,1}a_{2,2}a_{3,3} + a_{1,2}a_{2,3}a_{3,1} + a_{1,3}a_{2,1}a_{3,2} \\ & - a_{3,1}a_{2,2}a_{1,3} - a_{3,2}a_{2,3}a_{1,1} - a_{3,3}a_{2,1}a_{1,2} \end{aligned}$$

If

$$\mathbf{A} = \begin{bmatrix} 1 & 3 & 0 \\ -1 & 5 & 2 \\ 1 & 2 & 1 \end{bmatrix}$$

then $|\mathbf{A}|$ is equal to $5 + 6 + 0 - 0 - 4 - (-3)$, or 10.

A more involved process is necessary for computing determinants of matrices with more than three rows and columns. We do not include a discussion of the process for computing a general determinant here, because MATLAB will automatically compute a determinant using the **det** function, with a square matrix as its argument, as in **det(A)**.

6.2   SOLUTIONS TO SYSTEMS OF LINEAR EQUATIONS

Consider the following system of three equations with three unknowns:

$$\begin{aligned} 3x + 2y - z &= 10 \\ -x + 3y + 2z &= 5 \\ x - y - z &= -1 \end{aligned}$$

We can rewrite this system of equations using the following matrices:

$$\mathbf{A} = \begin{bmatrix} 3 & 2 & -1 \\ -1 & 3 & 2 \\ 1 & -1 & -1 \end{bmatrix} \qquad \mathbf{X} = \begin{bmatrix} x \\ y \\ z \end{bmatrix} \qquad \mathbf{B} = \begin{bmatrix} 10 \\ 5 \\ -1 \end{bmatrix}$$

Using matrix multiplication, the **system of equations** can then be written as $\mathbf{AX} = \mathbf{B}$. Go through the multiplication to convince yourself that this matrix equation yields the original set of equations.

To simplify the notation, we designate the variables as x_1, x_2, x_3, and so on. Rewriting the initial set of equations using this notation, we have

$$
\begin{array}{rrrcr}
3x_1 & +2x_2 & -x_3 & = & 10 \\
-x_1 & +3x_2 & +2x_3 & = & 5 \\
x_1 & -x_2 & -x_3 & = & -1
\end{array}
$$

This set of equations is then represented by the matrix equation $\mathbf{AX} = \mathbf{B}$, where $\mathbf{X}$ is the column vector $[x_1, x_2, x_3]^T$. We now present two methods for solving a system of N equations with N unknowns.

6.2.1   Solution Using the Matrix Inverse

One way to solve a system of equations is by using the matrix inverse. For example, assume that $\mathbf{A}$, $\mathbf{X}$, and $\mathbf{B}$ are the matrices defined earlier in this section:

$$
\mathbf{A} = \begin{bmatrix} 3 & 2 & -1 \\ -1 & 3 & 2 \\ 1 & -1 & -1 \end{bmatrix} \qquad \mathbf{X} = \begin{bmatrix} x_1 \\ x_2 \\ x_3 \end{bmatrix} \qquad \mathbf{B} = \begin{bmatrix} 10 \\ 5 \\ -1 \end{bmatrix}
$$

Then $\mathbf{AX} = \mathbf{B}$. If we premultiply both sides of this matrix equation by $\mathbf{A}^{-1}$, we have $\mathbf{A}^{-1}\mathbf{AX} = \mathbf{A}^{-1}\mathbf{B}$. However, because $\mathbf{A}^{-1}\mathbf{A}$ is equal to the identity matrix $\mathbf{I}$, we have $\mathbf{IX} = \mathbf{A}^{-1}\mathbf{B}$, or $\mathbf{X} = \mathbf{A}^{\wedge-1}\mathbf{B}$. In MATLAB, we can compute this solution with the following command:

```
X = inv(A)*B;
```

As an example, we will solve the following system of equations:

$$
\begin{array}{l}
3x_1 + 5x_2 = -7 \\
2x_1 - 4x_2 = 10
\end{array}
$$

Type the following MATLAB commands to define $\mathbf{A}$ and $\mathbf{B}$:

```
A = [3 5; 2 -4];
```

```
B = [-7 10]';
```

Now solve for $\mathbf{X}$ using the inverse of $\mathbf{A}$:

```
X = inv(A)*B;
```

MATLAB finds the following solution:

```
X =
         1.0000
        -2.0000
```

EXAMPLE 6.4

SOLVING SIMULTANEOUS EQUATIONS

Solving an electrical circuit problem quickly results in a large number of simultaneous equations. For example, consider the electrical circuit in Figure 6.3. It contains a single voltage source and five resistors. You can analyze this circuit by dividing it up into smaller pieces and applying two basic electrical facts:

$$\sum voltage \text{ around a circuit must be zero}$$

$$\text{Voltage} = \text{current} \times \text{resistance}, \; V = iR$$

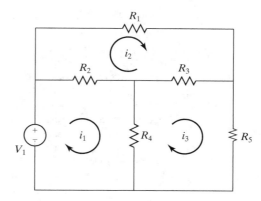

Figure 6.3. An electrical circuit.

Following the lower left-hand loop results in our first equation:

$$-V_1 + R_2(i_1 - i_2) + R_4(i_1 - i_3) = 0$$

Following the upper loop results in our second equation:

$$R_1 i_2 + R_3(i_2 - i_3) + R_2(i_2 - i_1) = 0$$

Finally, following the lower right-hand loop results in the last equation:

$$R_3(i_3 - i_2) + R_5 i_3 + R_4(i_3 - i_1) = 0$$

Since we know all the resistances (R values) and the voltage, we have three equations and three unknowns. Now we need to rearrange the equations so that they are in a form where we can perform a matrix solution—in other words, we need to isolate the i's:

$$(R_2 + R_4)i_1 + (-R_2)i_2 + (-R_4)i_3 = V_1$$
$$(-R_2)i_1 + (R_1 + R_2 + R_3)i_2 + (-R_3)i_3 = 0$$
$$(-R_4)i_1 + (-R_3)i_2 + (R_3 + R_4 + R_5)i_3 = 0$$

Create a MATLAB program to solve these equations, using the matrix inverse method. Allow the user to enter the five values of R and the voltage from the keyboard.

SOLUTION

1.   State the Problem

Find the three currents for the circuit shown.

2.   Describe the Input and Output

Input

Five resistances, R_1, R_2, R_3, R_4, R_5, and the voltage V provided from the keyboard

Output

Three current values, i_1, i_2, i_3

3.   Hand Example

If there is no applied voltage in a circuit, there can be no current. So if we enter any value for the resistances and enter zero for the voltage, the answer should be zero.

4.   Develop a MATLAB Solution

```
%Example 6.4
%Finding Currents
clear,clc
R1 = input('Input the value of R1');
R2 = input('Input the value of R2');
R3 = input('Input the value of R3');
R4 = input('Input the value of R4');
R5 = input('Input the value of R5');
V = input('Input the value of voltage, V');
coef = [(R2-R4), -R2, -R4;
        -R2, (R1 + R2 +R3), (-R3);
        -R4, - R3, (R3 + R4 + R5)]
result = [V; 0; 0]
I = inv(coef)*result
```

generates the following interaction in the command window:

```
Input the value of R1:  5
Input the value of R2:  5
Input the value of R3:  5
Input the value of R4:  5
Input the value of R5:  5
Input the value of voltage, V:  0
coef =
     0    -5    -5
    -5    15    -5
    -5    -5    15
result =
     0
     0
     0
I =
     0
     0
     0
```

5.   Test the Solution

We purposely chose to enter a voltage of zero to check our solution. Circuits without a driving force (voltage) cannot have a current flowing through them. Now try the program with other values:

```
Input the value of R1:  2
Input the value of R2:  4
Input the value of R3:  6
Input the value of R4:  8
Input the value of R5:  10
Input the value of voltage, V:  10
```

gives

```
I =
   -0.9906
   -0.5660
   -0.4717
```

The negative values for current indicate the current is flowing in a direction opposite to the one we chose as positive. Since our selection was arbitrary, this isn't surprising. ∎

6.2.2   Solution Using Matrix Left Division

A better way to solve a system of linear equations is to use the matrix division operator:

```
X = A\B;
```

This method produces the solution using Gaussian elimination, without forming the inverse. Using the matrix division operator is more efficient than using the matrix inverse and produces a greater numerical accuracy.

As an example, we will solve the same system of equations used in the previous example:

$$3x_1 + 5x_2 = -7$$
$$2x_1 - 4x_2 = 10$$

However, now solve for **X** by using matrix left division:

```
X = A\B;
```

Again, MATLAB finds the following solution:

```
X =
      1
     -2
```

To confirm that the values of **X** do indeed solve each equation, we can multiply **A** by **X** using the expression **A/X**. The result is the column vector $[-7, 10]^{T}$.

If there is not a unique solution to a system of equations, an error message is displayed. The solution vector may contain values of NaN, ∞, or $-\infty$, depending on the values of the matrices **A** and **B**.

6.3   SPECIAL MATRICES

MATLAB contains a group of functions that generate special matrices; we present some of these functions here.

6.3.1   Matrix of Zeros

The **zeros** function generates a matrix containing all zeros. If the argument to the function is a scalar, as in **zeros(6)**, the function will generate a square matrix using the argument as both the number of rows and the number of columns. If the function has two scalar arguments, as in **zeros(m,n)**, the function will generate a matrix with m rows and n columns. Because the **size** function returns two scalar arguments that represent the number of rows and columns in a matrix, we can use the size function to generate a matrix of zeros that is the same size as another matrix. The following statements illustrate these various cases:

```
A = zeros(3)
A =
      0    0    0
      0    0    0
      0    0    0

B = zeros(3,2)
```

```
B =
             0    0
             0    0
             0    0
C = [1, 2, 3 ; 4, 2, 5]
C =
             1    2    3
             4    2    5
D = zeros(size(C))
D =
             0    0    0
             0    0    0
```

6.3.2   Matrix of Ones

The **ones** function generates a matrix containing all ones, just as the **zeros** function generates a matrix containing all zeros. If the argument to the function is a scalar, as in **ones(6)**, the function will generate a square matrix using the argument as both the number of rows and the number of columns. If the function has two scalar arguments, as in **ones(m,n)**, the function will generate a matrix with m rows and n columns. To generate a matrix of ones that is the same size as another matrix, use the size function to determine the correct number of rows and columns. The following statements illustrate these various cases:

```
A = ones(3)
   A =
             1    1    1
             1    1    1
             1    1    1
B = ones(3,2)
B =
             1    1
             1    1
             1    1
C = [1, 2, 3 ; 4, 2, 5]
C =
             1    2    3
             4    2    5
D = ones(size(C))
D =
             1    1    1
             1    1    1
```

6.3.3   Identity Matrix

An identity matrix is a matrix with ones on the main diagonal and zeros everywhere else. For example, the following matrix is an identity matrix with four rows and four columns:

$$\begin{bmatrix} 1 & 0 & 0 & 0 \\ 0 & 1 & 0 & 0 \\ 0 & 0 & 1 & 0 \\ 0 & 0 & 0 & 1 \end{bmatrix}$$

Note that the main diagonal is the diagonal containing elements in which the row number is the same as the column number. Therefore, the subscripts for elements on the main diagonal are (1,1), (2,2), (3,3), and so on.

In MATLAB, identity matrices can be generated using the **eye** function. The arguments of the **eye** function are similar to those for the **zeros** and the **ones** functions. If the argument to the function is a scalar, as in **eye(6)**, the function will generate a square matrix using the argument as both the number of rows and the number of columns. If the function has two scalar arguments, as in **eye(m,n)**, the function will generate a matrix with m rows and n columns. To generate an identity matrix that is the same size as another matrix, use the **size** function to determine the correct number of rows and columns. Although most applications use a square identity matrix, the definition can be extended to nonsquare matrices. The following statements illustrate these various cases:

```
A = eye(3)
    A =
        1    0    0
        0    1    0
        0    0    1
B = eye(3,2)
B =
        1    0
        0    1
        0    0
C = [1, 2, 3 ; 4, 2, 5]
C =
        1    2    3
        4    2    5
D = eye(size(C))
D =
        1    0    0
        0    1    0
```

Hint: We recommend that you do not name an identity matrix i, because i will no longer represent $\sqrt{-1}$ in any statements that follow.

Recall that **A * inv(A)** equals the identity matrix. We can illustrate this with the following statements:

```
A=[1,0,2; -1, 4, -2; 5,2,1]
A =
        1        0        2
       -1        4       -2
        5        2        1
inv(A)
ans =
      -0.2222   -0.1111    0.2222
       0.2500    0.2500    0.0000
       0.6111    0.0556   -0.1111
A*inv(A)
ans =
       1.0000    0.0000    0.0000
      -0.0000    1.0000    0.0000
      -0.0000   -0.0000    1.0000
```

In general, for matrices,

$$A*B \neq B*A$$

However, for identity matrices,

$$A*I = I*A$$

which we can show with the following MATLAB code:

```
I = eye(3)
I =
     1    0    0
     0    1    0
     0    0    1
A*I
ans =
     1    0    2
    -1    4   -2
     5    2    1
I*A
ans =
     1    0    2
    -1    4   -2
     5    2    1
```

6.3.4   Diagonal Matrices

The **diag** function can be used to create a diagonal matrix or to extract one of the diagonals of a matrix. To extract the main diagonal from the foregoing matrix **A**, type

```
diag(A)
```

which generates the following matrix:

```
ans =
     1
     4
     1
```

Other diagonals can be saved by passing a second parameter k to **diag**. The second parameter denotes the position of the diagonal from the main diagonal ($k = 0$). Using the example matrix **A**,

```
diag(A,1)
```

returns

```
ans =
     0
    -2
```

If the first argument to **diag** is a vector, **V**, then this function generates a square matrix. If $k = 0$, then the elements of **V** are placed on the main diagonal, and if $k > 0$, they are placed above the main diagonal. If $k < 0$, they are placed below the main diagonal. Thus, we have

```
B=[1 2 3]
B =
     1    2    3
diag(B)
```

```
ans =
     1    0    0
     0    2    0
     0    0    3
diag(B,1)
ans =
     0    1    0    0
     0    0    2    0
     0    0    0    3
     0    0    0    0
```

6.3.5   Magic Matrices

MATLAB includes a matrix function called **magic** that generates a matrix with unusual properties. The sum of all of the columns is the same, as is the sum of all of the rows. For example, we might have

```
A=magic(4)
A =
    16    2    3   13
     5   11   10    8
     9    7    6   12
     4   14   15    1

sum(A)
ans =
    34    34    34    34
```

To find the sum of the rows, we need to transpose the matrix:

```
sum(A')
ans =
    34    34    34    34
```

Not only is the sum of all of the columns and rows the same; but also the sum of the diagonals is the same. The diagonal from left to right is

```
diag(A)
ans =
    16
    11
     6
     1
```

Finding the sum of the diagonal reveals the same number as the sum of the rows and columns:

```
sum(diag(A))
ans =
    34
```

Finally, to find the diagonal from lower left to upper right, we first have to flip the matrix and then find the sum of the diagonal:

```
fliplr(A)
ans =
    13    3    2   16
     8   10   11    5
    12    6    7    9
```

```
      1   15   14    4
diag(ans)
ans =
     13
     10
      7
      4
sum(ans)
ans =
     34
```

One of the earliest documented examples of a magic square is shown in Figure 6.4, by Albrecht Dürer, created in 1514. Scholars believe the square was a reference to alchemical concepts popular at the time. The date of the woodcut is included in the two middle squares of the bottom row.

Figure 6.4. Melancholia, by Albrect Dürer, 1514.

Magic squares have fascinated both professional and amateur mathematicians for centuries. For example, Benjamin Franklin experimented with magic squares. You can create magic squares of any size greater than 2×2, using MATLAB. However, other magic squares are possible—MATLAB's solution is not the only one.

SUMMARY

In this chapter we defined the transpose, the inverse, and the determinant of a matrix. We also defined the dot product (between two vectors) and a matrix product (between two matrices). Two methods for solving a system of N equations with N unknowns using matrix operations were presented. One method used matrix left division, and the other used the inverse of a matrix. We also presented several special matrix functions, **zeros, ones**, the identity matrix **eye**, the diagonal function **diag**, and magic squares.

MATLAB SUMMARY

This MATLAB summary lists and briefly describes all of the special characters, commands, and functions that were defined in this chapter:

Special Characters	
'	indicates a matrix transpose
*	matrix multiplication
\	matrix left division

Commands and Functions	
det	computes the determinate of a matrix
diag	extracts the diagonal from a matrix
	generates a matrix with the input on the diagonal
eye	generates an identity matrix
fliplr	flips a matrix from left to right
inv	computes the inverse of a matrix
magic	generates a magic square
ones	generates a matrix composed of ones
size	determines the number of rows and columns in a matrix
zeros	generates a matrix composed of zeros

KEY TERMS

determinant	inverse	transpose
dot product	matrix multiplication	magic square
identity matrix	system of equations	

Problems

1. Compute the dot product of the following pairs of vectors, and then show that

$$\mathbf{A} \cdot \mathbf{B} = \mathbf{B} \cdot \mathbf{A}$$

a. $\mathbf{A} = [1\ 3\ 5]$, $\mathbf{B} = [-3\ -2\ 4]$

b. $\mathbf{A} = [0\ -1\ -4\ -8]$, $\mathbf{B} = [4\ -2\ -3\ 24]$

2. Compute the total mass of the following components, using a dot product:

Component	Density	Volume
Propellant	1.2 g/cm^3	700 cm^3
Steel	7.8 g/cm^3	200 cm^3
Aluminum	2.7 g/cm^3	300 cm^3

3. Bomb calorimeters are used to determine the energy released during chemical reactions. The total heat capacity of a bomb calorimeter is defined as the sum of the product the mass of each component and the specific heat capacity of each component. That is,

$$CP = \sum_{i=1}^{n} m_i C_i$$

where

m_i is the mass of each component, g
C_i is the heat capacity of each component, J/gK
CP is the total heat capacity, J/K

Find the total heat capacity of a bomb calorimeter with the following components:

Component	Mass	Heat Capacity
Steel	250 g	0.45 J/gK
Water	100 g	4.2 J/gK
Aluminum	10 g	0.90 J/gK

4. Compute the matrix product **A**°**B** of the following pairs of matrices:
   a. **A** = [12 4; 3 −5], **B** = [2 12; 0 0]
   b. **A** = [1 3 5; 2 4 6], **B** = [−2 4; 3 8; 12 −2]

5. A series of experiments were performed with the bomb calorimeter from Problem 3. In each experiment, a different amount of water was used, as shown in the following table:

Experiment #	Mass of Water
1	110 g
2	100 g
3	101 g
4	98.6 g
5	99.4 g

Calculate the total heat capacity for the calorimeter for each of the experiments.

6. Given the array **A** = [−1 3; 4 2], raise **A** to the second power by array exponentiation. Raise **A** to the second power by matrix exponentiation. Explain why the answers are different.

7. Given the array $\mathbf{A} = [-1\ 3; 4\ 2]$, compute the determinant of A.

8. If $\mathbf{A}$ is conformable to $\mathbf{B}$ for addition, then a theorem states that $(\mathbf{A} + \mathbf{B})^\mathbf{T} = A^T + B^T$. Use MATLAB to test this theorem on the following matrices:

$$\mathbf{A} = \begin{bmatrix} 2 & 12 & -5 \\ -3 & 0 & -2 \\ 4 & 2 & -1 \end{bmatrix} \qquad \mathbf{B} = \begin{bmatrix} 4 & 0 & 12 \\ 2 & 2 & 0 \\ -6 & 3 & 0 \end{bmatrix}$$

9. Given that matrices $\mathbf{A}$, $\mathbf{B}$, and $\mathbf{C}$ are conformable for multiplication, the associative property holds; that is, $\mathbf{A}(\mathbf{BC}) = (\mathbf{AB})\mathbf{C}$. Test the associative property using matrices $\mathbf{A}$ and $\mathbf{B}$ from Problem 8, along with matrix $\mathbf{C}$:

$$\mathbf{C} = \begin{bmatrix} 4 \\ -3 \\ 0 \end{bmatrix}$$

10. Recall that not all matrices have an inverse. A matrix is singular (i.e., it doesn't have an inverse) if $|\mathbf{A}| = 0$. Test the following matrices using the determinant function to see if each has an inverse:

$$\mathbf{A} = \begin{bmatrix} 2 & -1 \\ 4 & 5 \end{bmatrix}, \qquad \mathbf{B} = \begin{bmatrix} 4 & 2 \\ 2 & 1 \end{bmatrix}, \qquad \mathbf{C} = \begin{bmatrix} 2 & 0 & 0 \\ 1 & 2 & 2 \\ 5 & -4 & 0 \end{bmatrix}$$

If an inverse exists, compute it.

11. Solve the following systems of equations using both the matrix left division and the inverse matrix methods:

a.
$$\begin{array}{rcr} -2x_1 & +x_2 & = & -3 \\ x_1 & +x_2 & = & 3 \end{array}$$

b.
$$\begin{array}{rrrcr} 10x_1 & -7x_2 & +0x_3 & = & 7 \\ -3x_1 & +2x_2 & +6x_3 & = & 4 \\ 5x_1 & +x_2 & +5x_3 & = & 6 \end{array}$$

c.
$$\begin{array}{rrrrcr} x_1 & +4x_2 & -x_3 & +x_4 & = & 2 \\ 2x_1 & +7x_2 & +x_3 & -2x_4 & = & 16 \\ x_1 & +4x_2 & -x_3 & +2x_4 & = & -15 \\ 3x_1 & -10x_2 & -2x_3 & +5x_4 & = & -15 \end{array}$$

12. Time each method you used in Problem 11 for part c by using the **clock** function and the **etime** function, the latter of which measures elapsed time. Which method is faster, left division or inverse matrix multiplication?

```
t0 = clock;
...
code to be timed
...
etime(clock, t0)
```

13. In Problem 4, we showed that the circuit shown in the figure could be described by the following set of linear equations:

$$(R_2 + R_4)i_1 + (-R_2)i_2 + (-R_4)i_3 = V_1$$
$$(-R_2)i_1 + (R_1 + R_2 + R_3)i_2 + (-R_3)i_3 = 0$$
$$(-R_4)i_1 + (-R_3)i_2 + (R_3 + R_4 + R_5)i_3 = 0$$

We solved this set of equations using the matrix inverse approach. Redo the problem, but this time use the left division approach.

14. **Amino Acids.** The amino acids in proteins contain molecules of oxygen (O), carbon (C), nitrogen (N), sulfur (S), and hydrogen (H), as shown in Table 6.1. The molecular weights for oxygen, carbon, nitrogen, sulfur, and hydrogen are as follows:

Oxygen	15.9994
Carbon	12.011
Nitrogen	14.00674
Sulfur	32.066
Hydrogen	1.00794

a. Write a program in which the user enters the number of oxygen atoms, carbon atoms, nitrogen atoms, sulfur atoms, and hydrogen atoms in an amino acid. Compute and print the corresponding molecular weight. Use a dot product to compute the molecular weight.

b. Write a program that computes the molecular weight of each amino acid in Table 6.1, assuming that the numeric information in this table is contained in a data file named **elements.dat**. Generate a new data file named **weights.dat** that contains the molecular weights of the amino acids. Use matrix multiplication to compute the molecular weights.

TABLE 6.1 Amino Acid Molecules

Amino Acid	O	C	N	S	H
Alanine	2	3	1	0	7
Arginine	2	6	4	0	15
Asparagine	3	4	2	0	8
Aspartic	4	4	1	0	6
Cysteine	2	3	1	1	7
Glutamic	4	5	1	0	8
Glutamine	3	5	2	0	10
Glycine	2	2	1	0	5
Histidine	2	6	3	0	10
Isoleucine	2	6	1	0	13
Leucine	2	6	1	0	13
Lysine	2	6	2	0	15
Methionine	2	5	1	1	11
Phenylanlanine	2	9	1	0	11
Proline	2	5	1	0	10
Serine	3	3	1	0	7
Threonine	3	4	1	0	9
Tryptophan	2	11	2	0	11
Tyrosine	3	9	1	9	11
Valine	2	5	1	0	11

7

Symbolic Mathematics

GRAND CHALLENGE: WEATHER PREDICTION

Weather balloons collect data from the upper atmosphere to use in developing weather models. The balloons, filled with helium, rise to an equilibrium point at which the difference between the density of the helium inside the balloon and the density of the air outside the balloon is just enough to support the weight of the balloon. During the day the sun warms the balloon, causing it to rise to a new equilibrium point; in the evening the balloon cools and descends to a lower altitude. The balloon can be used to measure the temperature, pressure, humidity, chemical concentrations, or other properties of the air around the balloon. A weather balloon may stay aloft for only a few hours, or as long as several years, collecting environmental data. The balloon falls back to earth as the helium leaks out or is released. Symbolic models of the balloon's elevation are often used to provide input to other calculations.

7.1   SYMBOLIC ALGEBRA

In addition to using numbers, we can use symbols to perform computations in MATLAB. This capability to manipulate mathematical expressions without using numbers can be very useful in solving certain types of engineering problems. The symbolic functions in MATLAB are based on the Maple 8 software package, which is published by Waterloo Maple, Inc., in Canada. A complete set of these symbolic functions is available in the Symbolic Math Toolbox. The professional version of MATLAB 7 includes the entire toolbox; a subset is included with the Student Edition. If you are using the student edition of MATLAB 6, release 12 or earlier, some of the examples in this section may not work.

SECTIONS

7.1   Symbolic Algebra
7.2   Equation Solving
7.3   Differentiation and Integration

OBJECTIVES

After reading this chapter, you should be able to

- create and manipulate symbolic variables
- factor and simplify mathematical expressions
- solve symbolic expressions
- solve systems of equations
- determine the symbolic derivative of an expression and integrate an expression

Symbolic algebra is used to factor and simplify mathematical expressions, to determine solutions to equations, and to perform integration and differentiation of mathematical expressions. Additional capabilities (not discussed here) include linear algebra functions for determining inverses, determinants, eigenvalues, and canonical forms of symbolic matrices; variable precision arithmetic for numerically evaluating mathematical expressions to any specified accuracy; symbolic and numerical solutions to differential equations; and special mathematical functions that evaluate functions such as Fourier transforms. For more details on these additional symbolic capabilities, refer to the **help** function; or to learn more about Maple, refer to *Introduction to Maple*® 8 by David Schwartz, Pearson Education, Inc., 2004.

7.1.1   Symbolic Expressions

A symbolic expression is stored in MATLAB as a character string. Single quotes are used to define the symbolic expression, which is entered as the argument of the **sym** function. For example,

```
S=sym('x^2 - 2*y^2 + 3*a')
```

returns

```
S =
x^2 - 2*y^2 + 3*a
```

Notice that symbolic results are not indented in the Command window. All of the calculations we have performed in previous chapters return an indented result, indicating that they are double-precision, floating-point numbers. Notice in the workspace window that **S** is identified as a symbolic variable. (See Figure 7.1.) Although **x**, **y** and **a** are part of the symbolic expression **S**, they are not listed individually in the workspace window.

To identify the variables in a symbolic expression or matrix, use the **findsym** function. The **findsym** function returns the variables of its single argument in alphabetical order:

```
findsym(S)
ans =
a, x, y
```

Notice again that the results are not indented and that **ans** is listed in the workspace window as a character variable.

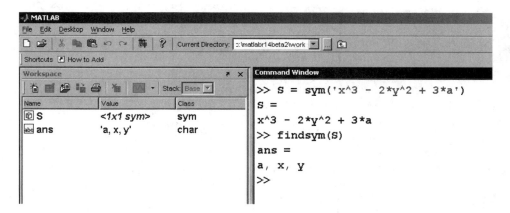

Figure 7.1.   Symbolic variables are stored in the workspace differently than character and numeric variables.

You can create complex expressions in two different ways: by defining the entire expression all at once as we've just done, or by defining each symbolic variable individually. You can use the **sym** command

```
a = sym('a')
```

which returns

```
a =
a
```

and define each variable one at a time, or you can use the **syms** command to define multiple symbolic variables all at once:

```
syms a x y
```

Obviously, the second approach is quicker because it requires less typing. Your workspace window should now reflect the fact that **a**, **x** and **y** are symbolic variables:

Name	Value	Size	Bytes	Class
S	$<1 \times 1$ sym$>$	1×4	156	sym
a	$<1 \times 1$ sym$>$	1×1	126	sym
ans	'a,x,y'	1×7	14	char
x	$<1 \times 1$ sym$>$	1×4	126	sym
y	$<1 \times 1$ sym$>$	1×4	126	sym

Hint: Your workspace window may not be set to include the size and class columns. Remember that you can adjust the workspace view from the menu bar. **Choose View → Choose by columns** and check the columns you would like shown.

Now you can use the symbolic variables to create new expressions:

```
S_new = x^2 - 2*y^2 + 3*a
```

To substitute variables or expressions within a symbolic expression, use the **subs** command. When used with three arguments, the syntax of **subs** is

```
subs(S, old, new)
```

S is a symbolic expression, and **old** is a symbolic variable or string that represents a variable name. **New** is a symbolic or numeric variable or expression. Multiple substitutions may be made by listing arguments within curly braces. For example, to substitute the variable **b** for variable **a** in the symbolic expression **S**, use

```
subs(S,'a','b')
```

which returns

```
ans =
x^2-2*y^2+3*(b)
```

To substitute the variables **q** and **r** for the variables **x** and **y**, respectively, type

```
subs(S,{'x','y'},{'q','r'})
```

giving

```
ans =
q^2-2*r^2+3*a
```

Note that neither of these commands stored the value of the new expression into **S**. For this reason, the first substitution was not reflected in the final answer after the second substitution.

Hint: If you define each variable separately using the **syms** command, you don't need the single quotes around the variable name when you use **subs**. For example, in **subs(S, x, 'q')**, **x** has been defined as a symbolic variable, but **q** has not.

Create symbolic objects **S1**, **S2**, **S3**, **S4**, and **S5** for the following mathematical expressions:

$$S1 = x^2 - 9$$
$$S2 = (x - 3)^2$$
$$S3 = \frac{x^2 - 3x - 10}{x + 2}$$
$$S4 = x^3 + 3x^2 - 13x - 15$$
$$S5 = 2x - 3y + 4x + 13b - 8y$$

Since **x** has already been defined as a symbolic variable, we can enter expressions **S1**, **S2**, **S3**, and **S4** either directly or with the **sym** function:

```
S1=x^2 -9
S1 =
x^2-9

S2=(x-3)^2
S2 =
(x-3)^2

S3=(x^2-3*x-10)/(x+2)
S3 =
(x^2-3*x-10)/(x+2)

S4=x^3 + 3*x^2 -13*x -15
S4 =
x^3+3*x^2-13*x-15
```

or

```
S1=sym('x^2 -9')
S1 =
x^2 -9
```

etc.

However, we'll need to use the variables **x**, **y**, and **b** in expression **S5**. Since **b** has not been defined as a symbolic variable, we'll either need to use the **sym** command or define **b** separately:

```
S5=sym('2*x - 3*y + 4*x + 13*b - 8*y')
S5 =
2*x - 3*y + 4*x + 13*b - 8*y
```

7.1.2 Symbolic Plotting

MATLAB includes a function called **ezplot** that generates a plot of a symbolic expression of one variable. (See Figure 7.2.) The independent variable ranges by default over the interval $[-2\pi, 2\pi]$. A second form of **ezplot** allows the user to specify the range. If the variable contains a singularity (i.e., a point at which the expression is not defined), that point is not plotted. The syntax for the **ezplot** function is described as follows:

ezplot(S) Generates a plot of **S** in the range $[-2\pi, 2\pi]$. **S** is assumed to be a function of one variable.

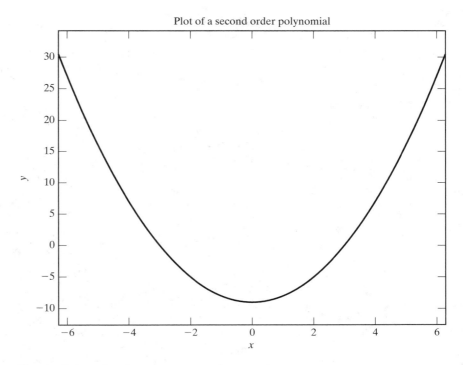

Figure 7.2. Plot of expression **S1**.

> **ezplot(S, [xmin, xmax])** Generates a plot of **S** in the range [xmin, xmax]. **S** is assumed to be a function of one variable.

We can use the symbolic expression **S1**, defined before, to demonstrate ezplot:

```
ezplot(S1)
```

You can add a title and labels in the usual way:

```
title('Plot of a second order polynomial')
xlabel('x'), ylabel('y')
```

7.1.3   Simplification of Mathematical Expressions

A number of functions are available for simplifying mathematical expressions by **collecting coefficients**, **expanding terms**, **factoring expressions**, or just making the expression simpler. A summary of these functions is as follows:

collect(S)	Collects coefficients of **S**
collect(S,'v')	Collects coefficients of **S** with respect to the independent variable **'v'**
expand(S)	Performs an expansion of **S**
factor(S)	Returns the factorization of **S**
simple(S)	Simplifies the form of **S** to a shorter form, if possible
simplify(S)	Simplifies **S** using Maple's simplification rules

To illustrate these functions, we will use the following symbolic expressions **S1**, . . . , **S5**:

```
factor(S1)
ans =
        (x-3)*(x+3)
```

```
expand(S2)
ans =
            x^2-6*x+9

simplify(S3)
ans =
            x-5

factor(S4)
ans =
            (x+5)*(x-3)*(x+1)

collect(S5)

ans =
        6*x-11*y+13*b
```

The **simple** function attempts to simplify a symbolic expression by using several different algebraic methods. Each method is displayed, along with its results. Finally, the shortest result is chosen as the answer.

As an example, we will use the **simple** function to find the simplest form of the following expression:

$$\frac{x^2 - 3x - 10}{x + 2}$$

First, create a symbolic expression **S3**:

```
S3 = sym('(x^2-3*x-10)/(x+2)');
```

Then call the **simple** function:

```
simple(S3)
```

The methods used and the various results are as follows:

```
simplify:          x-5
radsimp:           x-5
combine(trig):     x-5
factor:            x-5
expand:            1/(x+2)*x^2-3/(x+2)*x-10/(x+2)
combine:           (x^2-3*x-10)/(x+2)
convert(exp):      (x^2-3*x-10)/(x+2)
convert(sincos):   (x^2-3*x-10)/(x+2)
convert(tan):      (x^2-3*x-10)/(x+2)
collect(x):        (x^2-3*x-10)/(x+2)
ans =              x-5
```

7.1.4   Operations on Symbolic Expressions

The standard arithmetic operations can be applied to symbolic expressions. Addition, subtraction, multiplication, division, and raising an expression to a power are performed by using the standard arithmetic operators. This feature can best be illustrated with examples. Before proceeding with the examples, create symbolic objects **S6**, **S7**, and **S8** for the following expressions:

$$S6 = \frac{1}{y - 3}$$

$$S7 = \frac{3y}{y + 2}$$

$$S8 = (y + 4)(y - 3)y$$

We will multiply the symbolic objects for $\frac{1}{y-3}$ and $(y - 4)(y - 3)y$. Also, we will use the **pretty** function to display the results in typeset form:

    pretty(S6* S8)

The results are as follows:

    (y + 4)y

Similarly, we will raise the symbolic expression **S7** to the third power and use **pretty** to print the results:

    pretty(S7^3)

returns

```
              3
            y
    27 ---------------
              3
          (y + 2)
```

The **poly2sym** function converts a numerical vector to a symbolic expression. The symbolic representation is the polynomial whose coefficients are listed in the vector. The default independent variable is x, but another variable may be named as a second argument to the function. The **sym2poly** function creates a coefficient vector from the symbolic representation of a polynomial.

First, we create a vector containing the coefficients of the polynomial:

    V = [1 -4 0 2 45];

Then, we create a symbolic expression for the polynomial represented by **V**:

    poly2sym(V)

The result is

    ans =
         x^4-4*x^3+2*x+45

7.2 EQUATION SOLVING

Symbolic math functions can be used to solve a single equation, a system of equations, and differential equations. Brief descriptions of the functions for solving a single equation or a system of equations are as follows:

solve(f)   Solves the symbolic equation **f** for its symbolic variable. Solves the equation **f = 0** for its symbolic variable if **f** is a symbolic expression. If there are multiple variables, MATLAB solves for **x** preferentially.

solve(f1,...fn)   Solves the system of equations represented by **f1, ...fn.**
solve(f,'y')   Solves the symbolic equation **f**, for variable **y**. You don't need single quotes around the second argument if it has been explicitly defined as symbolic.

To illustrate the use of the **solve** function, assume that the following equations have been defined:

```
eq1 = sym('x-3=4');
eq2 = sym('x^2-x-6');
```

Notice that in **eq1** the symbolic expression is an equation, but in **eq2** the expression is not set equal to anything. In this case, MATLAB will assume that the expression is equal to zero:

```
eq3 = sym('x^2 + 2*x + 4 =0');
eq4 = sym('3*x + 2*y -z = 10');
eq5 = sym('-x + 3*y + 2*z = 5');
eq6 = sym('x - y - z = -1');
```

Reference	Function Value
`solve(eq1)`	ans = 7
`solve(eq2)`	ans = [3] [−2]
`solve(eq3)`	ans = [−21+i*3^(1/2)] [−21−i*3^(1/2)]
`solve(eq4)`	ans = 22/3*y+1/3*z+10/3 (solved for x)
`solve(eq4,y)`	ans = 23/2*x+1/2*z+5 (solved for y)
`solve(eq4,eq5,eq6)`	ans = x: [1 × 1 sym] y: [1 × 1 sym] z: [1 × 1 sym]
`[A,B,C]=solve(eq4,eq5,eq6)`	A= −2 B= 5 C= −6

When we attempt to solve the set of simultaneous equations, **eq4**, **eq5**, and **eq6**, the result is puzzling. It tells us that the results are 1×1 symbolic variables, but it doesn't reveal the value of those variables. To force the results to be displayed, we must assign them variables names:

[X1, X2, X3,…Xn] = solve(f1,…fn)

The results are assigned alphabetically. For example, if the variables used in your symbolic expressions are **q**, **x**, and **p**, the results will be returned in the order, **p**, **q**, **x**, independently of the names you have assigned for the results.

The result of the **solve** function is a symbolic variable, either **ans** or a user defined name. If you want to use that result in a MATLAB expression that requires a double-precision, floating-point input, you can change the variable type with the **double** function. For example,

```
double(x)
```

changes **x** from a symbolic variable to a matrix variable.

The function for solving ordinary differential equations is **dsolve**, but it is not discussed in this text. For more information, consult the MATLAB help files.

EXAMPLE 7.1	**USING SYMBOLIC MATH**

MATLAB's symbolic capability allows us to let the computer do the math. Recall the equation for diffusivity:

$$D = D_0 \exp\left(\frac{-Q}{RT}\right)$$

Solve the equation for Q, using MATLAB.

SOLUTION

1.   State the Problem

Find the equation for Q

2.   Describe the Input and Output

Input

   Equation for D

Output

   Equation for Q

3.   Hand Example

$$D = D_0 \exp\left(\frac{-Q}{RT}\right)$$

$$\frac{D}{D_0} = \exp\left(\frac{-Q}{RT}\right)$$

$$\ln\left(\frac{D}{D_0}\right) = \frac{-Q}{RT}$$

$$Q = RT \ln\left(\frac{D_0}{D}\right)$$

Notice that the minus sign caused the values inside of the natural logarithm to be inverted.

4.   Develop a MATLAB Solution

First, define a symbolic equation and give it a name. Notice that it's okay to put an equality inside of the expression:

```
X = sym('D = D0*exp(-Q/RT)')
X =
D = D0*exp(-Q/RT)
```

Now we just tell MATLAB to solve our equation. We need to tell it to solve for **Q**, and **Q** needs to be in single quotes because it has not been separately defined as a symbolic variable:

```
solve(X,'Q')
ans =
-log(D/D0)*RT
```

5.   Test the Solution

Compare the MATLAB solution with the hand solution. The only difference is that we pulled the minus sign inside of the logarithm. Notice that MATLAB (as well as most computer programs) represents the ln as **log**. Recall that **log**$_{10}$ is represented as **log10**.   ■

EXAMPLE 7.2

USING SYMBOLIC MATH TO SOLVE A BALLISTICS PROBLEM

We can use the symbolic math capabilities of MATLAB to explore the equations representing the path followed by an unpowered projectile, such as a cannon ball. (See Figure 7.3.)

We know from elementary physics that the distance a projectile travels horizontally is

$$d_x = v_0 t \cos(\theta)$$

and the distance traveled vertically is

$$d_y = v_0 t \sin(\theta) - \frac{1}{2}gt^2$$

where

v_0 is the velocity at launch
t is time
θ is the launch angle
g is the acceleration due to gravity

Use these equations and MATLAB's symbolic capability to derive an equation for the distance the projectile has traveled horizontally when it hits the ground (the range).

SOLUTION

1.   State the Problem

Find the range equation.

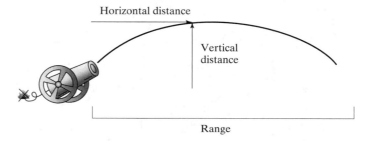

Figure 7.3.   The range of a projectile depends on the initial velocity and the launch angle.

2.   Describe the Input and Output

Input

Equations for horizontal and vertical distances

Output

Equation for range

3.   Hand Example

$$d_y = v_0 t \sin(\theta) - \frac{1}{2}gt^2 = 0$$

Rearrange to give

$$v_0 t \sin(\theta) = \frac{1}{2}gt^2$$

Divide by t and solve:

$$t = \frac{v_0 \sin(\theta) \times 2}{g}$$

Now substitute this expression for t into the horizontal distance formula:

$$d_x = v_0 t \cos(\theta)$$

$$\text{range} = v_0\left(\frac{v_0 \sin(\theta) \times 2}{g}\right)\cos(\theta)$$

We know from trigonometry that $\sin\theta \cos\theta$ is the same as $\sin(2\theta)$, which would allow a further simplification if we wanted it.

4.   Develop a MATLAB Solution

First, define the symbolic variables:

```
syms v0 t theta g
```

Define the symbolic expression for the vertical distance traveled:

```
Distancey = v0 * t *sin(theta) - 1/2*g*t^2;
```

Define the symbolic expression for the horizontal distance traveled:

```
Distancex = v0 * t *cos(theta);
```

Solve the vertical distance expression for the impact time, since the vertical distance is zero at impact:

```
impact_time = solve(Distancey,t)
```

The preceding returns two answers:

```
impact_time =
[          0]
[ 2*v0*sin(theta)/g]
```

This makes sense, since the vertical distance is zero at launch, and again at impact. Substitute impact time into the horizontal distance expression. Since we are only interested in the second time, we'll need to use **impact_time(2):**

```
impact_distance = subs(Distancex,t,impact_time(2))
```

The substitution results in an equation for the distance the projectile has traveled when it hits the ground:

```
impact_distance =
2*v0^2*sin(theta)/g*cos(theta)
```

5. Test the Solution

Compare the MATLAB solution with the hand solution. Both approaches give the same result and agree with the hand example.

MATLAB can simplify the result, although this is already pretty simple. We chose to use the **simple** command to demonstrate all the possibilities:

```
simple(impact_distance)
```

gives the following results:

```
simplify:          2*v0^2*sin(theta)/g*cos(theta)
radsimp:           2*v0^2*sin(theta)/g*cos(theta)
combine(trig):     v0^2*sin(2*theta)/g
factor:            2*v0^2*sin(theta)/g*cos(theta)
expand:            2*v0^2*sin(theta)/g*cos(theta)
combine:           v0^2*sin(2*theta)/g
convert(exp):      -i*v0^2*(exp(i*theta)-1/exp(i*theta))/
                   g*(1/2*exp(i*theta)+1/2/exp(i*theta))
convert(sincos):   2*v0^2*sin(theta)/g*cos(theta)
convert(tan):      4*v0^2*tan(1/2*theta)/
                   (1+tan(1/2*theta)^2)^2/
                   g*(1-tan(1/2*theta)^2)
collect(v0):       2*v0^2*sin(theta)/g*cos(theta)
mwcos2sin:         2*v0^2*sin(theta)/g*cos(theta)
ans =
v0^2*sin(2*theta)/g
```

■

EXAMPLE 7.3

USING SYMBOLIC MATH TO SOLVE A BALLISTICS PROBLEM

MATLAB's symbolic capabilities can be used to derive an equation for the distance a projectile travels before it hits the ground (Figure 7.4). The horizontal and vertical distance formulas

$$d_x = v_0 t \cos(\theta)$$

and

$$d_y = v_0 t \sin(\theta) - \frac{1}{2} g t^2$$

where

v_0 is the velocity at launch
t is time

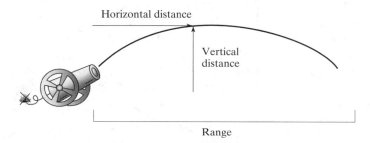

Horizontal distance

Vertical distance

Range

Figure 7.4. The range of a projectile depends on the initial velocity and the launch angle.

θ is the launch angle

g is the acceleration due to gravity

were combined to give

$$\text{range} = v_0 \left(\frac{v_0 \sin(\theta) \times 2}{g} \right) \cos(\theta)$$

Using MATLAB's symbolic plotting capability, create a plot showing the range traveled for angles from 0 to $\pi/2$. Assume an initial velocity of 100 m/s and an acceleration due to gravity of 9.8 m/s^2.

SOLUTION

1.   State the Problem

Plot the range as a function of launch angle.

2.   Describe the Input and Output

Input

Symbolic equation for range

$v_0 = 100$ m/s

$g = 9.8$ m/s^2

Output

Plot of range versus angle

3.   Hand Example

$$\text{range} = v_0 \left(\frac{v_0 \sin(\theta) \times 2}{g} \right) \cos(\theta)$$

We know from trigonometry that $\sin\theta \cos\theta$ equals $\sin(2\theta)/2$. We can thus simplify the result to

$$\text{range} = \frac{v_0^2}{g} \sin(2\theta)$$

Using this equation, we can easily calculate a few data points:

angle	range, m
0	0
pi/6	884
pi/4	1020
pi/3	884
pi/2	0

The range appears to increase with increasing angle, and then decrease back to zero when the cannon is pointed straight up.

4   Develop a MATLAB Solution

Recall from Example 7.2 that

```
impact_distance =
2*v0^2*sin(theta)/g*cos(theta)
```

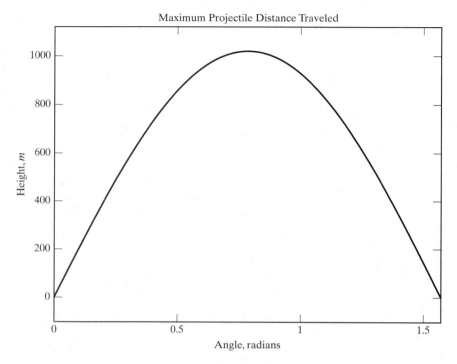

Figure 7.5. `Ezplot` of projectile range.

Use the **subs** function to substitute the numerical values of launch velocity **&** acceleration due to gravity into the equation

```
impact_100 = subs(impact_distance,{v0,g},{100, 9.8})
```

which returns

```
impact_100 =
100000/49*sin(theta)*cos(theta)
```

Finally, plot the results and add a title and labels:

```
ezplot(impact_100,[0, pi/2])
title('Maximum Projectile Distance Traveled')
xlabel('angle, radians')
ylabel('height, m')
```

which generates the plot in Figure 7.5.

5.   Test the Solution

The MATLAB solution agrees with the hand solution.   ∎

7.3   DIFFERENTIATION AND INTEGRATION

The operations of **differentiation** and **integration** are used extensively in solving engineering problems. In this section, we discuss the differentiation and integration of symbolic expressions.

7.3.1   Differentiation

The **diff** function is used to determine the symbolic derivative of a symbolic expression. There are four forms in which the **diff** function can be used to perform symbolic differentiation:

diff(f)	Returns the derivative of the expression **f** with respect to the default independent variable.
diff(f, 't')	Returns the derivative of the expression **f** with respect to the variable **t**.
diff(f,n)	Returns the **n**th derivative of the expression **f** with respect to the default independent variable.
diff(f,'t', n)	Returns the **n**th derivative of the expression **f** with respect to the variable **t**.

We now present several examples using the **diff** function for symbolic differentiation. First, we define the following symbolic expressions:

```
S1 = sym('6*x^3-4*x^2+b*x-5');
S2 = sym('sin(a)');
S3 = sym('(1-t^3)/(1+t^4)');
```

The following table shows function references and their corresponding values:

Reference	Function Value
diff(S1)	18*x^2 - 8*x+b
diff(S1,2)	36*x-8
diff(S1,'b')	x
diff(S2)	cos(a)
diff(S3)	-3*t^2/(1+t^4)-4*(1-t^3)/(1+t^4)^2*t^3
simplify(diff(S3))	t^2*(-3+t^4-4*t)/(1+t^4)^2

7.3.2   Integration

The **int** function is used to integrate a symbolic expression **f**. This function attempts to find the symbolic expression **F** such that **diff(F) = f**. It is possible that the integral (or antiderivative) may not exist in closed form or that MATLAB cannot find the integral. In such cases, the function will return the unevaluated command. The **int** function can be used in the following forms:

int(f)	Returns the integral of the expression **f** with respect to the default independent variable.
int(f,'t')	Returns the integral of the expression **f** with respect to the variable **t**.
int(f,a,b)	Returns the integral of the expression **f** with respect to the default independent variable evaluated over the interval **[a,b]**, where **a** and **b** are numeric expressions.
int(f,'t',a,b)	Returns the integral of the expression **f** with respect to the variable **t** evaluated over the interval **[a,b]**, where **a** and **b** are numeric expressions.
int(f,'m','n')	Returns the integral of the expression **f** with respect to the default independent variable evaluated over the interval **[m,n]**, where **m** and **n** are symbolic expressions.

We now present several examples that use the **int** function for symbolic integration. First, we define the following symbolic expressions:

```
S1 = sym('6*x^3-4*x^2+b*x-5');
S2 = sym('sin(a)');
S3 = sym('sqrt(x)');
```

The following table shows function references and their corresponding values:

Reference	Function Value
int(S1)	3/2*x^4-4/3*x^3+1/2*b*x^2-5*x
int(S2)	-cos(a)
int(S3)	2/3*x^(3/2)
int(S3,'a','b')	2/3*b^(3/2)-2/3*x^(3/2)
int(S3, 0.5, 0.6)	2/25*15^(1/2)-1/6*2^(1/2)
double(int(S3, 0.5, 0.6))	0.0741

EXAMPLE 7.4

USING SYMBOLIC MATH TO SOLVE A BALLISTICS PROBLEM

The symbolic plotting capability of MATLAB can be used to create a graph of range versus distance, based on the range formula

$$\text{range} = v_0 \left(\frac{v_0 {}^* \sin(\theta) \times 2}{g} \right) \cos(\theta)$$

where

v_0 is the velocity at launch, which we choose to be 100 m/s
θ is the launch angle
g is the acceleration due to gravity, which we choose to be 9.8 m/s²

Use MATLAB's symbolic capability to find the angle where the maximum range occurs, and to find the maximum range. (See Figure 7.6.)

SOLUTION

1. State the Problem

Find the angle where the maximum range occurs.
Find the maximum range.

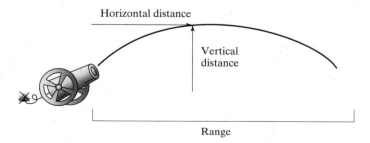

Horizontal distance

Vertical distance

Range

Figure 7.6. The range of a projectile depends on the initial velocity and the launch angle.

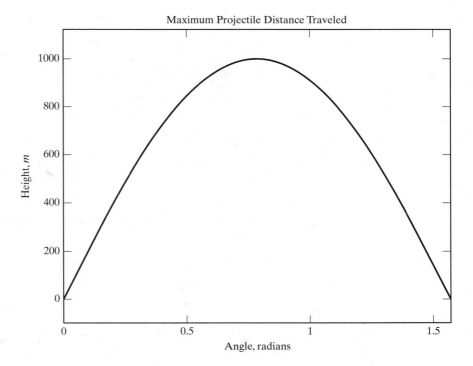

Figure 7.7. `Ezplot` of projectile range.

2.   Describe the Input and Output

Input

   Symbolic equation for range

   $v_0 = 100$ m/s

   $g = 9.8$ m/s^2

Output

   The angle where the max occurs

   The max range

3.   Hand Example

From the graph shown in Figure 7.7, the maximum range appears to occur at a launch angle of approximately 0.7 or 0.8 radian, and the maximum height appears to be approximately 1000 m.

4.   Develop a MATLAB Solution

Recall that the symbolic expression for the impact distance with v_0 and g defined as 100 m/s and 9.8 m/s^2, respectively, is

```
impact_100 =
100000/49*sin(theta)*cos(theta)
```

From the graph, we can see that the maximum distance occurs when the slope is equal to zero. The slope is the derivative of **impact_100**, so we need to set the derivative equal to zero and solve. Since MATLAB automatically assumes that an expression is equal to zero,

```
max_angle=solve(diff(impact_100))
```

returns the angle where the maximum height occurs:

```
max_angle =
[ -1/4*pi]
[  1/4*pi]
```

There are two results, but we are only interested in the second one, which can be substituted into the expression for the range:

```
max_distance = subs(impact_100,theta,max_angle(2))
max_distance =
50000/49
```

MATLAB returns to change the fraction because of the way the Maple engine performs calculations. To change the result to a decimal representation, we need to use the **double** function:

```
double(max_distance)
ans =
 1.0204e+003
```

5. Test the Solution

The hand solution suggested an angle of 0.7 to 0.8 radians. The calculated value of pi/4 is equal to 0.785 radians. The estimated maximum height was approximately 1000 meters, compared to the calculated 1024 meters. Try the problem again with different values of g (the acceleration due to gravity) and initial launch velocity. ∎

SUMMARY

In this chapter, we presented MATLAB's functions for performing symbolic mathematics. Examples were given to illustrate the simplification of expressions, the evaluation of operations with symbolic expressions, and the derivation of symbolic solutions to equations. In addition, we presented the MATLAB functions for determining the symbolic derivatives and integrals of expressions.

MATLAB SUMMARY

This MATLAB summary lists and briefly describes all of the special characters, commands, and functions that were defined in this chapter.

Special Character

'	used to enclose a symbolic expression

Commands and Functions

collect	collects coefficients of a symbolic expression
ciff	differentiates a symbolic expression
double	changes a symbolic variable into a double-precision, floating-point variable
expand	expands a symbolic expression
ezplot	generates a plot of a symbolic expression
factor	factors a symbolic expression
findsym	finds symbolic variables in a symbolic expression
int	integrates a symbolic expression

`numden`	returns the numerator and denominator expressions
`poly2sym`	converts a vector to a symbolic polynomial
`pretty`	prints a symbolic expression in typeset form
`simple`	shortens a symbolic expression
`simplify`	simplifies a symbolic expression
`solve`	solves an equation
`subs`	replaces variables in a symbolic expression
`sym2poly`	converts a symbolic expression to a coefficient vector

KEY TERMS

collecting coefficients	factoring expressions	symbolic expression
differentiation	integration	
expanding terms	symbolic algebra	

Problems

1. Create symbolic objects **S1** and **S2** for the following expression:

$$S1 = (x - 1)^2 + 2x - 1$$
$$S2 = x$$

2. Execute the **simple** function using **S1** as an argument. Which of the nine simplification methods succeeds in finding the simplest expression for **S1**?

3. What is the result of the symbolic division **S2/S1**? What is the result of `factor(S2/S1)`?

4. Solve the equation $$\frac{x - 1}{x^2 + 4} = 2.$$

5. Define a symbolic variable for each of the equations, and use MATLAB's symbolic capability to solve for each unknown.

$$x_1 - x_2 - x_3 - x_4 = 5$$
$$x_1 + 2x_2 + 3x_3 + x_4 = -2$$
$$2x_1 + 2x_3 + 3x_4 = 3$$
$$3x_1 + x_2 + 2x_4 = 1$$

6. Compare the amount of time it takes to solve Problem 5 with left division and with symbolic math, using the **tic** and **toc** functions:

```
tic
...
code to be timed
...
toc
```

7. Determine the first and second derivatives of the following functions, using MATLAB's symbolic functions:

a. $g(x) = x^3 - 5x^2 + 2x + 8$

b. $g_2(x) = (x^2 + 4x + 4) * (x - 1)$

c. $g_3(x) = (x^2 - 2x + 2)/(10x - 24)$

d. $g_4(x) = (x^5 - 4x^4 - 9x^3 + 32)^2$

8. Use MATLAB's symbolic functions to determine the values of the following integrals:

a. $\int_{0.5}^{0.6} |x| \, dx$

b. $\int_{0}^{1} |x| \, dx$

c. $\int_{-1}^{-0.5} |x| \, dx$

d. $\int_{-0.5}^{0.5} |x| \, dx$

Weather Balloons   Assume that the following polynomial represents the altitude in meters during the first 48 hours following the launch of a weather balloon:

$$h(t) = -0.12t^4 + 12t^3 - 380t^2 + 4100t + 220$$

Assume that the units of t are hours.

9. Use MATLAB to determine the equation for the velocity of the weather balloon, using the fact that the velocity is the derivative of the altitude.

10. Use MATLAB to determine the equation for the acceleration of the weather balloon, using the fact that acceleration is the derivative of the velocity, or the second derivative of the altitude.

11. Use MATLAB to determine when the balloon hits the ground. Because $h(t)$ is a fourth-order polynomial, there will be four answers. However, only one answer will be physically meaningful.

12. Use MATLAB's symbolic plotting capability to create plots of altitude, velocity, and acceleration from time zero until the balloon hits the ground. You'll need three separate plots, since altitude, velocity, and acceleration all have different units.

13. Determine the maximum height reached by the balloon. Use the fact that the velocity of the balloon is zero at the maximum height.

Water Flow   Assume that water is pumped into an initially empty tank. It is known that the rate of flow of water into the tank at time t (in seconds) is $50 - t$ liters per second. The amount of water Q that flows into the tank during the first x seconds can be shown to be equal to the integral of the expression $(50 - t)$ evaluated from 0 to x seconds.

14. Determine a symbolic equation that represents the amount of water in the tank after x seconds.

15. Determine the amount of water in the tank after 30 seconds.

16. Determine the amount of water that flowed into the tank between 10 seconds and 15 seconds after the flow was initiated.

Elastic Spring   Consider a spring with the left end held fixed and the right end free to move along the x-axis. We assume that the right end of the spring is at the origin $x = 0$, when the spring is at rest. When the spring is stretched, the right end of the spring is at some new value of x that is greater than zero. When the spring is compressed, the right end of the spring is at some value that is less than zero. Assume that a spring has a natural length of 1 ft and that a force of 10 lb_f is required to compress the spring to a length of 0.5 ft. It can then be shown that the work, in ft/lb_f done to stretch the spring from its natural length to a total of n ft, is equal to the integral of $20x$ over the interval from 0 to $n - 1$.

17. Use MATLAB to determine a symbolic expression that represents the amount of work necessary to stretch the spring to a total length of n ft.

18. What is the amount of work done to stretch the spring to a total of 2 ft?

19. If the amount of work exerted is 25 ft/lb_f, what is the length of the stretched spring?

8

Numerical Techniques

GRAND CHALLENGE

The design and construction of the Alaska pipeline presented numerous engineering challenges. One of the most important problems that had to be addressed was how to protect the permafrost (the perennially frozen subsoil in arctic or subarctic regions) from the heat of the pipeline itself. The oil flowing in the pipeline is warmed by pumping stations and by friction from the walls of the pipe such that the supports holding the pipeline have to be insulated or even cooled to keep them from melting the permafrost at their bases. Many such physical processes are difficult to predict theoretically, but equations representing their behavior can be modeled using numerical techniques such as the ones presented in this chapter. (See Figure 8.1.)

8.1 INTERPOLATION

Interpolation is a technique by which we estimate a variable's value between two known values. There are a number of different techniques for this, but in this section we present the two most common types of interpolation: linear interpolation and cubic-spline interpolation. In both techniques, we assume that we have a set of data points which represents a set of xy-coordinates for which y is a function of x; that is, $y = f(x)$. We then have a value of x that is not part of the data set for which we want to find the y value. (See Figure 8.2.)

8.1.1 Linear Interpolation

Linear Interpolation is one of the most common techniques for estimating data values between two given data points. With this technique, we assume that the function between the points can be estimated by a straight line drawn

SECTIONS

OBJECTIVES

After reading this chapter, you should be able to

- perform linear and cubic-spline interpolations
- calculate the best-fit straight line and polynomial to a set of data points
- use the basic fitting tool
- use the curve fitting toolbox
- perform numerical integrations
- perform numerical differentiations

Figure 8.1. A portion of the Alaska pipeline.

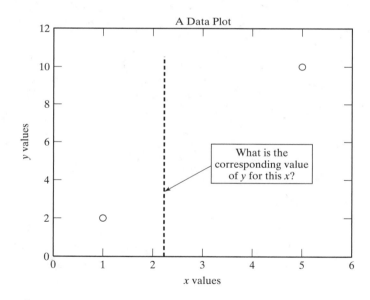

Figure 8.2. Interpolation between data points.

between the points. (See Figure 8.3.) If we find the equation of a straight line defined by the two known points, we can find y for any value of x. The closer together the points are, the more accurate our approximation is likely to be. Of course, we could use this equation to extrapolate points past our collected data. This is rarely wise, however, and often leads to large errors.

8.1.2   Cubic-Spline Interpolation

A cubic spline is a smooth curve constructed to go through a set of points. The curve between each pair of points is a third-degree polynomial (which has the general form $a_0x^3 + a_1x^2 + a_2x + a_3$) which is computed so that it provides a smooth curve between

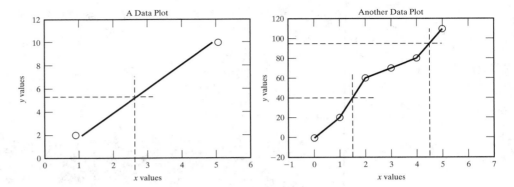

Figure 8.3. Linear interpolation—connect the points with a straight line to find y.

the two points and a smooth transition from the third-degree polynomial between the previous pair of points. (See Figure 8.4.)

8.1.3 interp1 Function

Hint: The last character in the function name **interp1** is a one. Depending on the font, it may look like the letter 'l'.

The MATLAB function that performs interpolation, **interp1**, has two forms. Each form assumes that vectors **x** and **y** contain the original data values and that another vector **x_new** contains the new point or points for which we want to compute interpolated **y_new** values. (The **x** values should be in ascending order, and the **x_new**

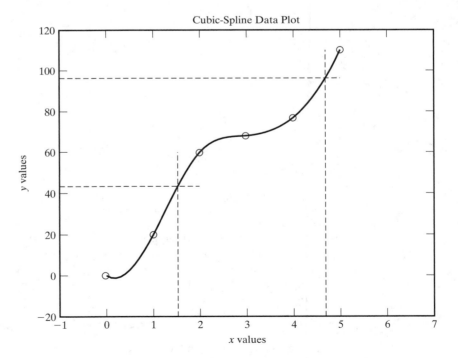

Figure 8.4. Cubic-spline interpolation—a total of five different cubic equations were used to generate this smooth function that joins all six points.

values should be within the range of the **x** values.) These forms are demonstrated in the following examples.

The points in Figures 8.3 and 8.4 were generated with the following commands:

```
x=0:5;
y=[0,20,60,68,77,110];
```

Suppose we would like to find a value for **y**, if $x = 1.5$. Unfortunately, 1.5 is not one of the elements in the **x** vector, so we'll need to perform an interpolation:

```
interp1(x,y,1.5)
```

returns

```
ans =
      40
```

We can see from Figure 8.3 that this answer corresponds to a linear interpolation between the **x, y** points at (1,20) and (2,60). The function **interp1** defaults to linear interpolation unless otherwise specified.

If, instead of a scalar value of new **x** values, we define an array of new **x** values, the function returns an array of new **y** values:

```
new_x = 0:0.2:5
new_y = interp1(x,y,new_x)
```

The new calculated points are plotted in Figure 8.5. They all fall on a straight line connecting the original data points. The commands to generate the graph are

```
plot(x,y,new_x,new_y,'o')
axis([-1,7,-20,120])
```

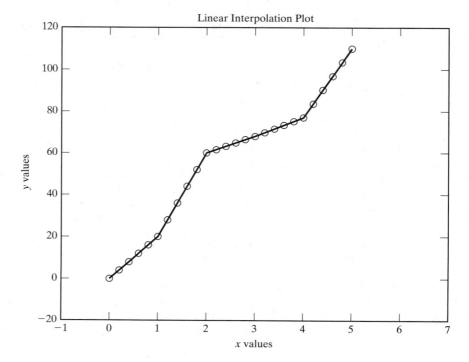

Figure 8.5.   Interpolated data points.

```
title('Linear Interpolation Plot')
xlabel('x values')
ylabel('y values')
```

If we wish to use a cubic spline interpolation approach, we must add a fourth argument to the **interp1** function. The argument must be a string. The choices are

'nearest'	nearest neighbor interpolation
'linear'	inear interpolation – which is the default
'spline'	piecewise cubic spline interpolation (SPLINE)
'pchip'	shape-preserving piecewise cubic interpolation
'cubic'	same as **'pchip'**
'v5cubic'	the cubic interpolation from MATLAB 5, which does not extrapolate and uses **'spline'** if X is not equally spaced.

To find the value of **y** at **x** = 1.5 using a cubic spline, type

```
interp1(x,y,1.5,'spline')
```

which returns

```
ans =
       42.2083
```

Referring to Figure 8.4, we see that this corresponds to our graph of a cubic spline. To generate a vector of new **y** values, we use the same procedure as before:

```
new_y = interp1(x,y,new_x, 'spline')
```

The results are plotted in Figure 8.6. The original points are connected with a straight line. The curved plot is constructed from the calculated points. (Remember, all MATLAB plots are constructed of straight line segments, but these are close enough together to approximate a curve.)

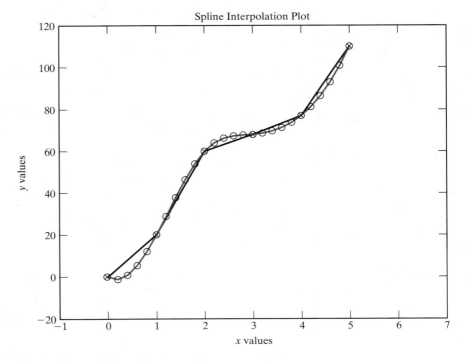

Figure 8.6. Cubic-spline interpolation.

The commands needed to generate Figure 8.6 are

```
plot(x,y,'-x',new_x,new_y,'-o')
axis([-1,7,-20,120])
title('Spline Interpolation Plot')
xlabel('x values')
ylabel('y values')
```

MATLAB provides two-dimensional (**interp2**) and three-dimensional (**interp3**) interpolation functions, which are not discussed here. Refer to the help feature for more information.

EXAMPLE 8.1

THERMODYNAMIC PROPERTIES— USING THE STEAM TABLES

The subject of thermodynamics makes extensive use of tables. Although many properties can be described by fairly simple equations, others either are poorly understood, or the equations describing their behavior are very complicated. It is much easier just to tabulate the data. For example, consider the data for steam at 0.1 MPa (approximately 1 atm), given in Table 8.1. These data could be used to analyze the geysers shown in Figure 8.7.

TABLE 8.1   Internal Energy as a Function of Temperature

Temperature, C	u, Internal Energy, kJ/kg
100	2506.7
150	2582.8
200	2658.1
250	2733.7
300	2810.4
400	2967.9
500	3131.6

Data from Steam Tables, SI units, by Joseph H. Keenan, Fredrick G. Keyes, Philip G Hill, and Joan G. Moore, New York, John Wiley and Sons, 1978.

Figure 8.7.   Geysers spray high temperature and high-pressure water and steam.

Use linear interpolation to determine the internal energy at 215° C.

Use linear interpolation to determine the temperature if the internal energy is 2600 kJ/kg.

SOLUTION

1. State the Problem

Using linear interpolation, find the internal energy of steam.

Using linear interpolation, find the temperature of the steam.

2. Describe the Input and Output

Input

Table of temperature and internal energy

U unknown

T unknown

Output

Internal energy

Temperature

3. Hand Example

In the first part of the problem, we need to find the internal energy at 215° C. The table includes values at 200° C and 250° C. First, we need to find what fraction of the way between 200 and 250 the value 215 falls:

$$\frac{215 - 200}{250 - 200} = 0.30$$

If we model the relationship between temperature and internal energy as linear, the internal energy should also be 30 percent of the distance between the tabulated values:

$$0.30 = \frac{U - 2658.1}{2733.7 - 2658.1}$$

Solving for *U* gives

$$U = 2680.78 \text{ kJ/kg}$$

4. Develop a MATLAB Solution

Create the MATLAB solution in an **m-file**, and then run it in the **command** environment:

```
%Example 8.1
%Thermodynamics
T=[100, 150, 200, 250, 300, 400, 500];
u = [2506.7, 2582.8, 2658.1, 2733.7, 2810.4, 2967.9, 3131.6];
newu=interp1(T,u,215)
newT=interp1(u,T,2600)
```

returns

```
newu =
      2680.78

newT =
      161.42
```

5.   Test the Solution

The MATLAB result matches the hand result. This approach could be used for any of the properties tabulated in the Steam Tables. The JANAF tables are a similar source of thermodynamic properties published by the National Institute of Standards and Technology.   ■

EXAMPLE 8.2

THERMODYNAMIC PROPERTIES— EXPANDING THE STEAM TABLES

Electric power plants use steam as a "working fluid" (see Figure 8.8). The science of thermodynamics makes extensive use of tables when systems such as a power plant are analyzed. Depending on the system of interest you may only need a portion of the table, such as Table 8.2.

Figure 8.8. Power plants use steam as a "working fluid".

TABLE 8.2 Properties of Superheated Steam

Properties of Superheated Steam at 0.1 MPa (approximately 1 atm)			
Temperatare, C	v, Specific Volume, m³/kg	u, Internal Energy, kJ/kg	h, Enthalpy kJ/kg
100	1.6958	2506.7	2676.2
150	1.9364	2582.8	2776.4
200	2.172	2658.1	2875.3
250	2.406	2733.7	2974.3
300	2.639	2810.4	3074.3
400	3.103	2967.9	3278.2
500	3.565	3131.6	3488.1

Data from Steam Tables, SI units, by Joseph H. Keenan, Fredrick G. Keyes, Philip G. Hill, and Joan G. Moore, New York, John Wiley and Sons, 1978.

Notice that this table is spaced at 50-degree intervals at first, and then at 100-degree intervals. Assume that you have a project that requires you to use this table, and you would prefer not to have to perform a linear interpolation every time you use it. Use MATLAB to create a table, applying linear interpolation, with a temperature spacing of 25 degrees.

SOLUTION

1. State the Problem

Find the specific volume, internal energy, and enthalpy every five degrees.

2. Describe the Input and Output

Input

Table of temperature and internal energy
New table interval of 5 degrees

Output

Table

3. Hand Example

We'll perform the calculations at 225°C:

$$\frac{225 - 200}{250 - 200} = 0.50 \quad \text{and} \quad 0.50 = \frac{U - 2658.1}{2733.7 - 2658.1}$$

solving for U gives

$$u = 2695.9 \text{ kJ/kg}$$

We can use this same calculation to confirm the calculations in the table we create.

4. Develop a MATLAB Solution

Create the MATLAB solution in an **m-file**, and then run it in the **command** environment:

```
%Example 8.2
%Thermodynamics
clear, clc
T = [100, 150, 200, 250, 300, 400, 500]';
u = [2506.7, 2582.8, 2658.1, 2733.7, 2810.4, 2967.9, 3131.6]';
h = [2676.2, 2776.4, 2875.3, 2974.3, 3074.3, 3278.2, 3488.1]';
v = [1.6958, 1.9364, 2.172, 2.406, 2.639, 3.103, 3.565]';
props=[v,u,h];
newT=[100:25:500]';
newprop=interp1(T,props,newT);
disp('Steam Properties at 0.1 MPa')
disp('Temp    Specific Volume  Internal Energy  Enthalpy')
disp(' C        m^3/kg           kJ/kg            kJ/kg')
fprintf('%6.0f  %10.4f     %8.1f       %8.1f \n',[newT,
   newprop]')
```

prints the table

```
Steam Properties at 0.1 MPa
Temp      Specific Volume  Internal Energy  Enthalpy
C         m^3/kg     kJ/kg      kJ/kg
   100    1.6958     2506.7     2676.2
   125    1.8161     2544.8     2726.3
   150    1.9364     2582.8     2776.4
   175    2.0542     2620.4     2825.9
   200    2.1720     2658.1     2875.3
   225    2.2890     2695.9     2924.8
   250    2.4060     2733.7     2974.3
   275    2.5225     2772.1     3024.3
   300    2.6390     2810.4     3074.3
   325    2.7550     2849.8     3125.3
   350    2.8710     2889.2     3176.3
   375    2.9870     2928.5     3227.2
   400    3.1030     2967.9     3278.2
   425    3.2185     3008.8     3330.7
   450    3.3340     3049.8     3383.1
   475    3.4495     3090.7     3435.6
   500    3.5650     3131.6     3488.1
```

5.   Test the Solution

The MATLAB result matches the hand result. Now that we know the program works, we can create more extensive tables by changing the definition of **newt** from

```
newT=[100:25:500]';
```

to a vector with a smaller temperature increment, such as

```
newT=[100:1:500]';
```

8.2   CURVE FITTING: LINEAR AND POLYNOMIAL REGRESSION

Assume that we have a set of data points collected from an experiment. After plotting the data points, we find that they generally fall in a straight line. However, if we were to try to draw a straight line through the points, only a couple of the points would probably fall exactly on the line. A least-squares curve fitting method could be used to find the straight line that is the closest to the points, by minimizing the distance from each point to the straight line. Although this line can be considered a "best fit" to the data points, it is possible that none of the points would actually fall on the line of best fit. (Note that this method is very different from interpolation, because the curves used in linear interpolation and cubic-spline interpolation actually contained all of the original data points.) In this section, we first discuss fitting a straight line to a set of data points, and then we discuss fitting a polynomial to a set of data points.

8.2.1   Linear Regression

Linear regression is the name given to the process that determines the linear equation which is the best fit to a set of data points, in terms of minimizing the sum of the squared distances between the line and the data points. To understand this process, we first consider the following set of data values:

```
x = 0.5;

y = [0, 20, 60, 68, 77, 110];
```

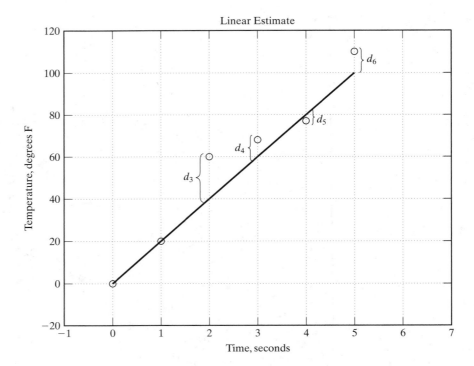

Figure 8.9. A linear estimate.

If we plot these points, it appears that a good estimate of a line through the points is $y = 20x$, as shown in Figure 8.9. This process is sometimes called "eyeballing it"—meaning that no calculations were done, but it looks like a good fit.

The following commands were issued to generate the plot:

```
y2=20*x;
plot(x,y,'o',x,y2)
axis([-1,7,-20,120])
title('Linear Estimate')
xlabel('Time,seconds')
ylabel('Temperature, degrees F')
grid
```

Looking at the plot, we can see that the first two points appear to fall exactly on the line, but the other points are off by varying amounts. To compare the quality of the fit of this line to other possible estimates, we find the difference between the actual y value and the value calculated from the estimate (in this case, $y = 20x$). (These values are listed in Table 8.3.)

TABLE 8.3 Difference Between Actual and Calculated Values

x	y (actual)	Y2 (calculated)	difference = y−y2
0	0	0	0
1	20	20	0
2	60	40	20
3	68	60	8
4	77	80	−3
5	110	100	10

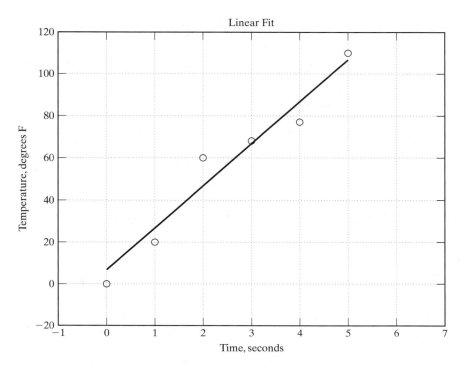

Figure 8.10.   Data and best-fit line.

If we sum the differences, some of the positive and negative values would cancel each other out and give a sum that is smaller than it should be. To avoid this problem, we could add the absolute value of the differences, or we could square them. The least squared technique uses the squared values. Therefore, the measure of the quality of the fit of this linear estimate is the sum of the squared distances between the points and the linear estimates. This sum can be computed with the following command:

```
sum_sq = sum((y-y2)^2)
```

For this set of data, the value of **sum_sq** is 573.

If we drew another line through the points, we could compute the sum of squares that corresponds to the new line. Of the two lines, the better fit is provided by the line with the smaller sum of squared distances. MATLAB uses techniques from calculus to minimize the sum of squared distances and arrive at the best-fit line. The MATLAB commands for doing this are described in Section 8.2.3. Figure 8.10 shows the best fit results of a linear regression analysis for our data. The corresponding sum of squares is 356.8190.

We call it linear regression when we derive the equation of a straight line, but more generally it is called **polynomial regression**. The linear equation used to model the data is a first-order polynomial.

8.2.2   Polynomial Regression

Linear regression is a special case of the polynomial regression technique. Recall that a polynomial with one variable can be written by using the following formula:

$$f(x) = a_0x^n + a_1x^{n-1} + a_2x^{n-2} + \cdots + a_{n-1}x + a_n$$

The degree of a polynomial is equal to the largest value used as an exponent. Therefore, the general form of a cubic (or third order) polynomial is

$$g(x) = a_0x^3 + a_1x^2 + a_2 + a_3$$

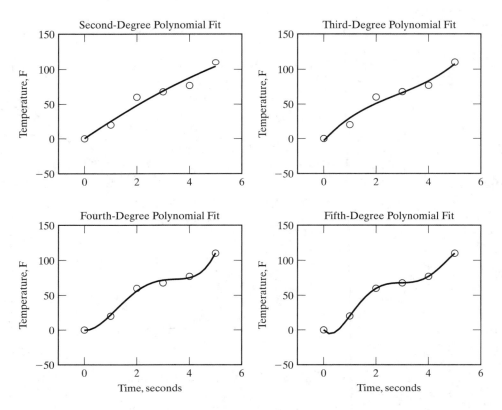

Figure 8.11. Polynomial fits.

Note that a linear equation is also a polynomial of degree one.

In Figure 8.11, we plot the original set of data points that we used in the linear regression example, along with plots of the best-fit polynomials with degrees two through five. Note that, as the degree of the polynomial increases, the number of points that fall on the curve also increases. If a set of $n + 1$ points is used to determine an nth degree polynomial, all n points will fall on the polynomial.

8.2.3 **polyfit** and **polyval** Functions

The MATLAB function for computing the best fit to a set of data with a polynomial is **polyfit**. This function has three arguments: the x coordinate of the data points, the y coordinate of the data points, and the degree n of the polynomial. The function returns the coefficients, in descending powers of x, of the nth degree polynomial used to model the data. For example, using the data

```
x=0:5;
y=[0,20,60,68,77,110]
```

the function

```
polyfit(x,y,1)
```

returns

```
ans =
     20.8286    3.7619
```

So the first-order polynomial that best fits our data is

$$f(x) = 20.8286x + 3.7619$$

Similarly, we can find other polynomials to fit the data by specifying a higher order in the **polyfit** equation. Thus,

```
polyfit(x,y,4)
```

returns

```
ans =
1.5625   -14.5231   38.6736   -3.4511   -0.3770
```

which corresponds to a fourth-order polynomial:

$$f(x) = 1.5625x^4 - 14.5231x^3 + 38.6736x^2 - 3.4511x - 0.3770$$

We could use these coefficients to create equations to calculate new values of y, for example,

```
y_first_order_fit = 20.8286* x + 3.7619;
```

and

```
y_fourth_order_fit = 1.5625*x.^4 -14.5231*x.^3 …
              + 38.6736*x.^2  -3.4511*x  -0.3770;
```

or we could use the function **polyval** provided by MATLAB to accomplish the same thing.

The **polyval** function is used to evaluate a polynomial at a set of data points. The first argument of the **polyval** function is a vector containing the coefficients of the polynomial (in an order corresponding to decreasing powers of **x**), and the second argument is the vector of **x** values for which we want to calculate corresponding **y** values.

Fortunately, the **polyfit** function can provide us the first input:

```
coef = polyfit(x,y,1)
y_first_order_fit = polyfit(coef,x)
```

These two lines of code could be shortened to one line by nesting functions:

```
y_first_order_fit = polyval(polyfit(x,y,1),x)
```

We can use our new understanding of the **polyfit** and **polyval** functions to write a program to create the plots in Figure 8.11:

```
y2=polyval(polyfit(x,y,2),new_x);
y3=polyval(polyfit(x,y,3),new_x);
y4=polyval(polyfit(x,y,4),new_x);
y5=polyval(polyfit(x,y,5),new_x);

subplot(2,2,1)
plot(x,y,'o',new_x,y2)

subplot(2,2,2)
plot(x,y,'o',new_x,y3)

subplot(2,2,3)
plot(x,y,'o',new_x,y4)

subplot(2,2,4)
plot(x,y,'o',new_x,y5)
```

The two new functions discussed in this section are summarized as follows:

polyfit(x,y,n)   Returns a vector of $n + 1$ coefficients that represents the best-fit polynomial of degree n for the x and y coordinates provided. The coefficient order corresponds to decreasing powers of x.

polyval(coef,x)   Returns a vector of polynomial values f(x) that correspond to the **x** vector values. The order of the coefficients corresponds to decreasing powers of x.

EXAMPLE 8.3

WATER IN A CULVERT

Determining how much water will flow through a culvert is not as easy as it might first seem (see Figure 8.12). The channel could have a nonuniform shape, obstructions might influence the flow, friction is important, etc. A numerical approach allows us to fold all of those concerns into a model of how the water actually behaves.

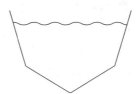

Figure 8.12.   Culverts do not necessarily have a uniform cross section.

Consider these data collected from an actual culvert:

Height, ft	Flow, ft³/s
0	0
1.7	2.6
1.95	3.6
2.60	4.03
2.92	6.45
4.04	11.22
5.24	30.61

Compute a best-fit linear, quadratic, and cubic fit for the data, and plot them on the same graph. Which model best represents the data? (Linear is first order, quadratic is second order, and cubic is third order.)

SOLUTION

1.   State the Problem

Perform a polynomial regression on the data, plot the results, and determine which order best represents the data.

2.   Describe the Input and Output

Input

Height and flow data

Output

Plot of the results

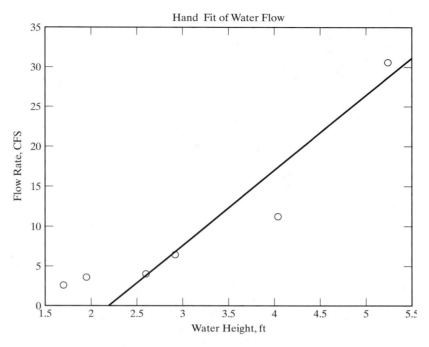

Figure 8.13. Hand fit of water flow.

3. Hand Example

Draw in an approximation of the curve by hand. Be sure to start at zero, because if the height of the water in the culvert is zero, no water should be flowing. (See Figure 8.13.)

4. Develop a MATLAB Solution

Create the MATLAB solution in an **m-file**, and then run it in the **command** environment:

```
%Example - Water in a Culvert

height = [1.7, 1.95, 2.6, 2.92, 4.04, 5.24];
flow = [2.6, 3.6, 4.03, 6.45, 11.22, 30.61];
new_height=0:0.5:6;
newflow1=polyval(polyfit(height,flow,1),new_height);
newflow2=polyval(polyfit(height,flow,2),new_height);
newflow3=polyval(polyfit(height,flow,3),new_height);
plot(height,flow,'o',new_height,newflow1,...
        new_height,newflow2,new_height,newflow3)
title('Fit of Water Flow')
xlabel('Water Height, ft')
ylabel('Flow Rate, CFS')
legend('Data','Linear Fit','Quadratic Fit', 'Cubic Fit')
```

generates the plot shown in Figure 8.14.

5. Test the Solution

The question of what line best represents the data is difficult to answer. The higher order polynomial approximation will follow the data points better, but it doesn't necessarily represent reality better.

The linear fit predicts that the water flow rate will be approximately −5 CFS at a height of zero, which doesn't match reality. The quadratic fit goes back up after a minimum

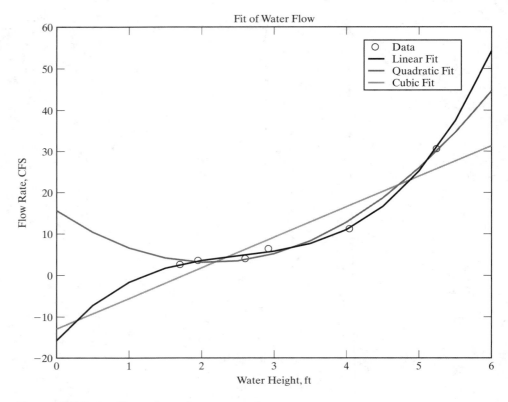

Figure 8.14. Different curve-fitting approaches.

at a height of approximately 1.5 meters—again, a result inconsistent with reality. The cubic (third-order) fit follows the points the best, and is probably the best polynomial fit.

We should also compare the result from the MATLAB solution to the hand solution. The third-order polynomial fit (cubic) approximately matches the hand solution. ∎

8.3   USING THE INTERACTIVE FITTING TOOLS

MATLAB 7 includes new interactive plotting tools that allow you to annotate your plots without using the command window. The software also includes basic curve fitting, more complicated curve fitting, and statistics tools.

8.3.1   Basic Fitting Tools

To access the basic fitting tools, first create a figure:

```
x=0:5;
y=[0,20,60,68,77,110]
plot(x,y,'o')
axis([-1,7,-20,120])
```

These commands create a graph (Figure 8.15) with the same data used in previous sections.

To activate the curve fitting tools, select **Tools-> Basic Fitting** from the menu bar on the figure. The **Basic Fitting** window opens on top of the plot. By checking **linear** and **cubic** (see Figure 8.15) and **show equations**, the plot shown in Figure 8.16 is generated.

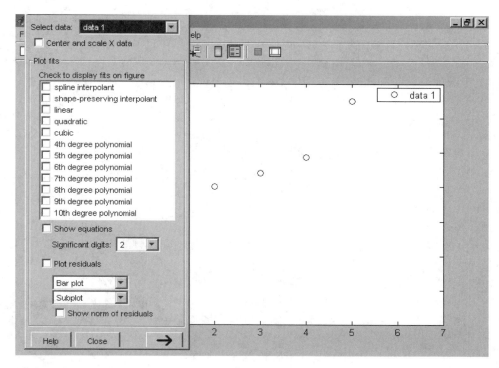

Figure 8.15. Interactive basic fitting window.

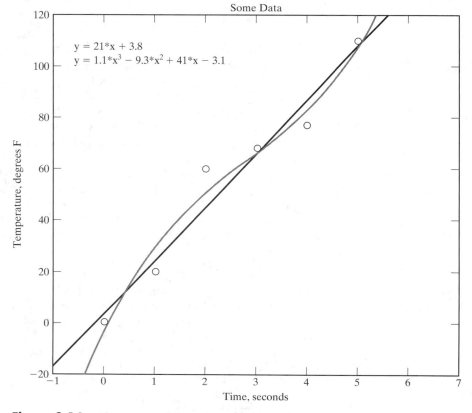

Figure 8.16. Plot generated using the **Basic Fitting** window.

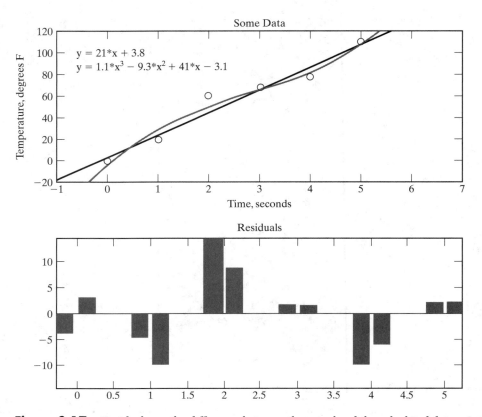

Figure 8.17. Residuals are the difference between the actual and the calculated data points.

Checking the **plot residuals** box generates a second plot, showing how far each data point is from the calculated line, as shown in Figure 8.17.

In the lower right-hand corner of the **Basic Fitting** window is an arrow button. Selecting that button twice opens the rest of the **Basic Fitting** window (Figure 8.18).

The center panel of the window shows the results of the curve fit and offers the option of saving those results into the workspace. The right-hand panel allows you to select x values and calculate y values based on the equation displayed in the center panel.

In addition to the **Basic Fitting** window, you can also access the **Data Statistics** window (Figure 8.19) from the figure menu bar. Select **Tools-> Data Statistics** from the figure window. This window allows you to calculate statistical functions interactively, such as mean and standard deviation, based on the data in the figure, and allows you to save the results to the workspace.

8.3.2   Curve Fitting Toolbox

In addition to the basic fitting utility, MATLAB contains toolboxes to help you perform more specialized statistical and data fitting operations. In particular, the **Curve Fitting toolbox** contains a GUI (graphical user interface) that allows you to fit curves with more tools than just polynomials.

Before you access the curve fitting toolbox, you'll need a set of data to analyze. We can use the following data:

```
x=0:5;
y=[0,20,60,68,77,110];
```

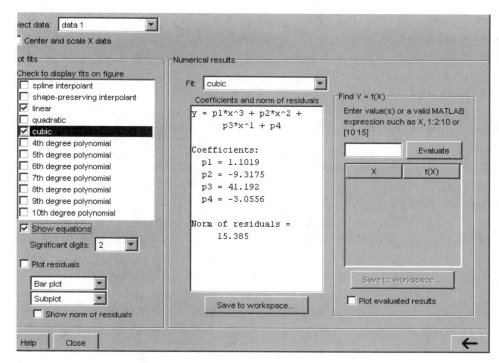

Figure 8.18. **Basic Fitting** window.

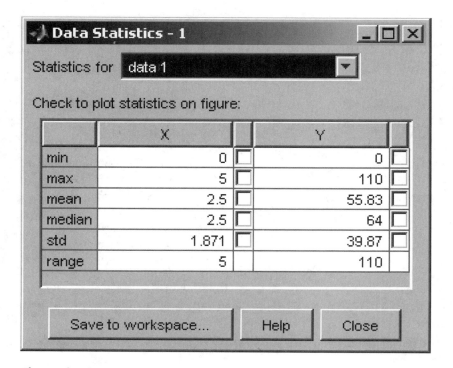

Figure 8.19. Data statistics window.

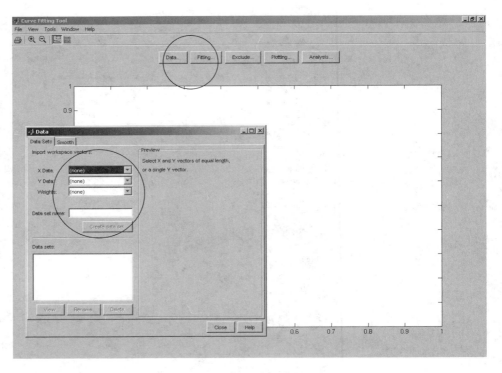

Figure 8.20. The **curve fitting** and **data** windows.

To open the curve fitting toolbox, type

```
cftool
```

This launches the curve fitting tool window. Now you'll need to tell the curve fitting tool what data to use. Select the **data** button, which will open a **data** window. The **data** window has access to the workspace and will let you select an independent (x) and dependent (y) variable from a drop-down list. (See Figure 8.20.)

In our example, from the drop-down lists, you should choose **x** and **y**, respectively. You can assign a data set name, or MATLAB will assign a name for you. Once you've chosen variables, MATLAB plots the data. At this point you can close the **data** window.

Going back to the **Curve Fitting Tool** window, you now select the **Fitting** button, which offers you choices of fitting algorithms. Select **New Fit**, and select a fit type from the **type of fit** list. You can experiment with fitting choices to find the best one for your graph. We chose an interpolated scheme, which forces the plot through all the points, and a third order polynomial. The results are shown in Figure 8.21.

EXAMPLE 8.4

POPULATION

The population of the earth is expanding rapidly, as is the population of the United States. (See Figure 8.22.) MATLAB includes a built-in data file, called **census**, that contains U.S. census data since 1790. The data file contains two variables, **cdate** which

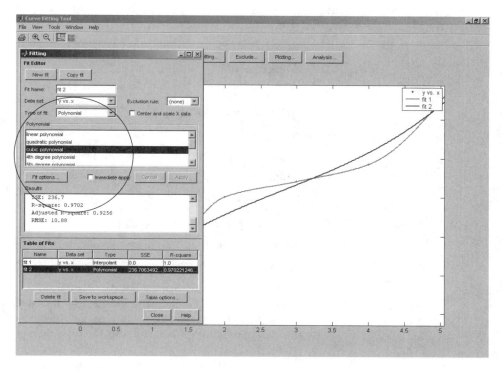

Figure 8.21. **Curve fitting** windows.

Figure 8.22. The earth's population is expanding.

contains the census dates, and **pop** which lists the population in millions. To load the file into your workspace, type

> `load census`

Use the **curve fitting** toolbox to find an equation that represents the data.

SOLUTION

1. State the Problem

Find an equation that represents the population growth in the United States

2. Describe the Input and Output

Input

Table of population data

Output

Equation representing the data

3. Hand Example

Plot the data by hand

4. Develop a MATLAB Solution

The **curve fitting** toolbox is an interactive utility, activated by typing

```
cftool
```

which opens the **curve fitting** window. Select the **data** button and choose **cdate** as the *x* value and **pop** as the *y* value. After closing the **data** window, select the **fitting** button.

Since we have always heard that population is growing exponentially, experiment with the exponential fit options. We also tried the polynomial option, and chose a third order (cubic) polynomial. Both approaches produced a good fit, but the polynomial was actually the best. We sent the **curve fitting** window graph to a figure window and added titles and labels (see Figure 8.23).

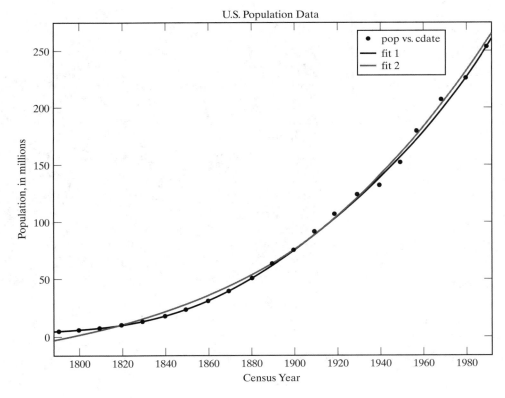

Figure 8.23. U.S. census data.

From the data in the **fitting** window we saw that the sum of the squares of the errors (SSE) was larger for the exponential fit, but that both approaches gave R values greater than 0.99. An R value of 1 indicates a perfect fit.

The results for the polynomial were

```
Linear model Poly3:
    f(x) = p1*x^3 + p2*x^2 + p3*x + p4
    where x is normalized by mean 1890 and std 62.05
Coefficients (with 95% confidence bounds):
    p1 =        0.921  (-0.9743, 2.816)
    p2 =        25.18  (23.57, 26.79)
    p3 =        73.86  (70.33, 77.39)
    p4 =        61.74  (59.69, 63.8)

Goodness of fit:
  SSE: 149.8
  R-square: 0.9988
  Adjusted R-square: 0.9986
  RMSE: 2.968
```

The x values used in the equation were normalized for a better fit by subtracting the mean and dividing by the standard deviation:

```
x = (cdate-mean(cdate))/std(cdate);
```

5. Test the Solution

Compare the fits by eye—they both appear to model the data adequately. It is important to remember that, just because a solution models the data well, it is rarely appropriate to extend the solution past the measured data. (See Figure 8.23.) ∎

8.4 NUMERICAL INTEGRATION

The integral of a function $f(x)$ over the interval $[a,b]$ is defined to be the area under the curve of $f(x)$ between a and b, as shown in Figure 8.24. If the value of this integral is K, the notation to represent the integral of $f(x)$ between a and b is

$$K = \int_a^b f(x)\, dx$$

For many functions, this integral can be computed analytically. However, for a number of functions, the integral cannot easily be computed analytically and thus requires a numerical technique to estimate its value. The numerical evaluation of an integral is also called quadrature, a term that comes from an ancient geometrical problem.

The numerical integration techniques estimate the function $f(x)$ by another function $g(x)$, where $g(x)$ is chosen so that we can easily compute the area under $g(x)$. Then, the better the estimate of $g(x)$ to $f(x)$, the better will be the estimate of the integral of $f(x)$. Two of the most common numerical integration techniques estimate $f(x)$ with a set of piecewise linear functions or with a set of piecewise parabolic functions. If we estimate the function with piecewise linear functions, we can then compute the area of the trapezoids that compose the area under the piecewise linear functions; this technique is called the **trapezoidal rule**. If we estimate the function with piecewise quadratic functions, we can then compute and add the areas of these components; this technique is called **Simpson's rule**.

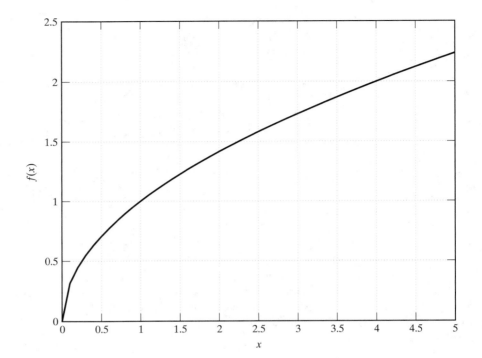

Figure 8.24. Square-root function.

8.4.1 Trapezoidal Rule and Simpson's Rule

If the area under a curve is represented by trapezoids and if the interval $[a,b]$ is divided into n equal sections, then the area can be approximated by the formula (trapezoidal rule)

$$K_T = \frac{b - a}{2n}(f(x_0) + 2f(x_1) + 2f(x_2) + \cdots + 2f(x_{n-1}) + f(x_n))$$

where the x_i values represent the endpoints of the trapezoids and where

$$x_0 = a \text{ and } x_n = b$$

If the area under a curve is represented by areas under quadratic sections of a curve, and if the interval $[a,b]$ is divided into $2n$ equal sections, then the area can be approximated by the formula (Simpson's rule)

$$K_s = \frac{h}{3}(f(x_0) + 4f(x_1) + 2f(x_2) + 4f(x_3) + \cdots + 2f(x_{2n-2}) + 4f(x_{2n-1}) + f(x_{2n}))$$

where the x_i values represent the end points of the sections and where

$$x_0 = a,$$
$$x_{2n} = b, \text{ and}$$
$$h = (b - a)/(2n)$$

If the piecewise components of the approximating function are higher degree functions (the trapezoidal rule uses linear functions, and Simpson's rule uses quadratic functions), the integration techniques are referred to as **Newton–Cotes integration techniques**.

The estimate of an integral improves as we use more components (such as trapezoids) to approximate the area under a curve. If we attempt to integrate a function with a singularity (a point at which the function or its derivatives are infinity or are not defined), we may not be able to get a satisfactory answer with a numerical integration technique.

8.4.2 MATLAB Quadrature Functions

MATLAB has two quadrature functions for performing numerical function integration. The **quad** function uses an adaptive form of Simpson's rule, whereas **quadl** uses an adaptive Lobatto quadrature. The **quadl** function is better at handling functions with certain types of singularities, such as

$$\int_0^1 \sqrt{x}\, dx$$

Both functions print a warning message if they detect a singularity, but an estimate of the integral is still returned.

The simplest form of the **quad** and **quadl** functions requires three arguments. The first argument is the name (in quotes) of the MATLAB function that returns a vector of values of $f(x)$ when given a vector of input values **x**. This function name can be the name of another MATLAB function, such as **sin**, or it can be the name of a user-written MATLAB function. The second and third arguments are the integral limits **a** and **b**. A summary of these functions is as follows:

quad('function',a,b)   Returns the area of the **'function'** between **a** and **b**, assuming that **'function'** is a MATLAB function.

quadl('function',a,b)   Returns the area of the **'function'** between **a** and **b**, assuming that **'function'** is a MATLAB function.

The script shown next can be used to compare the results of the **quad** and **quadl** functions with the analytically calculated results. The script prompts the user for a specified interval:

```
%    These statements compare the quad and quadl functions
%    with the analytical results for the integration of the
%    square root of x over an interval [a,b], where a and b
%    are nonnegative.
%
a = input('Enter left endpoint (nonnegative): ');
b = input('Enter right endpoint (nonnegative): ');
%
%    k is the computed analytical result
k = (2/3)*(b^(1.5) - a^(1.5));
```

```
%
%      The following two statements compute the quad and quad
%      functions from a to b
kquad=quad('sqrt',a,b);
kquadl=quadl('sqrt',a,b);
%
%      Display the results
fprintf('Analytical: %f \n',k);
fprintf('Quad: %f \n',kquad);
fprintf('Quadl: %f \n',kquadl);
```

These integration techniques can handle some singularities that occur at one or the other interval endpoints, but they cannot handle singularities that occur within the interval. For these cases, you should consider dividing the interval into subintervals and providing estimates of the singularities using other results, such as l'Hôpital's rule.

To illustrate, assume that we want to determine the integral of the square-root function for nonnegative values of a and b:

$$K_Q = \int_a^b \sqrt{x}\, dx$$

The square-root function $f(x) = \sqrt{x}$ is plotted in Figure 8.25 for the interval [0, 5]; the values of the function are complex for $x < 0$. This function can be integrated analytically to yield the following for nonnegative values of a and b:

$$K = \frac{2}{3}(b^{3/2} - a^{3/2})$$

You can cut and paste the preceding script into a file and test it. If you select an interval that contains a singularity, you will see a message similar to the following:

Recursion level limit reached in quad. Singularity likely.

The following example demonstrate the script's use:

```
Enter left endpoint (nonnegative): 1.5
Enter right endpoint (nonnegative): 15
Analytical: 37.505089
    Quad: 37.504990
    Quadl: 37.505088
Enter left endpoint (nonnegative): 0.2
Enter right endpoint (nonnegative): 5
Analytical: 7.393931
    Quad: 7.393905
    Quadl: 7.393926
```

The **quad** and **quadl** functions can also include a fourth argument, which represents a tolerance. If the tolerance is omitted, a default value of 0.001 is assumed. The integration function continues to refine its estimate for the integration until the relative error is less than the tolerance, using the following iterative test:

$$\frac{\text{previous estimate} - \text{current estimate}}{\text{previous estimate}} < \text{tolerance}$$

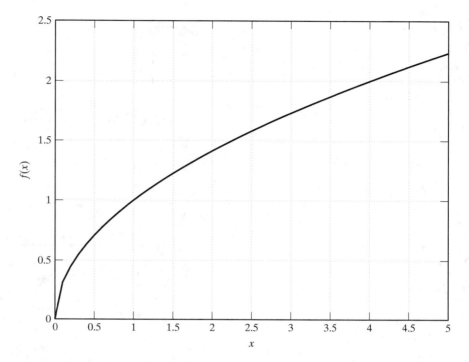

Figure 8.25. Velocity profile of flowing oil.

8.5   NUMERICAL DIFFERENTIATION

The derivative of a function $f(x)$ is defined to be a function $f'(x)$ that is equal to the rate of change of $f(x)$ with respect to x. The derivative can be expressed as a ratio, with the change in $f(x)$ indicated by $df(x)$ and the change in x indicated by dx, giving

$$f'(x) = \frac{df(x)}{dx}$$

There are many physical processes for which we want to measure the rate of change of a variable. For example, velocity is the rate of change of position (as in meters per second), and acceleration is the rate of change of velocity (as in meters per second squared). It can also be shown that the integral of acceleration is velocity and that the integral of velocity is position. Hence, integration and differentiation have a special relationship, in that they can be considered to be inverses of each other: The derivative of an integral returns the original function, and the integral of a derivative returns the original function, to within a constant value.

The derivative $f'(x)$ can be described graphically as the slope of the function $f(x)$, where the slope of $f(x)$ is defined to be the slope of the tangent line to the function at the specified point. Thus, the value of $f'(x)$ at the point a is $f'(a)$, and it is equal to the slope of the tangent line at the point a, as shown in Figure 8.26.

Because the derivative of a function at a point is the slope of the tangent line at the point, a value of zero for the derivative of a function at the point x_k indicates that the line is horizontal at that point. Points with derivatives of zero are called **critical points** and can represent either a horizontal region, a local maximum, or a local minimum of the function. (The point may also be the global maximum or global minimum, as shown in Figure 8.27, but more analysis of the entire function would be needed to determine this.)

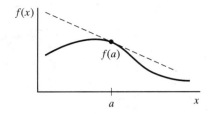

Figure 8.26. Derivative of (x) at $x = a$.

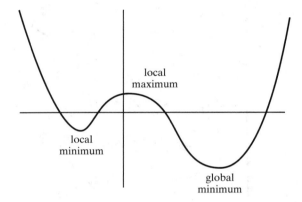

Figure 8.27. Example of function with critical points.

If we evaluate the derivative of a function at several points in an interval and we observe that the sign of the derivative changes, then a local maximum or a local minimum occurs in the interval. The second derivative [the derivative of $f'(x)$] can be used to determine whether or not the critical points represent local maxima or local minima. More specifically, if the second derivative of an **extrema point** is positive, then the value of the function at the extrema point is a local minimum; if the second derivative of an extrema point is negative, then the value of the function at the extrema point is a local maximum.

8.5.1 Difference Expressions

Numerical differentiation techniques estimate the derivative of a function at a point x_k by approximating the slope of the tangent line at x_k using values of the function at points near x_k. The approximation of the slope of the tangent line can be done in several ways, as shown in Figure 8.28.

Figure 8.28(a) assumes that the derivative at x_k is estimated by computing the slope of the line between $f(x_{k-1})$ and $f(x_k)$, as in

$$f'(x_k) = \frac{f(x_k) - f(x_{k-1})}{x_k - x_{k-1}}$$

This type of derivative approximation is called a **backward difference approximation**. Figure 8.28(b) assumes that the derivative at x_k is estimated by computing the slope of the line between $f(x_k)$ and $f(x_{k+1})$, as in

$$f'(x_k) = \frac{f(x_{k+1}) - f(x_k)}{x_{k+1} - x_k}$$

This type of derivative approximation is called a **forward difference approximation**.

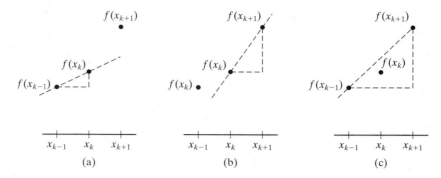

Figure 8.28. Techniques for computing $f'(x_k)$.

Figure 8.28(c) assumes that the derivative at x_k is estimated by computing the slope of the line between $f(x_{k-1})$ and $f(x_{k+1})$, as in

$$f'(x_k) = \frac{f(x_{k+1}) - f(x_{k-1})}{x_{k+1} - x_{k-1}}$$

This type of derivative approximation is called a **central difference approximation**, and we usually assume that x_k is halfway between x_{k-1} and x_{k+1}. The quality of all of these types of derivative computations depends on the distance between the points used to estimate the derivative; the estimate of the derivative improves as the distance between the two points decreases.

The second derivative of a function $f(x)$ is the derivative of the first derivative of the function:

$$f''(x) = \frac{df'(x)}{dx}$$

This function can be evaluated using slopes of the first derivative. Thus, if we use backward differences, we have

$$f''(x_k) = \frac{f'(x_k) - f'(x_{k-1})}{x_k - x_{k-1}}$$

Similar expressions can be derived for computing estimates of higher derivatives.

8.5.2 `diff` Function

The **diff** function computes differences between adjacent values in a vector, generating a new vector with one fewer value. If the **diff** function is applied to a matrix, it operates on the columns of the matrix as if each column were a vector. A second, optional argument specifies the number of times to recursively apply **diff**. Each time **diff** is applied, the length of the vector is reduced in size. A third, optional argument specifies the dimensions in which to apply the function. The forms of **diff** are summarized as follows:

```
diff(X)
```
For a vector **X**, **diff** returns
```
[X(2)-X(1) X(3)-X(2) … X(n)-X(n-1)].
```

```
diff(X)
```
For a matrix **X**, **diff** returns the matrix of column differences
```
[X(2:m,:)-X(1:m-1,:)]
```

```
diff(X,n,dim)
```

The general form of **diff** returns the **nth** difference function along dimension **dim** (a scalar). If $n >=$ the length of **dim**, then **diff** returns an empty array.

To illustrate, we define vectors **x**, **y**, and **z** as follows:

```
x = [0 1 2 3 4 5];
y = [2 3 1 5 8 10];
z = [1 3 5; 1 5 10];
```

Then the vector generated by **diff(x)** is

```
diff(x)
ans =
1    1       1       1       1
```

The vector generated by **diff(y)** is

```
diff(y)
ans =
1    -2      4       3       2
```

If you execute **diff** twice, the length of the returned vector is 4:

```
diff(y,2)
ans =
-3   6       -1      -1
```

The **diff** function can be applied to either dimension of matrix **z**:

```
diff(z,1,1)
ans =
0    2       5
diff(z,1,2)
ans =
2    2
4    5
```

An approximate derivative dy can be computed by using **diff(y)./diff(x)**. Note that these values of dy are correct for both the forward difference equation and the backward difference equation. The distinction between the two methods for computing the derivative is determined by the values of the vector **xd**, which correspond to the derivative dy. If the corresponding values of **xd** are [1,2,3,4,5], dy computes a backward difference. If the corresponding values of **xd** are [0,1,2,3,4], dy computes a forward difference.

As an example, consider the function given by the following polynomial:

$$f(x) = x^5 - 3x^4 - 11x^3 + 27x^2 + 10x - 24$$

A plot of this function is shown in Figure 8.29. Recall that the zeros of the derivative correspond to the points of local minima or local maxima of a function. The function in this example does not have a global minimum or global maximum, because the function ranges from $-\infty$ to ∞. The local minima and maxima (or critical points) of this function occur at -2.3, -0.2, 1.5, and 3.4. You can use the **find** function to identify the critical points of a function. Assume that we want to compute the derivative of this function over the interval $[-4,5]$. We can perform this operation using the **diff** function, as shown in the following script, where df represents **df** and xd represents the x values corresponding to the derivative:

```
%Evaluate f(x) and f'(x).
%
x = -4:0.1:5;
f = x.^5 - 3*x.^4 - 11*x.^3 + 27*x.^2 + 10*x - 24;
```

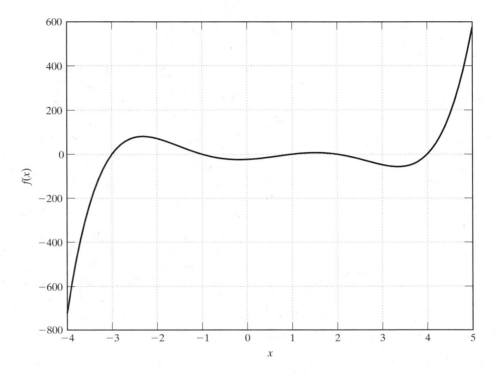

Figure 8.29. Fifth-degree polynomial.

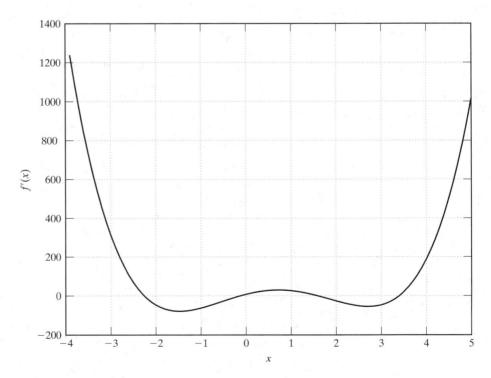

Figure 8.30. Derivative of fifth-degree polynomial.

```
df = diff(f)./diff(x);
xd = x(2:length(x));
plot(xd, df);
```

Using values of **df** and **xd** from the previous calculations, we can use the **find** function to determine the indices k of the locations in **product** for which **df(k)** is equal to zero. These indices are then used with the vector **xd** to print the approximation to the locations of the critical points:

```
%Find locations of critical points of f'(x).
%
product = df(1:length(df)-1).*df(2:length(df));
critical = xd(find(product<0))
critical =
-2.3000      -0.2000       1.5000 3.4000
```

In the example discussed in this section, we assumed that we had the equation of the function to be differentiated, and thus we could generate points of the function. In many engineering problems, the data to be differentiated are collected from experiments. Thus, we cannot choose the points to be close together to get a more accurate measure of the derivative. In these cases, it might be a good solution to use alternative techniques that allow us to determine an equation for a polynomial that fits a set of data and then compute points from the equation to use in computing values of the derivative.

SUMMARY

In this chapter, we explained the difference between interpolation and least-squares curve fitting. Two types of interpolation were presented: linear interpolation and cubic-spline interpolation. After presenting the MATLAB commands for performing these types of interpolations, we then turned to least-squared curve fitting using polynomials. This discussion explained how to determine the best fit to a set of data using a polynomial with a specified degree and then how to use the best-fit polynomial to generate new values of the function. Use of the interactive **basic fitting** window was also described to perform these same functions, as was the **curve fitting toolbox**. Techniques for numerical integration and numerical differentiation were also presented in this chapter.

MATLAB SUMMARY

This MATLAB summary lists and briefly describes all of the commands and functions that were defined in this chapter:

Commands and Functions	
cftool	opens the curve fitting graphical user interface
diff	computes the differences between adjacent values
interp1	computes linear and cubic interpolation
polyfit	computes a least-squares polynomial
polyval	evaluates a polynomial
quad	computes the integral under a curve (Simpson)
quadl	computes the integral under a curve (Lobatto)

KEY TERMS

approximation	derivative	linear interpolation
backward difference	extrema points	linear regression
central difference approximation	forward difference approximation	quadratic equation
critical points	graphical user interface (GUI)	quadrature
cubic equation	interpolation	Simpson's rule
cubic spline	least-squares	trapezoidal rule
degree of a polynomial		

Problems

1. Generate $f(x) = x^2$ for $x = [-3 -1\ 0\ 2\ 5\ 6]$.

   a. Compute and plot the linear and cubic-spline interpolation of the data points over the range $[-3:0.05:6]$.

   b. Compute the value of $f(4)$ using linear interpolation and cubic-spline interpolation. What are the respective errors when the answer is compared with the actual value of $f(4)$?

2. **Cylinder Head Temperatures.** Assume that the following set of temperature measurements is taken from the cylinder head in a new engine that is being tested for possible use in a race car:

Time, s	Temperature, °F
0.0	0.0
1.0	20.0
2.0	60.0
3.0	68.0
4.0	77.0
5.0	110.0

   a. Compare plots of these data, assuming linear interpolation and assuming cubic-spline interpolation for values between the data points, using time values from 0 to 5 in increments of 0.1 s.

   b. Using the data from part (a), find the time value for which there is the largest difference between its linear-interpolated temperature and its cubic-interpolated temperature.

3. Assume that we measure temperatures at three points around the cylinder head in the engine from Problem 2, instead of at just one point. The set of data is then the following:

Time, s	Temp1	Temp2	Temp3
0.0	0.0	0.0	0.0
1.0	20.0	25.0	52.0
2.0	60.0	62.0	90.0
3.0	68.0	67.0	91.0
4.0	77.0	82.0	93.0
5.0	110.0	103.0	96.0

   a. Assume that these data have been stored in a matrix with six rows and four columns. Determine interpolated values of temperature at the three points in the engine at 2.6 seconds, using linear interpolation.

   b. Using the information from part (a), determine the time that the temperature reached 75 degrees at each of the three points in the cylinder head.

4. **Spacecraft accelerometer.** The guidance and control system for a spacecraft often uses a sensor called an accelerometer, which is an electromechanical

device that produces an output voltage proportional to the applied acceleration. Assume that an experiment has yielded the following set of data:

Acceleration	Voltage
4	0.593
2	0.436
0	0.061
2	0.425
4	0.980
6	1.213
8	1.646
10	2.158

a. Determine the linear equation that best fits this set of data. Plot the data points and the linear equation.
b. Determine the sum of the squares of the distances of these points from the line of best fit determined in part (a).
c. Compare the error sum from part (b) with the same error sum computed from the best quadratic fit. What do these sums tell you about the two models for the data?

5. Compute $\tan(x)$ for $x = [-1:0.05:1]$.

a. Compute the best-fit polynomial of order four that approximates $\tan(x)$. Plot $\tan(x)$ and the generated polynomial on the same graph. What is the sum of square error of the polynomial approximation for the data points in x?
b. Compute $\tan(x)$ for $x = [-2:0.05:2]$. Using the polynomial generated in part (a), compute values of y from -2 to 2, corresponding to the **x** vector just defined. Plot $\tan(x)$ and the values generated from the polynomial on the same graph. Why aren't they the same shape?

6. **Sounding Rocket Trajectory.** The following data set represents the time and altitude values for a sounding rocket that is performing high-altitude atmospheric research on the ionosphere:

Time, s	Altitude, m
0	60
10	2,926
20	10,170
30	21,486
40	33,835
50	45,251
60	55,634
70	65,038
80	73,461
90	80,905
100	87,368
110	92,852
120	97,355
130	100,878
140	103,422
150	104,986
160	106,193
170	110,246

Time, s	Altitude, m
180	119,626
190	136,106
200	162,095
210	199,506
220	238,775
230	277,065
240	314,375
250	350,704

a. Determine an equation that represents the data, using the interactive curve fitting tools available in MATLAB 7.

b. Plot the altitude data. The velocity function is the derivative of the altitude function. Using numerical differentiation, compute the velocity values from these data, using a backward difference. Plot the velocity data. (Note that the rocket is a two-stage rocket.)

c. The acceleration function is the derivative of the velocity function. Using the velocity data determined from part (b), compute the acceleration data, using backward difference. Plot the acceleration data.

7. **Simple Root Finding.** Even though MATLAB makes it easy to find the roots of a function, sometimes all that is needed is a quick estimate. This can be done by plotting a function and zooming in very close to see where the function equals zero. Since MATLAB draws straight lines between data points in a plot, it is good to draw circles or stars at each data point, in addition to the straight lines connecting the points. Plot the following function, and zoom in to find the roots:

```
n = 5;
x = linspace(0,2*pi,n);
y = x .* sin(x) + cos(1/2*x).^2 - 1./(x - 7);
plot (x,y,'-o')
```

Increase the value of **n** to increase the accuracy of the estimate.

Consider the data points in the following two vectors:

$$\mathbf{X} = [0.1\ 0.3\ 5.0\ 6.0\ 23.0\ 24.0]$$
$$\mathbf{Y} = [2.8\ 2.6\ 18.1\ 26.8\ 486.1\ 530.0]$$

8. Determine the best-fit polynomial of order 2 for the data. Calculate the sum of squares for your results. Plot the best-fit polynomial for the six data points.

9. Generate a new **X** containing 250 uniform data points in increments of 0.1 from [0.1, 25.0]. Using the best-fit polynomial coefficients from the previous problem, generate a new **Y** containing 250 data points. Plot the results.

10. Compute an estimate of the derivative using the new X and the new Y generated in the previous problem. Compute the coefficients of the derivative. Plot the derivative.

11. **Function Analysis.** Let the function f be defined by the following equation:

$$f(x) = 4e^{-x}$$

Plot this function over the interval [0,1]. Use numerical integration techniques to estimate the integral of $f(x)$ over [0, 0.5], and over [0,1].

Appendix A
Special Characters, Commands and Functions

These tables are grouped according to category, which roughly parallels the chapter organization

Special Characters	Matrix Definition	Chapter
[ ]	Forms matrices	Chapter 2
( )	Used in statements to group operations Used with a matrix name to identify specific elements	Chapter 2
,	Separates subscripts or matrix elements	Chapter 2
;	Separates rows in a matrix definition Suppresses output when used in commands	Chapter 2
:	Used to generate matrices Indicates all rows or all columns	Chapter 2

Special Characters	Operators used in MATLAB calculations (scalar and array)	Chapter
=	assignment operator–assigns a value to a memory location–not the same as an equality	Chapter 2
%	Indicates a comment in an M-file	Chapter 2
+	Scalar and array addition	Chapter 2
−	Scalar and array subtraction	Chapter 2
°	Scalar multiplication	Chapter 2
.°	Array multiplication	Chapter 2
/	Scalar division	Chapter 2
./	Array division	Chapter 2
^	Scalar exponentiation	Chapter 2
.^	Array exponentiation	Chapter 2

Commands	Formatting	Chapter
format +	sets format to plus and minus signs only	Chapter 2
format compact	sets format to compact form	Chapter 2
format long	sets format to 14 decimal places	Chapter 2
format long e	sets format to 14 exponential places	Chapter 2
format loose	sets format back to default, non compact form	Chapter 2
format short	sets format back to default, 4 decimal places	Chapter 2
format short e	sets format to 4 exponential places	Chapter 2

Commands	Basic Workspace Control	Chapter
ans	Default variable name for results of MATLAB calculations	Chapter 2
clc	clears command screen	Chapter 2
clear	clears workspace	Chapter 2
exit	terminates MATLAB	Chapter 2
help	invokes help utility	Chapter 2
load	loads matrices from a file	Chapter 2
quit	terminates MATLAB	Chapter 2
save	saves variables in a file	Chapter 2
who	lists variables in memory	Chapter 2
whos	lists variables and their sizes	Chapter 2

Special Functions	Functions with special meaning, that do not require an input	Chapter
eps	smallest difference recognized	Chapter 3
i	imaginary number	Chapter 3
Inf	infinity	Chapter 3
j	imaginary number	Chapter 3
Nan	Not a number	Chapter 3
pi	numeric approximation of the value of π	Chapter 2 and 3

Functions	Elementary Math	Chapter
abs	computes the absolute value	Chapter 3
ceil	rounds to the nearest integer toward positive infinity	Chapter 3
erf	calculates the error function	Chapter 3
exp	computes the value of e^x	Chapter 3
fix	rounds to the nearest integer toward zero	Chapter 3
floor	rounds to the nearest integer toward minus infinity	Chapter 3
log	computes the natural log	Chapter 3
log10	computes the log base 10	Chapter 3
log2	computes the log base 2	Chapter 3
rem	calculates the remainder in a division problem	Chapter 3
round	rounds to the nearest integer	Chapter 3
sign	determines the sign (positive or negative)	Chapter 3
sqrt	calculates the square root of a number	Chapter 3

Functions	Trigonometry	Chapter
asin	computes the inverse sine (arcsine)	Chapter 3
cos	computes the cosine	Chapter 3
sin	computes the sine	Chapter 3
sinh	computes the hyperbolic sine	Chapter 3
tan	computes the tangent	Chapter 3
	MATLAB includes all the common trigonometric functions. Only the most common are listed here	

Functions	Data Analysis	Chapter
cumprod	computes a cumulative product of the values in an array	Chapter 3
cumsum	computes a cumulative sum of the values in an array	Chapter 3
max	finds the maximum value in an array, and determines which element stores the maximum value	Chapter 3
mean	computes the average of the elements in an array	Chapter 3
median	finds the median of the elements in an array	Chapter 3
min	finds the minimum value in an array, and determines which element stores the minimum vale	Chapter 3
prod	multiplies the values in an array	Chapter 3
std	determines the standard deviation	Chapter 3
sum	sums the values in an array	Chapter 3

Functions	Random Numbers	Chapter
rand	calculates evenly distributed random numbers	Chapter 3
randn	calculates normally distributed (Gaussian) random numbers	Chapter 3

Functions	Two-Dimensional Plots	Chapter
bar	generates a bar graph	Chapter 4
barh	generates a horizontal bar graph	Chapter 4
contour	generates a contour plot	Chapter 4
hist	generates a histogram	Chapter 4
loglog	generates an x-y plot, with both axes scaled logarithmically	Chapter 4
pie	generates a pie chart	Chapter 4
plot	creates an x-y plot	Chapter 4
polar	creates a polar plot	Chapter 4
semilogx	generates an x-y plot, with the x-axis scaled logarithmically	Chapter 4
semilogy	generates an x-y plot, with the y-axis scaled logarithmically	Chapter 4

Functions	Three-Dimensional Plots	Chapter
bar3	generates a three-dimensional bar graph	Chapter 4
barh3	generates a horizontal three-dimensional bar graph	Chapter 4

mesh	generates a mesh plot of a surface	Chapter 4
peaks	Creates a sample matrix used to demonstrate graphing functions	Chapter 4
pie3	generates a three-dimensional pie chart	Chapter 4
plot3	generates a three dimensional line plot	Chapter 4
sphere	example function used to demonstrate graphing	Chapter 4
surf	generates a surface plot	Chapter 4
surfc	generates a combination surface and contour plot	Chapter 4

Special Characters	Control of Plot Appearance	Chapter
Indicator	**Line Type**	Chapter 4
–	solid	Chapter 4
:	dotted	Chapter 4
–.	dash-dot	Chapter 4
–	dashed	Chapter 4
		Chapter 4
Indicator	**Point Type**	Chapter 4
.	point	Chapter 4
o	circle	Chapter 4
x	x-mark	Chapter 4
+	plus	Chapter 4
°	star	Chapter 4
s	square	Chapter 4
d	diamond	Chapter 4
v	triangle down	Chapter 4
∧	triangle up	Chapter 4
<	triangle left	Chapter 4
>	triangle right	Chapter 4
p	pentagram	Chapter 4
h	hexagram	Chapter 4
Indicator	**Color**	
b	blue	Chapter 4
g	green	Chapter 4
r	red	Chapter 4
c	cyan	Chapter 4
m	magenta	Chapter 4
y	yellow	Chapter 4
k	black	Chapter 4

Functions	Figure Control	Chapter
axis	Freezes the current axis scaling for subsequent plots or specifies the axis dimensions	Chapter 4
figure	opens a new figure window	Chapter 4
grid off	turns the grid off	Chapter 4
grid on	adds a grid to the current and all subsequent graphs in the current figure	Chapter 4

hold off	instructs MATLAB **to** erase figure contents before adding new information	Chapter 4
hold on	instructs MATLAB **not to** erase figure contents before adding new information	Chapter 4
legend	Adds a legend to a graph	Chapter 4
shading flat	shades a surface plot with one color per grid section	Chapter 4
shading interp	shades a surface plot by interpolation	Chapter 4
subplot	divides the graphics window up into sections available for plotting	Chapter 4
text	Adds a textbox to a graph	Chapter 4
title	adds a title to a plot	Chapter 4
xlabel	adds a label to the x-axis	Chapter 4
ylabel	adds a label to the y-axis	Chapter 4
zlabel	adds a label to the z -axis	Chapter 4

Functions	**Figure Color Schemes**	**Chapter**
autumn	optional colormap used in surface plots	Chapter 4
bone	optional colormap used in surface plots	Chapter 4
colorcube	optional colormap used in surface plots	Chapter 4
cool	optional colormap used in surface plots	Chapter 4
copper	optional colormap used in surface plots	Chapter 4
flag	optional colormap used in surface plots	Chapter 4
hot	optional colormap used in surface plots	Chapter 4
hsv	optional colormap used in surface plots	Chapter 4
jet	default colormap used in surface plots	Chapter 4
pink	optional colormap used in surface plots	Chapter 4
prism	optional colormap used in surface plots	Chapter 4
spring	optional colormap used in surface plots	Chapter 4
summer	optional colormap used in surface plots	Chapter 4
summer	optional colormap used in surface plots	Chapter 4
white	optional colormap used in surface plots	Chapter 4
winter	optional colormap used in surface plots	Chapter 4

Special Characters	**Comparison Operators**	**Chapter**
$<$	less than	Chapter 5
$<=$	less than or equal to	Chapter 5
$>$	greater than	Chapter 5
$>=$	greater than or equal to	Chapter 5
$==$	equal to	Chapter 5
$\sim=$	not equal to	Chapter 5

Special Characters	**Logical Operators**	**Chapter**
&	and	Chapter 5
|	or	Chapter 5
$\sim$	not	Chapter 5

Special Characters	Format Control	Chapter
%f	fixed point, or decimal notation	Chapter 5
%e	exponential notation	Chapter 5
%g	either fixed point or exponential notation	Chapter 5
\n	linefeed	Chapter 5
\r	carriage return	Chapter 5
\t	tab	Chapter 5
\b	backspace	Chapter 5

Functions	Input/Output (I/O) Control	Chapter
disp	displays matrix or text	Chapter 5
fprintf	prints formatted information	Chapter 5
input	prompts the user to enter a value	Chapter 5
num2string	converts an array into a string	Chapter 5
pause	pauses the execution of a program, until any key is hit	Chapter 4 and 5

Functions	Control Structures	Chapter
else	defines the path if the result of an if statement is false	Chapter 5
elseif	defines the path if the result of an if statement is false, and specifies a new logical test	Chapter 5
end	identifies the end of a control structure	Chapter 5
find	determines which elements in a matrix meet the input criteria	Chapter 5
for	generates a loop structure	Chapter 5
if	tests a logical expression	Chapter 5
while	generates a loop structure	Chapter 5

Functions	Timing	Chapter
clock	determines the current time on the CPU clock	Chapter 5
etime	finds elapsed time	Chapter 5
tic	starts a timing sequence	Chapter 5
toc	stops a timing sequence	Chapter 5

Functions	Function Definition	Chapter
function	identifies an M-file as a function	Chapter 5
help	invokes help utility	Chapter 2
nargin	determines the number of input arguments in a function	Chapter 5
nargout	determines the number of output arguments from a function	Chapter 5

Functions	Matrix Definition, Manipulation and Analysis	Chapter
det	computes the determinate of a matrix	Chapter 6
diag	extracts the diagonal from a matrix generates a matrix with the input on the diagonal	Chapter 6
eye	generates an identity matrix	Chapter 6
fliplr	flips a matrix from left to right	Chapter 6
inv	computes the inverse of a matrix	Chapter 6
length	determines the largest dimension of an array	Chapter 3
linspace	defines a linearly spaced vector	Chapter 2
magic	generates a magic square	Chapter 6
meshgrid	maps each of two vectors into separate two-dimensional matrices, the size of which is determined by the source vectors	Chapter 4 & 5
ones	generates a matrix composed of ones	Chapter 6
size	determines the number of rows and columns in an array	Chapter 3
size	determines the number of rows and columns in a matrix	Chapter 6
sort	sorts the elements of a vector into ascending order	Chapter 3
zeros	generates a matrix composed of zeros	Chapter 6

Special Characters	Matrix Operations	Chapter
'	used to enclose a symbolic expression	Chapter 7
°	symbolic multiplication	Chapter 7
/	symbolic division	Chapter 7
−	symbolic subtraction	Chapter 7
+	symbolic addition	Chapter 7
^	symbolic exponentiation	Chapter 7

Functions	Functions used with Symbolic Expressions	Chapter
collect	collects coefficients of a symbolic expression	Chapter 7
diff	differentiates a symbolic expression	Chapter 7
double	changes a symbolic variable into a double precision floating point variable	Chapter 7
expand	expands a symbolic expression	Chapter 7
ezplot	generates a plot of a symbolic expression	Chapter 7
factor	factors a symbolic expression	Chapter 7
findsym	find symbolic variables in a symbolic expression	Chapter 7
int	integrates a symbolic expression	Chapter 7
numden	returns the numerator and denominator of an expression	Chapter 7
poly2sym	converts a vector to a symbolic polynomial	Chapter 7
pretty	prints a symbolic expression in typeset form	Chapter 7
simple	simplifies a symbolic expression	Chapter 7
simplify	simplifies a symbolic expression	Chapter 7
solve	solves an equation	Chapter 7
subs	replace variables in a symbolic expression	Chapter 7
sym2poly	converts a symbolic expression to a coefficient vector	Chapter 7

Functions	Numerical Calculus	Chapter
diff	computes the differences between adjacent values in a vector	Chapter 8
quad	computes the integral under a curve (Simpson) defined by a vector	Chapter 8
quad1	computes the integral under a curve (Lobatto) defined by a vector	Chapter 8

Functions	Numerical Techniques	Chapter
cftool	opens the curve fitting graphical user interface	Chapter 8
interp1	computes linear and cubic interpolation	Chapter 8
linear	used with **interp1** to perform a linear interpolation	Chapter 8
polyfit	computes a least-squares polynomial	Chapter 8
polyval	evaluates a polynomial	Chapter 8
spline	used with **interp1** to perform a cubic spline interpolation	Chapter 8

Index

while function, 180, 271
while loops, 172, 175–177
    calculating factorials using (example), 176–177
white function, 136, 270
who command, 51, 267
whos command, 43, 51, 267
width field, 152
Wind tunnels, 16
winter function, 136, 270
Word processors, 6
WordPerfect, 6, 45
Workspace window, MATLAB, 18, 20–22, 75
Workstations, 4

X

x (x-mark), 134, 269
x-coordinate, matrices, 26

xlabel function, 136, 270
x-y coordinate, matrices, 26
x-y plot, 100–101

Y

y (yellow), 134, 269
y-coordinate, matrices, 26
Year 2000 (Y2K) programming bug, 9
ylabel function, 136, 270

Z

zeros function, 180, 199, 205, 272
Zeros, matrix of, 199–200
zlabel function, 136, 270